MARRIAGE DIVORCE
AND THE CHURCH

MARRIAGE DIVORCE AND THE CHURCH

The Report of a Commission appointed by the
Archbishop of Canterbury to prepare a statement
on the Christian Doctrine of Marriage

LONDON **SPCK** 1972

First published in 1971
Third impression 1972
S.P.C.K.
Holy Trinity Church
Marylebone Road
London NW1 4DU

Made and printed offset in Great Britain by
The Camelot Press Ltd,
London and Southampton

NOTE
Corrections made for the second impression
included two of substance which are referred to
on pages 156 and 166.
The Regulations Concerning Marriage and Divorce
made by the Convocation of Canterbury in
May 1957 are reprinted for information in the third
impression (Appendix 9)
An additional note to Appendix 1 *Jesus on Divorce
and Remarriage* appears on p. 169.

SBN 281 02711 0

CONTENTS

MEMBERS OF THE COMMISSION   ix
ACKNOWLEDGEMENTS   x
THE REPORT   xi

1 WHY A REPORT WAS NEEDED   1
  ANGLICAN OPINION   4
  CHURCH AND STATE   8
  UNDERLYING QUESTIONS   12

2 MARRIAGE AS RELATIONSHIP   14
  THE NEEDS WHICH MARRIAGE MEETS   15
  Sexual Fulfilment   15
  Maturation of Personality   18
  Children   20
  MARRIAGE AS A NATURAL STATE   23
  THE REALIZATION OF MARRIAGE   26
  THE CHARACTERISTICS OF MARRIAGE   28
  Exclusiveness   28
  Commitment   32
  Permanency   35
  THE SINGLE STATE   41
  MARRIAGE IN CHURCH   42

3 THE INSTITUTION OF MARRIAGE   45
  PERSONAL AND INSTITUTIONAL FACTORS   46
  THE ROLE OF THE STATE   48
  THE INTERESTS OF THE STATE IN THE FAMILY   51
  PASTORAL AND LITURGICAL CONSIDERATIONS   52

4 THE STRENGTHENING OF MARRIAGE   60
  THE MEDIEVAL VIEW OF INDISSOLUBILITY   62
  PRESENT PRACTICE IN THE CHURCH OF ENGLAND   64
  THE EASTERN ORTHODOX CHURCH   66
  SOME UNACCEPTABLE PROPOSALS   67
  THE PROMISES   70
  THE QUESTION OF MORAL CONSENSUS   71
  A POSSIBLE COURSE OF ACTION   73

Appendices

1 JESUS ON DIVORCE AND REMARRIAGE   79
by Hugh Montefiore

2 THE CORRELATION OF THEOLOGICAL AND EMPIRICAL MEANING   96
by J. W. Bowker

3 THE SACRAMENT OF MARRIAGE IN   113
   EASTERN CHRISTIANITY
   by A. M. Allchin

4 MARRIAGE AS ILLUSTRATING SOME   126
   CHRISTIAN DOCTRINES
   by Helen Oppenheimer

5 VOWS   131
   by Helen Oppenheimer and Hugh Montefiore

6 MARITAL BREAKDOWN   142
   by J. Dominian
   APPENDED NOTE ON "AN INSTITUTE FOR THE FAMILY"   150

7 MARRIAGE AND DIVORCE IN THE   152
   ANGLICAN COMMUNION
   by Herbert Waddams
   APPENDED NOTE ON THE ANGLICAN CHURCH OF CANADA   158

8 EPISCOPAL DISCRETION AND THE CLERGY   165

9 REGULATIONS CONCERNING MARRIAGE AND DIVORCE   167
   Convocation of Canterbury, May 1957

ADDITIONAL NOTE TO APPENDIX 1   169

THE MEMBERS OF THE COMMISSION

HOWARD ROOT (*Chairman*)
Canon Theologian of Winchester Cathedral, Professor of Theology in the
University of Southampton.

HUGH MONTEFIORE
Bishop of Kingston-upon-Thames.

A. M. ALLCHIN
Warden, The Convent of the Incarnation, Fairacres, Oxford.

J. W. BOWKER
Fellow of Corpus Christi College, Lecturer in Divinity, Cambridge
University.

G. R. DUNSTAN
Canon Theologian of Leicester Cathedral, F. D. Maurice Professor of
Moral and Social Theology at King's College, London.

MRS T. B. HEATON
For many years Secretary and Counsellor of the Oxford Marriage
Guidance Council.

LADY OPPENHEIMER
Writer on moral and philosophical theology, and until recently lecturer in
Christian Ethics at Cuddesdon Theological College.

HERBERT WADDAMS
Canon Residentiary of Canterbury Cathedral.

Consultant to the Commission
DR J. DOMINIAN, M.A., M.B., B.CHIR., M.R.C.P.Ed., D.P.M.
Consultant Psychiatrist at the Central Middlesex and Shenley Hospitals.

Secretarial Assistant
MISS R. D. WATLING

ACKNOWLEDGEMENTS

Thanks are due to the following for permission to quote from copyright sources:

Delachaux et Niestlé: *L'Orthodoxie*, by Paul Evdokimov.

The Faith Press Ltd: *Marriage and Divorce in accordance with the Canon Law of the Orthodox Church*, by H. S. Alivisatos.

The Faith Press Ltd and World Publishing Co., Cleveland, U.S.A.: *Said or Sung*, by Austin Farrer.

Monastère de Chevetogne: *Le Marriage dans les Eglises d'Orient* by A. Raes, S. J.

Morehouse–Barlow Co. Inc.: *Parents and Priests of the Redemption*, by Athenagoras Kokkinakis.

A. R. Mowbray & Co. Ltd: *The Church and Divorce*, by A. R. Winnett.

Lady Namier and the Editor of *The Listener*: article by Lady Namier (Julia de Beausobre).

Papadimitriou: *Honest to Orthodoxy*, by Christos Yannaras.

THE REPORT

YOUR GRACE,

We, the undersigned, were appointed under the terms of a Resolution passed by the Convocation of Canterbury in 1967. We were constituted by your Grace as a Commission in the spring of 1968, and we met for the first time in the summer of that year. Our terms of reference were "to prepare a statement on the Christian doctrine of marriage". This statement was to be prepared against the background of a debate in the Convocation of Canterbury "as to whether there might be occasions for relaxing the present rule of the Convocations whereby a divorced person with a former partner living may not have on remarrying a marriage service in Church".

These terms of reference caused us difficulty, since the composition of our Commission and the time available to us precluded a full investigation into marriage, which would require, with much else, the assistance of an anthropologist, a sociologist, and a lawyer among others. On the other hand, we were aware that much more is required today from theologians than a retracing of the ways in which historically the Church has understood marriage. We hope that the type of report which we now submit accords with your Grace's own interpretation of our terms of reference when we referred them back verbally to your Grace for elucidation.

We have completed our work under what have appeared to us to be heavy pressures. Although we were constituted as an independent Commission, we have been expected to consult with the Doctrine Commission (with which we have overlapping membership); and this we have done on two occasions. The consideration and passing of the Divorce Reform Act, after we had begun our work, and the prospect of its coming into operation on 1 January 1971, have increased the difficulties under which we have worked. The situation has been such that your Grace has, together with the Archbishop of York, circulated a Pastoral Letter on this subject to the clergy of the Church of England, in advance of the publication of our report. In the ordinary way we should have hoped to be in a position to publish our report in 1972; but we have brought it forward so as to make it available as early as possible in 1971. This is not to suggest that our report is ill-considered, for we were coming to a common mind about its shape early in 1970. But we believe that we could have produced a more finished report had we worked in our own time. Further, we found that the subject of our report—the Christian doctrine of marriage—had been debated independently in the Church Assembly at its summer meeting of 1970, and there were mistakes about our membership in its official publication. Later we discovered that, on the initiative of the Convocation of York, a Joint Consultation of the Canterbury and York Convocations had been set up (without prior consultation or agreement with us) to consult with us in the closing stages of the drafting of our report. We have attempted to co-operate with them also; but we must emphasize to your Grace that the report which we now submit is the product of our own thinking, and we make it on our own responsibility. While we are grateful to members of the Doctrine Commission and the Joint Consultation for the positive suggestions which they have made, our work is our own.

We have called the fourth chapter "The Strengthening of Marriage" in the hope that to face the realities of marriage breakdown and remarriage, and to think out theologically principled procedures for dealing with them, will help to strengthen the institution of matrimony.

It may be that interest in our report will centre on Chapter 4, with its suggestions about the possibility of the marriage in church of divorced persons—it was certainly against the background of a debate on this very matter that the decision to constitute this Commission was taken; and some of us wish that this had been made clearer in our initial terms of reference. We have reported first on the Christian doctrine of marriage, since without such a basis conclusions about divorce and remarriage could not be formulated. We hope that what we have written about marriage as a relationship and as an institution may be found helpful by the Church.

We would point out that in this fourth chapter we do not presume to tell the Church of England what it ought to do. Our proposal is more modest. We ask the competent authorities to discover, by appropriate means, whether there now exists within the Church of England a moral consensus about the propriety, in certain circumstances, of the marriage in church of divorced persons. It came to be our unanimous conclusion, after prolonged discussions, much heart-searching, and in some cases a conscientious change of mind, that, if the Church of England reached such a moral consensus, it would be compatible with reason, the word of God in Scripture, and theological tradition.

Our report carries only the authority of the Commission which prepared it. The appendices, which are integral to the report and to which the report makes frequent reference, are the responsibility of their authors. They have not been embodied in the report itself, partly because of our concern to keep the report short, and partly because we did not all share the specialized knowledge that enabled their authors to compose them.

We would draw attention to the appendix on "Episcopal Discretion and the Clergy". Although this matter, strictly speaking, falls outside our terms of reference, we came across it in the course of our work, and we include it because we believe that—quite apart from our own recommendations— this matter should be investigated by the appropriate authorities in view of its immediate practical importance.

We gratefully acknowledge many who have helped us: numerous correspondents in this country and elsewhere, and in particular those bishops of the Anglican Communion who were able to meet some of our members during the Lambeth Conference of 1968. We are grateful for written memoranda from Mr David Faull and the Worshipful Chancellor the Reverend E. Garth Moore.

We met ten times; eight meetings were residential. At these meetings we received much kindness, not least from the Sisters of Bethany at Bournemouth and the Benedictine community of West Malling. We are grateful also to our Consultant, Dr Dominian, who, as a specialist in matters concerning marriage and marital breakdown, has made a valuable contribution to our work. As members of the Church of England, we welcomed a Roman Catholic to help us, and we have benefited from the arguments which he has been able to advance concerning some parts of our report.

The Reverend John Bowker was appointed to act as Secretary to the Commission, but before we had progressed very far ill health forced him to resign this post; happily he has been able to attend a number of times including the two final meetings. Miss Dawn Watling, who has acted as Secretarial Assistant, has had in consequence to shoulder a heavy load of work, and to her we express our thanks.

We have pleasure in submitting our report, and we hope that we have discharged our commission to your Grace's satisfaction.

signed   Howard Root (*Chairman*)

Hugh Montefiore
Bishop of Kingston-upon-Thames

A. M. Allchin

J. W. Bowker

G. R. Dunstan

Irene Heaton

Helen Oppenheimer

Herbert Waddams

1
Why a Report was needed

1 Marriage is under scrutiny. Because it has a central place in personal and social life, marriage is a subject of universal interest and concern. For this reason it is affected by changes in people's outlook and conditions of life. It is because these changes have been so rapid and widespread that fundamental issues have recently been raised about marriage both as a relationship and as an institution. For example, the question has been asked whether marriage, if not outmoded, is becoming so, although there is no sociological evidence that this is the case. More information about marriage, and in particular about attitudes and behaviour within marriage, is beginning to become available. There is increased knowledge about marital breakdown as well as increased incidence of, and new legal grounds for, divorce. In some circles all this has led to a certain nervousness and anxiety about the future of marriage.

2 In this situation there have been various reactions among Christians. There has been a desire for a plain and authoritative statement of Christian teaching on marriage so that, amid contemporary uncertainties, Christians at least can see their way clear. There has also been a realization that such a statement should take into account the secular realities of marriage and divorce as these are now known, and in particular the many hard cases of personal tragedy and broken marriage which have beset Christians as well as others. There has been a further development in the attitudes of some Christians towards this situation. Personal experience of Christian men and women whose marriages have broken down and who have later decided in good conscience to remarry has led some to question the Church's present discipline of marriage. Many provinces of the Anglican Communion have modified or are reconsidering their regulations. In October 1967 a debate was initiated in the Convocation of Canterbury by the then Bishop of Worcester (L. M. Charles-Edwards) in the hope of reconsidering the present discipline of the

Church of England so that, in certain cases, it would be possible for the remarriage of a divorced person, who still had a former partner living, to be solemnized in church. The motion was lost in the House of Bishops. The bishops held that it would be inopportune to consider altering the Church's discipline of marriage until there had been a proper examination of the Church's doctrine of marriage. The Convocation of Canterbury thereupon asked the Archbishop to set up a small group "to present a statement of the Christian doctrine of marriage". This commission was the result; and it is against this background that this report is presented.

3 This report is therefore concerned with the Christian understanding of marriage and divorce; in this respect it is to be distinguished from an earlier report which dealt with the law of divorce in a secular society. In 1966 the Archbishop caused a report to be published under the title *Putting Asunder*.[1] It was the work of another group which he had appointed, under the chairmanship of the Bishop of Exeter, which recommended a radical reform of the legal basis for divorce in the law of the land: it proposed that the matrimonial offence as the ground of action for divorce be abolished, and that the recognition of an irretrievable breakdown of marriage be put in its place. The Law Commission, established by Parliament to review such areas of the law as were remitted to it by the Lord Chancellor, was interesting itself in the divorce law at the same time. It studied *Putting Asunder* carefully, and in *The Field of Choice*[2] published its own comments on it, appreciative of the argument for establishing the divorce law upon a new ground, but critical of the court procedures proposed. The two documents were debated together in the House of Lords, and the Government of the day made it known that it would support legislation to embody an acceptable compromise, accommodating the principle expounded in *Putting Asunder* to court procedures which, in the opinion of the Law Commission, would not make divorce proceedings more expensive or protracted than they were already.

4 Accordingly, the legislative processes began which resulted in the Divorce Reform Act of 1969, to come into operation on 1 January 1971. This Act abolished the matrimonial offence as the ground of action, and with it the old, disputed, but pragmatically useful distinction between the "innocent" and the "guilty" partner. It enacted that "the sole ground on which a petition for divorce may be presented to

---

[1] S.P.C.K. 1966.   [2] H.M.S.O. 1966, Cmd. 3123.

the court by either party to a marriage shall be that the marriage has broken down irretrievably" (S.1). What were formerly "matrimonial offences" become matrimonial situations, with the legal notion of "offence" taken out of them; they are to be set before the court as facts upon which to ground the presumption that the marriage had irretrievably broken down; if the presumption is not rebutted, the court will pronounce the marriage to have broken down and the parties freed from their mutual marital obligations. The much disputed section 2(1)(e) of the Act will allow the partner who, in terms of the old law, was technically in desertion to initiate proceedings for the dissolution of the marriage against the will of the spouse deserted; and, unless rebutted, the fact of their having lived apart for five years will be accepted by the court as presumptive evidence of irretrievable breakdown of the marriage; the marriage will be dissolved against the wish of the deserted spouse, unless the court is of the opinion that "the dissolution of the marriage will result in grave financial or other hardship to the respondent and that it would in all the circumstances be wrong to dissolve the marriage" (S.4). In future, after the Act has come into force, the form of words required will be that "the marriage has been dissolved"; it will not be accurate to say that "A has divorced B", or that "B has been divorced by A". While there are elements in the Act which have been strongly criticized in the Church, it is important to note that the substitution of the concept of irretrievable breakdown for that of the matrimonial offence has been regarded by many as a great gain from the Christian point of view.

5 To these developments the Church of England has contributed, through the publication of *Putting Asunder* and the consequent discussions between the Bishop of Exeter's Group and the Law Commission, and by the approbation of the principle set out in *Putting Asunder* by the affirmative vote in a debate in the Church Assembly on 16 February 1967.[1] The authors of *Putting Asunder* had said expressly that their appointed task was to consider the law necessary in "secular society" and not the matrimonial doctrine and discipline of the Church of England: they neither made nor implied any recommendation concerning them.[2] Nevertheless, it was said both within and outside the Church that the Church was bound to take cognizance of this recommendation for the secular law, and to examine its own practice, and even its own doctrine, accordingly.

[1] *Church Assembly—Report of Proceedings*, vol. XLVII, no. 2., pp. 230 ff.
[2] *Putting Asunder*, p. 4.

Anglican Opinion

6 Earlier, in 1958, the spirit of inquiry and even of unease was expressed in the Lambeth Conference, in the cautious language of the final Resolutions. Committee 5 of the Conference was responsible for one of the main topics, "The Family in Contemporary Society". Its major preoccupations were the problems facing family life, particularly in countries and regions undergoing rapid economic, industrial, and social development, and also the problems of population growth and contraception. In affirming its unqualified faith in lifelong monogamy as the essence of marriage, and in the duty of the Church to witness to this, it had to face also the related questions of polygamy and divorce. The whole conference, therefore, grounding itself on the Report of Committee 5, enunciated the two following Resolutions:

118. The Conference recognizes that divorce is granted by the secular authority in many lands on grounds which the Church cannot acknowledge, and recognizes also that in certain cases, where a decree of divorce has been sought and may even have been granted, there may in fact have been no marital bond in the eyes of the Church. It therefore commends for further consideration by the Churches and Provinces of the Anglican Communion a procedure for defining marital status, such as already exists in some of its Provinces.

119. The Conference believes that the Resolutions of the 1948 Lambeth Conference concerning marriage discipline have been of great value as witnessing to Christ's teaching about the life-long nature of marriage, and urges that these Resolutions, and their implications, should continue to be studied in every Province.[1]

7 The unease of the Conference shows itself in the concluding words of each Resolution. Resolution 118 suggests an investigation of the idea and practice of nullity, the way in which in practice the Roman Catholic Church has sought to mitigate the rigour of the doctrine of the absolute indissolubility of marriage, which it upholds in principle. If the marriage bond can in no circumstances be dissolved, the only way open to find relief from a marriage which has become intolerable, apart from legal separation, is to ask whether there is any possible reason for declaring that the bond has never been. Resolution 119 pays tribute to Resolutions of the Conference of 1948—one of which (no. 94) recommended the denial of remarriage in church to any divorced person with a partner still living—and then commended the Resolutions for further study—a fact which of itself suggests that their content and implication was not judged to be altogether satisfactory.

[1] *The Lambeth Conference 1958* (S.P.C.K. 1958), pt. 1, p. 58.

8 Resolutions 92 and 94 of 1948,[1] in fact, marked the fullest development of the indissolubilist view of marriage, and of one treatment of the problem of divorce. This view had hitherto coexisted with other views in the Church of England and in the Anglican Communion. When the 1857 Divorce Act was passed, the prevailing understanding of the "Matthaean exception"[2] still allowed many churchmen to accept the idea of divorce in cases of adultery. The Lambeth Conference of 1888, however, resolved against the admission of "guilty partners" to remarriage in church, and already by the turn of the century it was keenly debated whether "innocent partners" should be excluded also.[3] The increasing ascendency of the exclusive view is seen in the career of Mandell Creighton, Bishop successively of Peterborough and London. In 1895, while Bishop of Peterborough, he could advise an inquiring clergyman as follows: "The only possible principle concerning marriage is that it is indissoluble", he wrote, "But all principles are set aside by sin," as our Lord himself had recognized in the Matthaean exception. He was reluctant to set the Church against the State

on such a point as the interpretation of the latitude to be assigned to the permission of dissolution which our Lord's words imply. . . . Is the Church on this point to admit of no equity? . . . We as Christians abhor divorce; but when a divorce has been adjudged necessary, are we to refuse any liberty to the innocent and wronged party? It seems to me a matter for our discretion on equitable grounds in each case. I should not advise any of my clergy to refuse to solemnize a marriage of an innocent person who genuinely desired God's blessing. I prefer to err on the side of charity.[4]

This appears to be a genuine expression of the dilemma faced by intelligent, just, and sensitive men at the turn of the century, and it hardly differs at all in principle from the case that has been urged consistently against the Church ever since, and is urged against it today. Nevertheless, Creighton as Bishop of London, presenting in July 1898 the Report of a Committee of Convocation on this subject,

---

[1] Resolution 92 called on Anglicans to maintain "the Church's standard of discipline" and implored "those whose marriage, perhaps through no fault of their own, is unhappy to remain steadfastly faithful to their marriage vows".
Resolution 94 read: "The Conference affirms that the marriage of one whose former partner is still living may not be celebrated according to the rites of the Church, unless it has been established that there exists no marriage bond recognized by the Church."
[2] Matt. 5.32: "Whosoever shall put away his wife, saving for the cause of fornication. . . ." (Also Matt. 19.9.)
[3] *The Lambeth Conference 1888*, Resolution 4, (A) and (B).
[4] *The Life and Letters of Mandell Creighton* (Longmans, Green 1904) II, pp. 68f; cf. p. 275, where, in 1897, as Bishop of London, he writes to an incumbent faced with a similar case that he himself could only lay down principles, "and leave the decision to your discretion with a full knowledge of the circumstances".

appeared to have made that Committee's recommendation his own
when he said

If any Christian, conscientiously believing himself or herself permitted by
our Lord's words to remarry, determine to do so, we recommend that then
endeavour should be made to dissuade such person from seeking marriage
with the rites of the church, legal provision having been made for marriage
by civil process.[1]

9 Lying behind the debate on this subject during the last decade of the
nineteenth century was the question of absolute indissolubility.
Despite a strong and growing tendency to bring Anglican teaching
into line with that of the Roman Catholic Church on this point, a
number of eminent High Churchmen still maintained the opposite
position. For example, William Bright, the church historian and
liturgist, could write on the basis of his reading of the patristic
evidence, "I am convinced that the Canon Law doctrine [of
absolute indissolubility] does not rest on Catholic consent."[2] A
similar stand was taken by Edward King, Bishop of Lincoln. Appealing to the Matthaean exception and to the teaching and practice of
the undivided Church, he affirmed in his Charge of 1895, "I am
unable to accept the conclusions of those who make marriage
absolutely indissoluble, and so forbid the remarriage of those who
have been separated, under any circumstances."[3] Still more interesting
is King's judgement on the way in which the question should be
approached:

Many writers on this subject appear to me to start from a wrong point of
view. Wishing to maintain the indissolubility of marriage, they begin by
saying that God has himself determined the point, by declaring "they are
no longer two but one flesh"; and more to the same effect. But this only
declares what God's original antecedent Will is with regard to marriage; of
which there can be no doubt. But the question for us to consider is not
what is the ideal view of Holy Matrimony, but what is the duty of the
Church with regard to the practice of Divorce which she finds in existence.
The point of view then from which we should consider this question is not
ideal but practical, ethical, remedial. We are not saying what ought to be
the normal conditions of married life, but what may be done under the
head of equity and mercy to save man from the worse results of his own
folly. This is not the point of view from which many writers have lately
written, in their zeal to uphold the ideal state of Holy Matrimony; but it is,
I believe, the point of view from which Divorce is regarded both in the Old
Testament and in the New, and by many of the Councils and Fathers of
the Church.[4]

[1] *The Life and Letters of Mandell Creighton*, II, p. 323.
[2] *Letters of William Bright*, ed. B. J. Kidd (London 1903), p. 12.
[3] Edward King, *Charge 1895*, p. 42.
[4] Ibid., p. 34.

These words have the greater weight as coming from a man who had not only been a professor of pastoral theology, but was also universally acknowledged as a pastor of exceptional gifts and experience.

10 None the less, from this period onwards, the opinion that no divorced person, "innocent" or "guilty", could remarry in church has gained ground, for it is held that innocent and guilty alike are still married in the sight of God, so that a second marriage must be an empty ceremony. The Lambeth Conference in 1908 resolved (by a majority of three votes) that it was "undesirable" to bless in church the marriage of such an "innocent" person.[1] In 1930 the Conference resolved that "the marriage of one, whose former partner is still living, should not be celebrated according to the rites of the Church".[2] In 1938 the Convocations of Canterbury and York both resolved that the Church of England should not permit the use of the marriage service in the case of anyone who had a former partner still living.[3] In the Canterbury Convocation on 1 October 1957 this Resolution formed part of a statement declared to be an Act of Convocation.

11 It should be said at once that these rules, though of strong moral authority, have no legal effect, for no decision of Convocation can take away a liberty granted by a Statute of the Realm. The Matrimonial Causes Act of 1937, for which Sir Alan Herbert was responsible, gave the clergy unlimited discretion, hitherto denied them, not only whether themselves to remarry divorced persons in church or not, but also whether or not to lend their churches for the solemnization of such marriages by another clergyman willing to do so. The effect of the Resolutions of Convocation was to require the clergy to use this discretion, in all cases, negatively. The bishops of the day, and those since, whether they accepted the principle behind the Resolutions or not (and some expressly did not), agreed to support the Resolutions in their dioceses; they could exercise strong moral suasion on their clergy, though, again, they could not compel them, nor proceed against them formally if they chose to act upon a liberty allowed them by the law. The policy was successful, in the sense that it achieved the end intended; and it undoubtedly had the support of the majority of the clergy. It is seldom now that a divorced person is married in church in the lifetime of a former spouse; and the belief has often been expressed that this discipline has been "of great value

---

[1] Resolution 40.   [2] Resolution 11.
[3] *Acts of the Convocations of Canterbury and York* (S.P.C.K. 1961), p. 61.

as witnessing to Christ's teaching about the lifelong nature of marriage".[1]

12 The statistics for England and Wales afford no evidence of any direct effect of such witness on the incidence of divorce: after achieving a post-war low level figure of 28,542 petitions for divorce in 1960, petitions climbed steadily and with increasing rapidity to 55,007 in 1968, a figure higher than any yet reported, even in the high peak period after the Second World War, and one which is no longer explicable as being relative only to the larger and longer-living married population. The rise is now absolute.

13 The question raised in Convocation, in October 1967, and referred to this Commission, is, therefore, part of a debate which has actively engaged the Church of England for the last hundred years. It goes still further back.[2] In his book *Divorce and Remarriage in Anglicanism* (Macmillan 1958) Dr A. R. Winnett traced two main theological traditions which have persisted in the Church of England since the Reformation: he calls them the "indissolubilist" and "non-indissolubilist" respectively. The one denies the theological possibility of a divorce *a vinculo matrimonii* (from the bond of matrimony), and so denies also the possibility of remarriage to the divorced; the other would permit, theologically, remarriage after divorce on the ground of the Matthaean exception and, for some theologians, on the ground of desertion as well. Both traditions have continued into the twentieth century: the Resolutions of Convocation and of the Lambeth Conferences which we have quoted represent the ascendency, in two generations, of one view over the other; a subsequent generation is not absolved from its duty of examining afresh both their theological and historical presuppositions and their practical effects.

Church and State

14 The ambiguity of the theological tradition had only a very limited opportunity to express itself in practice until after the enactment of the first Matrimonial Causes Act in 1857, because practice was controlled by what the law allowed, and until 1857 the law of England in this respect was virtually that of the canon law of the medieval Western Church. At the Reformation the Church of England

---

[1] *Lambeth Conference 1948*, Resolution 92, pt. 1, p. 49.
[2] See Appendix 3, pp. 113f below.

inherited from the Church of Rome the doctrine of the strict indissolubility of a marriage between two baptized persons, validly
solemnized and consummated. In practice the Reformers had never
seen this doctrine worked out in its full rigour, because of the widespread practice of granting decrees of nullity. The prohibited degrees
of kindred and affinity were much more extensive in the pre-Triden-
tine Roman Church than they are now; they were multiplied by the
addition of spiritual relationships, entered into by baptism, so that
sponsorship at holy baptism—that is, acting as a godparent—set up a
pattern of prohibited degrees between the two families as though
they were related by kindred and affinity. It followed from this, first,
that it was difficult in small urban or village communities to marry
with any degree of certainty that the marriage was not within one of
the many prohibited degrees; secondly, that if there should arise a
need or wish to secure release from a marriage so made, a search
could probably discover a ground for its nullity. The Reformers cut
back the prohibited degrees to what they regarded as scriptural proportion—to the table formerly annexed to the Book of Common
Prayer.[1] In doing so they left themselves with the strictest doctrine of
marriage in Christendom, and without the means by which its rigour
had formerly been mitigated in practice. The utmost relief that the
courts could allow was (apart from a decree of nullity for a very
limited range of causes) separation *a mensa et thoro* (from bed and
board), a relief which carried with it a prohibition of marriage
during the lifetime of either spouse. Resort to the High Court of
Parliament after the prosecution of a successful suit for separation
in the ecclesiastical court, and other proceedings for what was in
effect a dispensation from this prohibition by a private Act of
Parliament enabled some 317 wealthy and powerful persons to
marry again, between the close of the seventeenth century and the
middle of the nineteenth. These marriages could have been solemnized,
as things then were, in no other way than with the rites of the Church.

15 The motion in Canterbury Convocation, therefore, to reopen this
question of the discipline of the Church concerning those who have
had marriages dissolved in a manner permitted by the statute law must
be seen as the contemporary stirring of a debate—not an academic
debate only, but one with consequences of profound personal importance to those involved—which is as old as the English Reformation,

[1] A revised table, promulgated by the Convocations in Canon B 31, has now replaced
the old one, and is to be exhibited in churches.

and which has its roots in the Western Church from which the Church of England derived. It may not properly be dismissed as another challenge of "permissiveness" to the Church, a mere provocation to jettison established moral standards or to betray eternal truths.[1] Neither may it properly be said that the Church is being dragged along, lamely and complacently, at the heels of the State, accommodating its "ideals" to the requirements of the new law of divorce. The whole history of the matrimonial and divorce jurisdiction of this country has been wrought out in engagement between Church and State, and no doubt it will continue to be so. For it is precisely in the engagement of the Church and the world that the Church is made aware of, and called to, its multiple duty. This duty is so to witness to the truth of the gospel as to minister healing and restoration, forgiveness and re-creation to the needs of fallen man. Theology is not wrought in a vacuum; neither are complex personal situations—which are in fact moral problems personally embodied—resolved by the application of simple formulas, however "orthodox" in letter and intent.

16 The Church of England does not stand alone in this inquiry. In a second book, *The Church and Divorce; A Factual Survey* (Mowbray 1968), Dr Winnett carried his inquiry forward from the close of his first to the eve of the 1968 Lambeth Conference. Again he had to report the continuing double tradition, throughout the Anglican Communion. On the one side there are Anglican Churches normally excluding divorced persons from remarriage in church, but admitting them, in varying manners, to the Holy Communion and to the holding of lay office in the churches. On the other side he reports other Anglican Churches which had provided, or were in the process of providing, for a discretionary admission of some such persons to remarriage in church, after procedures designed to assure that their intentions, in such a subsequent marriage, are those of a lifelong and exclusive union which alone the Church regards as the intention of God as confirmed by Christ.[2]

17 The Protestant Episcopal Church in the U.S.A. has, since 1946,

---

[1] The same charge was refuted over three centuries ago by John Milton when he wrote: "Not that licence, and levity, and unconsented breach of faith should herein be countenanced, but that some conscionable and tender pity might be had of those who have unwarily, in a thing they never practised before, made themselves the bondmen of a luckless and helpless matrimony" (*The Doctrine and Discipline of Divorce*, Book I, Preface).

[2] Particulars and details of these developments, for example, in Canada and New Zealand, are to be found in Appendix 7, pp. 152f below.

operated not only a canon on divorce but also a canon based on an "extension of nullity"[1]—an approach not dissimilar to that which it is thought has the most probable immediate future in the development of Roman Catholic thinking and practice. This extension of nullity would imply that in many cases where it had been assumed that a marriage existed, because the canonical formalities had been observed, it would be possible to assume that there had not been sufficient mutual giving towards a *consortium totius vitae* (a sharing of the whole of life) and therefore no marriage, and no impediment to a further marriage with the rites of the Church.

18 There is a growing ferment in the Roman Catholic Church on the subject of divorce and remarriage and a dissatisfaction with its present practice based on nullity. This was evidenced by interventions at the Second Vatican Council, and it is shown not only by popular books such as that of M. West and R. Francis, *Scandal in the Assembly* (William Heinemann, Pan Books 1970), but also by more scholarly studies like that of V. J. Pospishill, *Divorce and Remarriage; Towards a New Catholic Teaching* (Burns and Oates 1967). The doctrine and discipline of marriage are under keen and lively discussion by theologians, canonists, and moral theologians, and many fresh ideas are being formulated.[2]

19 The Churches of the Reformation, and the Evangelical Churches which originated in the eighteenth century, have, in general, not followed the strictly indissolubilist line of the late medieval Western Church, preferring to guide themselves by rules derived from the scriptural treatment of the Matthaean exception and the Pauline privilege,[3] and to distinguish, though not universally, between the "innocent" and the "guilty" partner. Here too developments parallel to those elsewhere can be seen. While the conscience of ministers is safeguarded in the Free Churches, remarriage of divorced persons in church is generally permitted subject to inquiries and considerations of a pastoral character. The Church of Scotland has given the whole question prolonged consideration and published more than one valuable report on the subject.[4] Reference is made to these facts in

---

[1] Winnett, *The Church and Divorce*, pp. 40f.
[2] Volumes of *The Jurist* (January 1970), *Concilium* (May 1970), and the *Heythrop Journal* (July 1970) have been concerned with these themes. See particularly an article in the latter by G. Vass, s.j., "Divorce and Remarriage in the Light of Recent Publications".
[3] See Appendix 1, pp. 79f below.
[4] For example, *Church of Scotland Report of the Special Committee on Remarriage of Divorced Persons (1957).*

Appendix 7. Thus the Church of England has not been alone in considering the subject afresh.

Underlying Questions

20 The inquiry must go behind the particulars of the Church's discipline to its understanding of the nature of marriage itself. The necessity of this may cause surprise. Is not the nature of marriage fully understood? Has it not been clarified once and for all, at least for Christians, in the word of Jesus confirming God's creative word in Genesis? Does not the Book of Common Prayer declare it in its preamble to the marriage service, and, even more definitely, in the affirmations and vows exchanged and in the prayers? Can it not be seen, persuasively, in the lives of happily married Christian people and in their families? The answer to all these questions is, in a sense, Yes; yet the questions remain. The society in which we live has been overtaken by rapid and extensive changes, scientific, social, cultural, economic, technical, which, though they may not have affected the inner core of the marriage relationship, have affected profoundly the outward living of it.

21 The full meaning of this relationship will be discussed later in this report. Here it is enough merely to indicate two examples of the changes which, in this generation, prompt people to ask such questions, as What is marriage? Why marry?, and which oblige the Church at the present time to respect such inquiries and to answer them. First, the widespread acceptance and use of contraception and the trend to dissociate sexual intercourse from conception have had important psychological effects. These require consideration of the relation of sexuality to marriage. The Church may, at the end of the inquiry, confirm its traditional teaching that the full physical expression of sexuality is properly confined within a heterosexual marital relationship; it must nevertheless undertake the inquiry, and it should inevitably dispel some erroneous notions, and so remove some unnecessary burdens, as it does so. Secondly, the social revolution following upon industrialization, and the prevalence of the urban economy and the urban way of life, have an inevitable effect on the nature of family obligations, on relationships within the family, and on the shape, structure, and quality of family life. It was, in one sense, one of the major achievements of the Victorian age that it

could identify the Christian family structure with its own characteristic social product. A price was paid for that identification; and it
left a later age with the task of discriminating in discussion between
something essentially Christian and something which is socially
grounded. This task too has to be attempted. Our health requires the
exercise; without it, there can be no true conversation between the
generations, no mutuality between those who incline to the security
of what they have known and those who stretch out for a freedom in
which they aspire to live.

22 This is no new exercise for the Church. This generation has no cause
for self-pity, or for pride, in what it has to undertake. The perennial
task of Christian theology is to interpret God and the things of God
to every generation of men and, in so doing, to interpret men to
themselves, to help them to find their identity, their place, their
purpose, in their own time. Theology is thus wrought out, as
Jacob's understanding was, in a wrestling with the powers encountered in the way, with the culture given in every age. Flight from this
task is apostasy, whether the flight be into unconcern with the slow
movements or convulsive changes of the world, or into a facile,
proud, or comforting identification of the Church of this age with
that of an earlier age—even of the earliest, the missionary Church of
the Apostles in the Graeco-Roman Empire. There we must look for
their testimony to Jesus, for their record of what the Incarnate Lord
was and did to them, and for all men, on earth. But fidelity to their
witness, and to him to whom they witnessed, binds us not to copy but
to reason; to reason morally, pastorally, and as a Church together,
about the testimony to which Jesus calls us in our own generation. It
is as a small contribution to this task that this report is written and
offered to the Church.

2
Marriage as Relationship

23 A statement on the Christian doctrine of marriage must relate the given Christian revelation to the actual situations in which people find themselves. Theology is the articulation of our response to the word of God, and of our awareness of his grace. This response is made in the context of our contemporary problems and experience; yet man's experience, both of life and of grace, is older than ours, and our own is partly shaped by what has gone before.

24 In the present situation in England, which is often described as one of widespread secularization, there is a strong inclination to regard marriage as simply a descriptive term covering a large variety of different relationships, "estates of life", or merely contractual obligations, which have in themselves no right or wrong about them. But this would be gravely mistaken, for it would suggest that the name "Christian" would mark off Christian marriage from all other forms of marriage. It would deny recognition to the secular reality of marriage as an almost universal way of life for men and women; and it would thereby suggest that the providence and purposes of God cannot be discerned within the natural world. Christians experience marriage "in the Lord" and its true nature and meaning are for them expressed in Christian terms; but this is not to deny in any way the reality of marriage among those outside the Christian Church. Matrimony, in the words of the Prayer Book, is "to be honourable among all men". Testimony must be given to the plain fact that Christian insights and the experienced reality of being "in Christ" have transformed the lives of married Christians. But, on the other hand, there is no such entity as "Christian marriage", except in the sense of the marriage of Christian men and women. God is generous in bestowing grace, and he does not confine his gifts within the Christian dispensation, and so what matrimony is may sometimes be as clearly seen in a non-Christian marriage as in a Christian one.

25 It is natural that this should be a time when people are asking radical questions about marriage. The new freedom of men and women to experiment tends to make them look afresh at old and well-tried relationships and institutions. Is marriage a way of life no longer suited to, or necessary for, most men and women? Is it possible to adventure into new and more flexible forms of relationship between the sexes? There is need for Christians to look again at their own insights into the true nature of marriage, and into the way in which it meets so many universal human needs.

26 Some needs have changed. In our present culture marriage is not strictly essential either to safeguard the status of women or to protect them economically. As these and other social and economic necessities recede, the inner needs of people become prominent and demand attention. These include the proper ordering and realization of the sexual potential of both sexes, the maturation of their personalities, and the full development of their children. Through these marriage contributes to the well-being of society as a whole and to the continuity of culture.

The Needs which Marriage Meets

Sexual Fulfilment

27 Marriage is the normal means for the maturing of adult sexuality. Its success can be marred by human frailty and by negative attitudes. It is a commonplace that the powerful sexual drive can not only express the highest and noblest feelings of mutual love and affection but can also be the vehicle (within as well as outside marriage) of greed, domination, indifference, hate, and most of the other destructive attitudes of mankind. There may be one-sided exploitation or, more commonly, a subtle mutual exploitation in which partners treat each other as things rather than as persons.

28 In the past there has been a strong tradition within Christian thinking which, despite the positive nature of biblical insights, has tended to regard the sexual act as sinful in itself. The feelings of guilt and fear which in all cultures are apt to be associated with sexuality may have been society's protection against the anxiety of being overwhelmed by something powerful and uncontrollable. Both in reaction against such feelings and in haste to liberate sex from the negative attitudes of the more immediate past, there has been a tendency to go to the other extreme. Tendencies to exalt within, before, and outside marriage, the purely physical aspect of sex, with its sensation of exquisite pleasure and bodily satisfaction, may be encouraged by the mass media and by cheap contraceptives. In fact, the humanizing of sex, that which distinguishes it from animal mating, is the realization and insistence that the physical relationship is properly part of a wider one involving the whole person, including feelings, imagination, reason, and will. In erotic love as, for instance, it is celebrated in the poetry of the Song of Songs in the Bible and in Christian poetry of love, all of these faculties are to be found.

29 It is precisely this regard for the dignity of the whole person that distinguishes human behaviour and prevents it from being reduced to that of "brute beasts that have no understanding", to which reference is made in the old Prayer Book service: their mating is different from man's, not because it is "bestial" in the modern, derogatory, sense of the word, but because it is "without understanding" of the totality of the human erotic encounter. It is in this inclusive sense that sexual love has its proper and honoured place in the Jewish and Christian tradition; its rejection has been a feature of dualistic or materialistic interpretations of life which were, in origin, neither Jewish nor Christian.

30 To remain human man cannot rest content with mere excitation. If human beings treat sexual encounter as merely the opportunity for sensation, however vivid and pleasurable it may be, they are thereby surrendering their humanity. For it is a characteristic of human beings that they are persons for whom the deepest personal relationships are expressed by physical means.[1] Indeed the revulsion felt by some young people against the whole institution of marriage and the tendency in favour of less well-defined sexual liaisons may not be simply a reaction against the impersonal structures of modern society, but, more specifically, a protest against loveless unions seen in their homes and elsewhere, in which sex is devoid of affection or personal significance.

31 Sexual experience then, for human beings, can never be just a physical experience; it is laden with meaning. It may express lust, or fear, or

---

[1] Conversely some of these more profound aspects of relationship cannot be realized without physical expression. See Appendix 4, pp. 126f below.

domination, or much else; but it can also symbolize and express the complete committing of one human being to another. So understood, its function may constructively be compared with the function of the Christian sacraments. Part of the description of a sacrament in the Prayer Book Catechism is "an outward and visible sign of an inward and spiritual grace given". Both in Christian life and in married life, the role of a specific physical action is to express and enact the spiritual reality. Without the spiritual, the meaning of the physical is distorted; without the physical, the spiritual may be hard to apprehend. The sacramental character of Christian belief is very comprehensive. Those who believe that God himself was made flesh in a physical body, and that his presence is made known to his people through material things, should find it congruous that in his providence it is likewise a physical action which within the total relationship of marriage most fully effects and expresses the union of two human beings.

32 Once the sexual act is recognized as the means of declaring the deepest and most complete personal exchange of love, its significance can best be experienced and expressed in a lifelong commitment. Without this it has the potential to wound either or both partners, as, for example, by arousing expectations of love without the capacity or the intention of fulfilling them. Even if this does not happen, the act itself is misused because it is made to express less than it fully symbolizes, and so it is prevented from effecting what it naturally signifies. Within this total commitment (total, that is, within the capabilities of both partners) it can strengthen and enhance the very relationship which it expresses. Within the union of marriage it can release for the spouses unexpected reserves of energy, cure the inner loneliness of each, confirm and enhance their sexual identity.

33 Thus man and wife can become "one flesh", one organism, as it were, belonging to one another in such a way that without each other they are less than themselves. The biblical phrase "one flesh" expresses a social and relational unit; in personal terms this does not mean that they lose their identities, or that the one becomes a copy of the other, but rather that they complement each other: each needs the other to be himself or herself, and when divided from each other they are divided from themselves. This relationship is not easy to realize within the institution of matrimony and marriages vary greatly in the degree to which it is attained.

34 It is sometimes said that this unity in duality is "biological" in nature, as though there were created a new physical organism. Within the union of marriage two very ordinary people, who are neither mature saints nor great lovers, can become so much part of one another, physically, emotionally, and intellectually, that to separate them seems to be a kind of amputation; but to claim "biological" union is to misinterpret and misuse a biblical image. The phrase "one flesh", although it had sexual overtones, probably originally described the new social unity that marriage effected.[1] In one Pauline use of the phrase the sexual side seems to have predominated. In 1 Cor. 6.16–17, St Paul wrote:

Know ye not that he which is joined to an harlot is one body? For two, saith he, shall be one flesh. But he that is joined unto the Lord is one spirit.

But it is very doubtful if there is any question here of a "biological" union. On the contrary, there is a contrast between the transitory and merely sexual union of a man with a harlot and the abiding spiritual union of a Christian with Christ as one of his members. In Eph. 5.31f the same text from Genesis concerning husband and wife is cited: "They two shall be one flesh". The main point of this citation, however, is to point to the indissoluble unity between Christ and his Church, which elsewhere in Pauline thought is frequently spoken of as his body.

35 This mystery of union in duality in marriage is illuminated by, and itself illuminates, the divine mystery of how God is present and works in man. Theologians have wrestled with ways of understanding and expressing how man's will can be free and yet man be assisted by the grace of God. It has baffled direct logical expression, and requires a variety of languages for the exploration of a known and experienced reality; so too with the union of two married persons. A further parallel may even be made with the central mysteries of the Christian faith, classically expressed in the formulas of Christ as "two natures in one person", and of the Trinity as "three Persons and one God", two phrases also attempting to express mysteries of coinherence.[2]

Maturation of Personality

36 Marriage, as has been pointed out, is also one of the central means through which the continuation of the development of the personality occurs. In order to understand this more fully a deeper analysis of

---

[1] Cf. Appendix 1, pp. 79f below.   [2] See Appendix 4, pp. 127–8 below.

human development in terms of a dynamic psychology is required. Human growth is a complex phenomenon which can be succinctly described as a process of gradual separation between child and parents. The closeness of mother and child, which takes its origin in the processes of reproduction and nurturing, is a basic fact of human experience. When this closeness is denied, broken, or harshly interrupted in infancy and childhood without adequate replacement, it can have gravely damaging effects.

37 In the intimacy of the attachment between child and mother, and a little later on between itself and both parents, the child learns the meaning of trust and security as well as experiencing the feelings of being wanted and appreciated. These, in short, are the foundations of self-esteem. Trust, acceptance, the ability to give and to receive, gradual independence combined with security, are all acquired in this first intimate relationship whose single and most important feature is permanency. It is in the secure permanency of the parent–child relationship that the child can slowly emerge and discover himself or herself as a separate person.

38 In the course of development every person will also experience conflict, ambivalence, the capacity to feel love and anger towards the same person, envy and admiration, jealousy and hostility. Alienation is, to a greater or lesser degree, an inevitable part of the process of becoming mature. It reaches its culmination in adolescence when the young men or women have to detach themselves from their parents. After an interval of a few years, necessary to discover and confirm their separate identity, they will be ready to form a reattachment, and after courtship to enter into marriage which is the second and only other comparable intimate close relationship in life. Marriage seen in this way does not only provide the means of sustaining a couple through their various needs but also acts as a stimulus for continuous growth of their personalities as well as furnishing, in the intimacy of the sexual relationship, the means of repairing the wounds or compensating the defects of the first relationship of childhood. If healing and growth are to be promoted in this way through marriage, then the husband–wife relationship needs permanency through mature life as the child–parent relationship needs it through childhood.

39 Permanency offers three characteristics present in the child–parent relationship and equally in the husband–wife relationship. First of all

B

it offers continuity. Both types of relationship have to face the problems of conflict, aggression, and alienation, which are the other side
of the coin of harmony, unity, and love. Only continuity allows the
resolution of conflict through forgiveness and reparation and, when
necessary, adaptation and change to avoid further conflict. Secondly,
it provides reliability. All intimate closeness is threatened by the
anxiety of loss, of being abandoned. Marriage can hardly continue
without some degree of reliability. Finally, to continuity and reliability, predictability must be added. This quality ensures that the
couples live their lives on the basis of the experiences which they have
shared together, forming foundations of predictable behaviour for
the future.

40 Marriage, considered not merely sexually, but also in its psychological aspects, can meet the deepest human needs because it
contains the basic ingredients of a relationship within which each
partner can discover himself or herself through the other, and each
can offer to the other the opportunity for healing and growth on
the basis of progressive mutual completion.

Children

41 The resultant fulfilment and stability of the husband and wife is not
only important for themselves but is also vital for the maturing of
their children. Evidence has accumulated in recent decades which
strongly suggests that those who lack the appropriate parental love
usually emerge from childhood with a limited capacity for relationship. By the time they reach twenty most children have been able to
progress from total dependency to separate identity; and those who
do not are frequently found to have a disturbed parental background.
A child requires sufficient self-esteem and self-acceptance to develop
normally to maturity. For this the secure love and affection of parents
is most important. Lack of parental stability in particular makes it
difficult for a child to achieve self-identification within his or her
sexual role. For these reasons a stable husband–wife relationship is
of vital importance to the development of a child's personality.[1]

42 The well-being of children is given early emphasis in the purposes
of marriage set out in the Book of Common Prayer, "First, It was
ordained for the procreation of children, to be brought up in the

---

[1] See Appendix 6, pp. 142f.

fear and nurture of the Lord, and to the praise of his holy name".[1] In the previous discussion the unitive aspect of marriage has been considered as primary, since it provides the necessary background for the provisions of procreation and education of children. Certainly if the development of marriage is traced from the mating of primates to the holy estate of matrimony, the continuance and well-being of the species has been the most obvious factor in forming the drives towards copulation and parenthood. But as the species evolved, so there emerged the primacy of the personal. The point is well put in the Encyclical *Humanae vitae*:

> Marriage, then, is far from being the effect of chance or the result of the blind evolution of natural forces. It is in reality the wide and provident institution of God the Creator, whose purpose was to establish in man his loving design. As a consequence, husband and wife, through that mutual gift of themselves, which is specific and exclusive to them alone, develop that union of two persons in which they perfect one another, in order to co-operate with God in the generation and education of new lives.[2]

The biological drive towards reproduction is satisfied functionally in the process of begetting, conception, and birth. Thereafter the care and nurture of the child becomes primarily a social process, involving (in ways differing in different cultures) the family group, and chiefly, in Western culture, the father and mother themselves. In Christian doctrine nurture is as important as procreation, because man is created for fellowship, and, as his true end, for fellowship with God. The primacy of the personal is particularly emphasized in the teaching of Jesus. When he spoke of the nature of matrimony, he is not recorded as speaking of the duty of parenthood; in his day it was regarded as the prime duty of every male to produce an heir. What Jesus stressed in his quotation from Genesis was the unitive nature of matrimony: "They two shall become one flesh". The leading desire, therefore, of a man and a woman to live their lives together, while it issues biologically in the procreation of their children, issues also socially in the creation of that unity of persons which gives the children the security which they need for personal growth.

43 Love itself is creative. Two people deeply in love normally want to have children. They need to give to others as well as to each other. Looked at from one point of view, the need can be seen as an urge implanted in the species through the process of evolution. But this

[1] Book of Common Prayer, The Form of Solemnization of Matrimony.
[2] Section 8.

urge is also expressive of profound theological principle. God has given to his creatures a share in his creative activity. In those beings in whom moral consciousness has evolved, this task should become a matter of responsible stewardship. The relationship of love and creation takes us into the very mystery of the Divine Being himself. The doctrine of the Trinity symbolizes God's inner being and self-sufficient perfection, and from it proceeds the doctrine of the creation, symbolizing the overflowing of his love into the creation of beings which can share in his life. For this to mean anything, one must be able to say that God has a life of his own to share, that love exists, not only in its creative activity, but in its own right. God in his essence is in one sense unknown to us, for human beings know God through his actions; but his concern for his universe is only one aspect of the mystery of his being. So also in marriage parenthood forms only a part in the whole series of relationships. Human fatherhood is an image of the fatherhood of God, and the relation of children to their parents is parallel to that between the children of God and their Father in heaven "of whom every family in heaven and earth is named" (Eph. 3.15).[1]

44 There is a natural pleasure in fertility. Today, however, the well-being of the species seems to demand the curtailment rather than the encouragement of the drive towards parenthood. The introduction of a degree of "death control" without a corresponding degree of "birth control" is producing an ecological imbalance which is potentially disastrous. The bishops of the Anglican Communion have already articulated the moral obligation of parents to regulate births by means acceptable to the husband and wife.[2] Contraception, however, is only one aspect of man's increasing control over the reproductive process. Medical technology is likely to open up many other new possibilities in the future in this sphere. These new discoveries need to be used with thought for the meaning of marriage and the dignity of man.[3] Most of these techniques seem directed towards increasing fertility rather than to limiting it; and although much is now written about contraception, both within and outside marriage, the Registrar General's statistics show that the number of illegitimate births has considerably increased over the last few years, a trend that may be checked by widespread abortion. Perhaps

[1] See Appendix 4, p. 130 below.
[2] *The Lambeth Conference 1968*, Resolution 115.
[3] See *Human Reproduction* (British Council of Churches 1962).

publicity accorded to new techniques, rather than the techniques themselves, encourages a trivializing attitude towards sex. Whatever new medical advances hold in store, in the foreseeable future children naturally conceived and born are likely to remain a characteristic of marriage. Christians have understood this relationship of parenthood not only as a parable of divine mysteries but as part of the providence of God. "Be fruitful and multiply" does not signify an unlimited licence to procreate large families and so "overfill" the earth, nor does it imply that a couple have the right to as many children as they desire for themselves. But the command does assert the fundamental goodness and propriety of the ordinary means of human reproduction.

45 There are marriages firmly based but without children, some from choice, some despite strong desire. The choice of childlessness may be prudential, for reasons of health; it may be vocational, in the interest of freedom for some life of particular service incompatible with parenthood; it may be temperamental, springing from a feeling, not necessarily reliable, in both partners of a rooted unsuitability to rear children; it may be merely casual, a day-to-day procrastination while lesser ends are pursued or lesser freedoms enjoyed. The discernment of motives in such matters is for the persons themselves; the pastoral office is to help them in their judgement, not to make it. Granted the inner connection between marital love, commitment, and creativity, the natural expectation is that the refusal of parenthood, rather than its acceptance, would require the strongest reasons for its justification. Persons entering upon marriage are right to assume an intention of parenthood on both sides, unless the circumstances are very special. A refusal of parenthood by one partner, against the wish of the other, must subject their marriage to the severest of strains. Christians ought, for themselves, to make all such decisions as part of their life of prayer and of pursuit of the guidance of God.

Marriage as a Natural State

46 Marriage and the family provide the appropriate milieu for meeting the fundamental needs of men and women as individuals, as couples, and as parents who are responsible for the physical, emotional, social, and spiritual requirements of their children. What is true for married partners and for children is true also for society as a whole. The

emotional and psychic health of all citizens, whether they be adult or
adolescent or as yet only children, is a matter of vital concern for
society. Marriage with its natural concomitant, the family, is a
necessary part of the structure of society, giving cohesion to the
formation of community.

47 These are the empirical reasons why marriage meets the deepest
needs of humanity. Speaking from faith one can see it as part of
God's plan and purpose for humanity. God has acted throughout
the natural sequence of events which has moulded the nature and
being of *homo sapiens,* so that for most people the need for marriage
is built into their being. Marriage is God's gracious gift to meet the
needs of men and women whom he has created. The mutuality of
man and woman and their mutual dependence is given theological
expression in the second chapter of Genesis;

And the rib, which the Lord God had taken from man, made he a woman,
and brought her unto the man. And Adam said, This is now bone of my
bones and flesh of my flesh; she shall be called Woman, because she was
taken out of Man. Therefore shall a man leave his father and his mother,
and shall cleave unto his wife; and they shall be one flesh (Gen. 2.22–4).

The same theological point is made more allusively in the previous
chapter of Genesis:

So God created man in his own image, in the image of God created he
him: male and female created he them (Gen. 1.27).

As Jesus said, "From the beginning of the creation God made them
male and female" (Mark 10.6). For this reason marriage was instituted, in the words of the *Homily of the State of Matrimony,*[1] so
that "man and woman should live lawfully in a perpetual friendly
fellowship".

48 There have been times in the history of the Church when marriage
has been regarded as a second-best option; and there are some words
of St Paul (1 Cor. 7.8) which have been taken to support this.[2] The
Scriptures do not assert that the unmarried state is inherently superior
to the married. But St Paul is not lightly to be dismissed, as sometimes he is, in an age impatient with negative judgements upon
sexual fulfilment. "The present distress" (1 Cor. 7. 26) is always with
us in the sense that, until God's new creation replaces this present,
deeply disordered one, there are always situations calling for service
so totally demanding that it excludes the possibility of commitment
to marriage at the same time. Those who choose to accept the free-

---

[1] See B.C.P., Article xxxv.   [2] See Appendix 2, pp. 96f below.

dom of the unmarried state in order to give themselves to these demands are rightly honoured in Christian tradition; the world has indeed known God through their service.

49 The Prayer Book phrase speaks of marriage as not only "instituted of God", but as "instituted of God in the time of man's innocency". This additional phrase expresses the faith that marriage is part of God's fundamental purpose for man, and that, though it is affected by sin, as is the whole of human life, it is not to be understood only as a remedy for sin. There can be about it something of the innocence depicted in the garden of Eden, a hint of the glory which belongs to the marriage of the Lamb. The primary factor in marriage should be the desire of the couple to be together and to be known to be together, and the union of the couple recapitulates the unity of all nature in the will of God. In fact, marriage could be expounded as a form of worship with its own sacramental expression;[1] and worship here signifies not self-abasing praise but the expression of adoration, wonder, and love.

50 The gaiety and joy of marriage have been better described by the poet and the novelist than by the theologian. This aspect of marriage by its nature is and remains a mystery, pointing towards the ultimate mystery of goodness and joy in participating in life as a child of God, and summing up all the goodness and joy of creation. In this connection it is irrelevant whether "romantic love" did or did not become closely associated with marriage until the Middle Ages, or whether a marriage has taken place without the couple concerned having already fallen in love. In the first place, romantic love is not necessarily to be equated with that gaiety and joy which is the proper expression of married chastity; and, in the second place, even in prearranged marriages, the quality of "blessedness" has often emerged after the marriage has taken place even when the "hint of glory" was absent in the beginning. What matters is that it should be there, for it invests marriage with a heavenly splendour and a primary worth.

51 This quality is splendidly recognized in the Jewish tradition with its traditional *Seven Blessings of the Bride and Bridegroom*:

Blessed art thou, O Lord, King of the Universe, who hast created everything to thy glory . . . who causest the bride and bridegroom to rejoice . . . who hast created joy and gladness, bridegroom and bride, love and fellowship, delight and pleasure, peace and unity. . . .

[1] See para. 31 above; also Appendix 4, pp. 128–9 below.

Within Christianity the exuberant joy expressed in the marriage liturgies of the Orthodox Churches witnesses to the same truth.[1] Indeed it may be said that in the Eastern Churches mutual devotion is the only adequate cause of matrimony.

The Realization of Marriage

52 It is one thing to describe the possibilities inherent in marriage; it is another thing to experience their realization. Marriages vary between the heights and the depths, or they may just go on going on. There is a tremendous range of possibilities between two married people, from joy and ecstasy to deadening and boring dreariness, or sheer misery. Love may turn to hate, faith may turn to mistrust, hope may become despair. Marriage can be a foretaste of heaven or an anticipation of hell. For many it can be more like a purgatory; for some it may be a mere remedy against fornication. There is no need to spell out the bitterness, disillusion, and pain of some marriages. That has been done in fiction and is all too well known in fact. There is no easy theological interpretation of distressing marital disaster any more than there is of profound marital fulfilment. Christians, however, are bound to look for some key to an understanding in two things central to the Christian faith: the cross of Christ and the vision of God. On the one hand, a marriage fulfilled gives some kind of foretaste of our final union with God, but that very fulfilment will almost certainly be costly in terms of suffering and sacrifice. On the other a miserable marriage is painful, but even the pain need not be sheer waste. No one comes to God without needy hands, and the vision of God may come through a life of painful self-sacrifice; there is no resurrection without death. Both happy and unhappy marriages must know "death" in this sense. And by God's grace no one is barred from sharing in resurrection. A doctrine of marriage must be adequate to encompass the depths as well as the heights of union; it must be able to interpret the whole range of possibilities within the marriage relationship.

53 The vows are unconditional: "for better for worse, for richer for poorer, in sickness and in health . . . till death us do part".[2] They envisage possibilities as wide as life itself. It is because of life's catastrophes as well as its joys that the partners need "the mutual

---

[1] See Appendix 3, pp. 113f below.
[2] See Appendix 5, pp. 131f below.

society, help and comfort that the one ought to have of the other, both in prosperity and in adversity". Sin and selfishness can ruin any human relationship, particularly one so close, intimate, and exclusive as marriage. If it is true that people cannot really know what unselfishness is like until they are married, precisely the same can be said of selfishness.

54 More frequent perhaps even than the failures due to sin and selfishness are the miseries which arise from an interior inadequacy on the part of one or both partners. It is a comparatively common experience among married couples that, on account of childhood privation, or distortion of personal relationships, or for other causes, a spouse finds himself incapable, through no fault of his own, of making the kind of response to his partner that is desired. The degree of incapacity, and so of frustration, can vary very greatly; and it may call for the exercise of great compassion. In particular, those who suffer from various kinds of psychological disorder may find that these greatly hinder them in making the kind of marital relationship that they want and hope to make; indeed, they may prevent the establishment of any stable marital relationship at all. There are some who have offered and exposed their love and loyalty again and again in their marriage and found it trampled upon. There are others who have not been able to give love and loyalty; or, if they have, their partner has not been able to respond. The shorthand description of this may be "incompatibility". The cross displays what happens when love incarnate offers and exposes himself to the world. One form of suffering may be to find that one has no love to offer, or when he does offer it, to find that his partner is unable, through interior incapacity, to respond. Hazards to marriage, whether sexual, temperamental, or environmental in origin, may not always be discovered before the wedding, even though the couple enter upon their union not "unadvisedly, lightly or wantonly", but, "reverently, discreetly . . . and in the fear of God".[1] There are some for whom marriage has meant and does mean ravaged lives, years of unhappiness, suffered both by the partners and by their offspring, unhealed wounds of frustration and quarrelling and hate. Both those whose marriage relationships have been ruined by sin and selfishness and those whose marital miseries arise, through no fault of their own, from interior inadequacies, are victims of what St Paul called *sarx*.

[1] Book of Common Prayer, The Form of Solemnization of Matrimony.

For I know that in me (that is, in my flesh), dwelleth no good thing: for to will is present with me; but how to perform that which is good I find not. For the good that I would I do not: but the evil which I would not, that I do (Rom. 7.18–19).

Sarx is inadequately rendered "the flesh" or "the lower nature". To live *kata sarka* ("after the flesh") is to be subject to all the frailties to which man is prone: distortion, disease, weakness, sensuality, sin, and death. For those caught in the toils of *sarx* marital suffering may seem insupportable.

55 This leads to critical questions. Which is the more important, the institution of marriage or the welfare of the two people concerned? To what extent are people called upon to endure what seems to be unendurable? How, in such circumstances, can the institution of marriage best be strengthened as well as the welfare of the two people promoted? To these problems we return in our final chapter. At this point we need to look at certain characteristics of relationship, without which marriage as it arises in human nature cannot exist, namely exclusiveness, commitment, and permanency.

The Characteristics of Marriage

Exclusiveness

56 The question arises as to precisely how exclusive this relationship is. The marriage promise speaks of "forsaking all other, keep thee only unto her, so long as ye both shall live". What does *all other* mean in this context? What does *only unto her* mean? And why is there one single condition to the total exclusiveness of this relation, *so long as ye both shall live*? Before examining the notion of exclusiveness, we first ask: Why this single but important exception?

57 According to the teaching of Jesus, there is no marrying or giving in marriage after this life, but human beings become *isangeloi*, like angels.[1] In the Jewish tradition angels are neuter, and it may be therefore that Jesus, by the use of this phrase, was implying that there is no sexual differentiation in the resurrection life. In our present experience we have physical bodies, and physical closeness brings sexual awareness. But in so far as the body is a part of the total reality of man it shares in whatever is promised to man in the

[1] See Appendix 2, pp. 96f below.

resurrection. In one sense therefore the marriage also ends at death—but not the relationship of the two people who are married. The conditions of life after death are unknown to us, and we can only speculate. The whole Christian tradition has thought of the life of heaven as that of a communion of love in which the relationships of this world have become universalized without losing their specific character. If this be so, then marriage may be seen as a sign pointing towards this more universal relationship between persons after death. To use more sacramental language, "the consecration of a part marks the destiny of the whole", so that the unique relationship between partners is not destroyed by death. It still remains, but it is no longer exclusive. It points to the ultimate destiny of all relationships. So marriage may be called "holy" because two people are set apart to signify a relationship which will hereafter become universal.

58 If the exclusiveness of marriage is modified by its restriction to this life, what are the limits to its exclusiveness within this life itself? One aspect of marital exclusiveness is found in the operation of incest taboos. Marriage must be exclusive of incest. In the Church of England the prohibited degrees are set out, in revised form in "A Table of Kindred and Affinity", to be found in Canon B 31; and all marriages purported to be made within these degrees are void. The origin of incest taboos is lost in prehistory. The only such taboo which seems universal is the prohibition of sexual relations between mother and son. A ban on sexual relations between brother and sister is nearly universal (although there are puzzling exceptions) but father–daughter relations, although usually disapproved, are not always considered to be heinous. Sex relations with other more distant kin are also usually forbidden but the pattern of extension beyond the boundaries of the elementary family shows great variation between different cultures. The original cause of these taboos is a matter of debate among anthropologists. Much is now known about the way in which diseases may be transmitted through dominant and recessive genes; and some think that incest rules represent a "folk knowledge" of the fact that in-breeding can be deleterious. If so, it remains obscure why these rules should be so varied. In any event efficient contraception means that a total ban on incestuous relations is no longer justifiable solely for this reason. Another view is that incestuous behaviour interrupts family solidarity. In the report of the Archbishop's Commission on *Kindred and Affinity as Impediments* *to Marriage*, published in 1940, there was an appendix by Malinowski in which he wrote:

A group leading a joint life with the intimacy of daily concerns, with the need of an organized authority and unselfish devotion, cannot tolerate within its framework the possibility of sexual approaches, for these act as a competitive and disruptive force incompatible with the even tenor and stability of the family.[1]

Such a view does not go uncontested. Some anthropologists hold that the incest taboo, far from prohibiting what men's feelings incline them to do, is on the contrary an expression of what men regard as the natural order. They claim that there is good evidence that the experience of weaning may generate adult feelings of sexual aversion between a son and his mother and that children of opposite sex brought up in close association as infants will be disinclined to engage in sex relations as adults. Other anthropologists find it hard to account for the development of the incest taboo, which is so strong and universal, if feelings of sexual aversion are naturally generated in this way. However, the fact that anthropologists can offer no single agreed explanation for incest prohibitions does not alter the fact that in one form or another such prohibitions are universal. It is not always the case that taboos against sex relations between near kin are exactly coincident with rules relating to the prohibition of marriage, but in our Western culture today the prohibited degrees, as specified in Judaeo-Christian tradition, are commonly held to provide the proper boundaries both for tolerated sex relations and for marriage. In the Bible and in Christian tradition any breach of these rules is strongly condemned and, although the details of the prohibited degrees vary as between one society and another, the universality of an incest taboo has to be recognized. Even though this universality cannot be satisfactorily explained, its existence must be respected.

59 How exclusive should marriage be of other relationships? Since there may be a sexual element in all relationships, should marriage mean the exclusion of all other close friendships, especially those with the opposite sex? There is a natural complementarity between man and woman, and this expresses itself in various ways which society has developed in order to observe the prudential limits required by the fundamental respect due to persons themselves, but

[1] P. 105.

which are none the less manifestations of gender. Today many of these conventional proprieties are under attack. Nevertheless, it remains true that the nature of the relationship should determine the manner of expression. For example, it has been argued above that there is one mode of expression of sexuality that is proper to marriage, namely the consummation in full physical union. It therefore follows that propriety demands that friendships or contacts between two people of the opposite sex who are not married to each other should not endanger the exclusive relationship of marriage, either by putting one partner under temptation, or by provoking the other to jealousy. Close relationships with others, particularly in the pursuit of a profession, are likely to arise. In a stable marriage relationship there is greater scope (for each partner) in friendships with the opposite sex. For less mature people this could lead to the endangering of the marriage relationship itself.

60 What has been promised at marriage is a mutual and exclusive consent to each other's person, so that "the wife hath not power of her own body, but the husband; and likewise also the husband hath not power of his own body, but the wife" (1 Cor. 7.4). These promises need not be impaired by close friendships of either partner with a third party, so long as they do not affect the close trust and love that each partner is to have for the other. To enjoy the complementarity of man and woman, in whatever mode of expression is proper to a given relationship, is to live as God ordained at creation, provided that the enjoyment is integral to the relationship and subordinated to the general obligation of charity, which is to serve the other's good. Here that good consists in mutual help towards that ripening of character and relationship to which all are called in Christ. Sin may spoil it, as when a lustful glance sees the other not as a person in a relationship, but as a sexual stimulus; but grace may restore it. Human sexuality may be universally affirmed, not by emphasizing only the exclusiveness of the marriage relationship, but by looking outward from marriage upon all men and women in their full humanity and affirming the value of each and all in ways appropriate to the relationship between them. The relationship between husband and wife remains unique and permanent. What at first sight might seem to detract from it in fact confirms it. Here a parallel may be suggested. At first sight the communion of saints might seem to detract from the uniqueness of Christ; but on closer inspection the

doctrine of the communion of saints, far from removing him from
the centre of devotion, only serves to enhance his glory because it is
reflected in the saints who are commemorated. If this is true of the
Bridegroom, so in a different mode it may be true of earthly relationships between married people and friends.

Commitment

61 Although infidelity has always been a risk of marriage itself, it is
also a symptom of the stresses and strains imposed on marriages
whose characteristics have changed substantially as a result of the
social changes of our day. The prolongation of life together with
earlier marriage means that couples can anticipate fifty years or more
of wedlock. Such longevity with the availability of more effective
means of contraception and the reduction in infant mortality means
that a great deal of time and energy has been released for activities
other than those traditionally associated with childbearing and caring
for children. Furthermore, whereas in the past widowhood often
occurred speedily after the departure of the last child from home,
spouses have now the opportunity of a new phase of marriage of
many years after their last child has left them.

62 These changes in longevity and health have been occurring in a
century which has witnessed, at least in the West, other important
changes in the material standards of living, in social mobility, and in
the "emancipation" of women. All this has brought out a rising
standard of expectation in personal fulfilment. Such fulfilment in
marriage is seen less and less as the simple discharge of a contractual
agreement but increasingly as the matching of mutual needs, changing with the various phases of marriage which have to be recognized
and met in an ongoing intimate relationship. Thus marriage, seen
primarily as a relationship, implies a recognition that allowances
must be made for change and growth, which are essential features of
the human personality and which can be dealt with only through a
flexible and dynamic interpersonal relationship.

63 To achieve this end commitment becomes an essential characteristic
of marriage. This is evidenced in the marriage vows and promises
which are made at its inauguration, and which, after centuries of
discussion, are still generally agreed to constitute the marriage:
nuptias consensus non concubitus facit (mutual consent, not intercourse, effects a marriage).

I ... take thee ... to my wedded wife, to have and to hold from this day forward, for better for worse, for richer for poorer, in sickness and in health, to love and to cherish, till death us do part ...

Apart from the limitation of death, the commitment is absolute. The spelling out of some possibilities implies the acceptance of all; only an unreserved vow meets the requirements of a total commitment. The words mean more than timeless affirmation of an existential experience. They are expressed in severely temporal language, *from this day forward*. A commitment that is limited to depth and does not extend in time is far less than total. That is why there is a need between lovers to vow eternal fidelity, and that is why a couple find strength in articulating, within a formal setting, the promises which spell out their unreserved and mutual self-commitment.

64 What does this commitment imply? It is not merely a matter of emotion; and, although it contains intellectual elements (for example, it can be apprehended), it affects the personality at a far deeper level than the intellect. There is a structure of commitment between husband and wife which deepens and ripens as the marriage matures. There is obedience, fidelity, companionship, affection, passion, and a determination of the will to seek the good of the beloved. It is the combination of all these that makes it possible for one to promise to *continue* to love the other, stimulating the mind, firing the imagination, and stirring the will. There is a parallel between marital and religious commitment, so that they mutually illuminate one another.[1] A marriage based only on emotion is as precarious as a religion based only on feelings. A marriage of mere convenience is as defective as a religion which consists only of conventional obligation. Just as there is a whole structure of commitment in matrimony, so too religious commitment has its own structure of constancy, fidelity, dependency, and love. It is significant that in the Bible the word used for God's relationship with Israel, *b'rith*, covenant, is also used of the institution of marriage.

65 Within this structure of commitment are faith, love, and hope. Husband and wife characteristically accept each other as they are. Their faith in each other's regard for them is not based on their own worth or right, but on the other's acceptance of them just as they are. It is hard to think of any other relationship (except perhaps within a religious community) where acceptance could be so unreserved, and,

[1] See Appendix 4, pp. 128–9 below.

because unreserved, so productive of mutual health and growth. Parents often find it hard to accept their children as adult; they continue to think of them as children. Similarly, children often find it hard to establish an adult relationship with their parents. Friends can know each other intimately, but differently from husband and wife. A married partner, who shares intimately in all life, can know the other's failings and frailties as well as his virtues and value. People need to forgive and to be forgiven; they need to love and to be loved; they need to accept and to be accepted. Here, theologically speaking, is a reflection of the central Christian truth of justification through faith.[1] It is because God through Christ has accepted us just as we are that we can begin to accept ourselves; and, because we can accept ourselves, we can begin to be the kind of people whom God calls us to be. It is because God has forgiven what we have been and accepted what we are, that he can make us what he wills us to be. Since life is not an even progression but a succession of fresh starts from different starting places, our response to God's acceptance of us recurs again and again. It is the same in marriage.

66 It is characteristic of marriage that one partner should believe in the other. A couple planning to marry cannot know what marriage will be like until they marry. This is true even if they have anticipated their marriage sexually; for the circumstances differ from those of marriage itself. When two people marry they venture into the unknown, as in an act of religious faith. They do not before marriage know each other as husband and wife, but they know enough about each other to make this venture. This is a reflection, after its different mode, of man's faith in God. No man has seen God at any time. But he can know enough about him to make an act of faith, and in his commitment he can verify his faith in a way which he could never anticipate before. Yet faith is itself a form of knowledge, the mode appropriate to God. God can never be proved; he can only be known through faith. There is a parallel here to the relationship between husband and wife. This too can never be proved; it can, however, be verified and deepened by continuing commitment.

67 If faith is characteristic of matrimony, so too is love. This love is experienced as a gift. The experience cannot be exhaustively explained merely in terms of chemical changes in the blood. When two people deeply love one another, they feel that they are bound together

[1] See Appendix 4, pp. 126f below.

by something which, though it may by others be described in reduc-
tionist terms, they know as an insight into the very nature of reality.[1]
It is through human love, and especially the love that issues in marriage and which ripens within marriage, that many people come to
experience and to acknowledge the reality of the love of God. There
is a distinction to be made between *agape*—self-giving love—and *eros*
—passionate yearning and involvement—just as there is a distinction
between God and man. But some theologians have tended to make
the distinction absolute and to deny to God any quality of *eros* and
to natural man a capacity for *agape*. God's love, like human love, is
experienced as a gift; it is received not as a right but as a grace; and
since God is love, human love gives us an insight into the nature of
God.

68 Love and faith project themselves into the future as hope. Hope is
certainly a characteristic of marriage. Where it is alive, the partners
are seized by the conviction that what they give to and receive from
each other in the present they will continue to give and receive in the
future, and that their relationship will deepen and grow. "Journeys
end in lovers' meeting." This is a reflection of Christian hope, for on
the basis of faith in what God is doing, and of love that is a response
to God's love, Christians dare to hope that their relationship with
God may be deepened and made permanent through all eternity.

Permanency

69 It has been shown how permanency fits in with the psychological
requirements of a personal relationship. Permanency as a characteristic of marriage has been clearly stated in Christian tradition. For
example, Canon B 30 of the canon law of the Church of England
states:

The Church of England affirms, according to our Lord's teaching, that
marriage is in its nature a union permanent and lifelong. . . .

It is evident, surveying the wreckage and breakdown of many marriages, that they have died without attaining their full nature; and
a similar tragedy is seen in those loveless unions which still retain the
outward formalities of marriage, but which can no longer in any
personal sense be designated unions of husband and wife. A married
couple can be parted from one another relationally, just as a brother
can be parted in this way from his sister or from any member

[1] See Appendix 2, pp. 96f below.

of the family with whom his relationship has irretrievably broken down. The couple will always remain people who have been married to one another; nothing can alter that fact, just as nothing can alter the facts of family kinship. Final marriage breakdown is precisely what occurs when two people who have been validly married (something that is a fact) suffer a complete and irretrievable dissolution of their matrimonial relationship (something which is no less a fact).

70 Despite marriage breakdown the permanence of marriage is a part of its true "nature"; and Christians are not concerned to assert that their marriages alone are and must be permanent, but rather that they have been given a true insight into the nature of all marriage. A marriage which grows and deepens so that it attains fully to its nature, "becomes what it is", a lifelong union. Just as it is possible for any organism to wither and die before it has grown into its full nature, so too marriage may break down before it has grown into what it should become. This does not mean that marriage is not permanent in nature, only that a particular marriage has failed to attain the fullness of that nature.

71 Various theological concepts have been used to express this insight into marriage. A word long used in Eastern and Western thought has been sacrament. This was given conciliar definition in the Council of Trent, and although marriage is not included as a dominical sacrament in the Thirty-nine Articles (nor, by implication, in the Church Catechism), yet the language remains popular and not without reason. A sacrament is God's instrument for leading men to holiness; rightly received, it is a sure and certain means of grace; both these things may be said of marriage. Sacraments are signs of Christ, ways of partaking in his death and rising; and so, for Christians, is marriage. Sacraments witness to the permanence and unchangeability of Christ's relationship with his Church. They rest on God's promise, and they are irrevocable because he has made them secure. Since sacraments signify what they represent, the sacrament of marriage, if this language is used, signifies the marriage of the Church as the Bride of Christ.

72 These truths, associated with the concept of marriage as a sacrament, explain why sacramental language is often retained. Yet the Tridentine doctrine of marriage as a sacrament has not been accepted by the Church of England; and for good reasons. Christians may be assisted by grace towards the perfection of life to which their marriage tends, but it is not always possible by empirical observation to discriminate *in kind* between the marriages of those who are baptized and those of the unbaptized. Marriage stands in the order of nature: grace perfects it. In the marriages of those who are baptized into Christ's dying and rising, a new way of response to God is opened up. This response brings with it into the life of the partners a series of human dimensions of motive, support, effort, and sacrifice, all of which are elements in this life of response to God and in which grace is vitally involved. This new possibility, which opens up within marriage, does not necessarily imply that mutual consent in the marriage of the baptized effects something which is wholly lacking for the unbaptized. The doctrine that mutual consent by two baptized persons of itself involves the creation of an indivisible *vinculum* or bond (in contrast to the unions of the unbaptized) is not biblical; nor is it a tradition of the universal Church; nor does it accord with the empirical evidence of matrimonial breakdown. If marriage be in this sense a sacrament, it hardly fits in with the typical structure of sacramental language. Marriage belongs to the order of creation rather than that of redemption. Acceptance of marriage as a sacramental reality, welcome because of the verities which this language can imply, has been accompanied among many Anglicans by a very profound unease about its definition as one of the seven sacraments. Among the implications of the doctrine is the belief that the "secondary" sacrament of matrimony can only be for those who have received the "primary" sacrament of baptism. To this must be contrasted the view which some hold that, since solemnization of matrimony exhibits the true nature of marriage and helps people to make it their own, it could be, in certain circumstances, available for those who are not baptized. The main objection to the Tridentine doctrine of marriage, however, is that it forecloses the question of indissolubility. If this question is to be critically examined, a return to the original sources becomes necessary, and that means a return to the New Testament.

73 The New Testament evidence is considered in some detail elsewhere.[1] Here, it must be emphasized that "a return to the New Testament" is not a simple procedure. It is certainly not a case simply of turning to passages in which such words as "marriage" and "divorce" are

---

[1] Appendix 1, pp. 79f and Appendix 2, pp. 96f below.

mentioned, and finding in those passages definitive and self-evident rulings. On the contrary, the Church must ask, and continue to ask, while time endures, what those passages *mean*, both in themselves and in the context of all that the New Testament gives us to know of the nature of God. The final and definitive "meaning" of passages in Scripture can never be attained, nor are the words of the New Testament self-evidently and timelessly clear, precisely because they cannot be abstracted from their temporal and spatial context, any more than the life of Jesus can be abstracted from *its* context.[1] Thus, although to some it seems to be the case that Jesus affirmed the indissolubility of marriage in such sayings as "What God hath joined together, let not man put asunder", and, "Whosoever shall put away his wife, and marry another, committeth adultery against her", the fact remains that this is not the only possible, or the only defensible, meaning of these texts. Equally, there is no doubt that what Jesus is recorded as having taught about marriage and divorce, and what he demanded of his followers as the standards of marriage, left them amazed. This is not to say, however, that he meant that marriage cannot be dissolved, or that in every conceivable circumstance it would be wrong to remarry. The fact that there can be much genuine uncertainty and disagreement among biblical exegetes on these points is of profound theological importance. It is a direct consequence of the way in which God reveals himself to the world in the realities of time and space. Scripture, equally, is offered to us as a means of grace in the conditions in which we are. Argument about the meaning of Scripture is a necessary consequence of the reality of incarnation. But equally, of course, the fact must be emphasized that Christian decisions *are* made, and that the process through which they are made is a part of the work and meaning of the Church. The point is that this is a persistent and living process, in which the resources of Christian theological meaning, in both Scripture and tradition, are kept constantly in relation to particular empirical circumstances; and in a sense the very existence of this Commission and its report is an example of this process.

74 In the context of this quest for meaning it is clear that marriage is of central importance in some New Testament passages, both in its own right, and as an insight into divine reality. In Eph. 5.31 the author cites Gen. 2.23: "For this cause shall a man leave his father and mother, and shall be joined unto his wife, and they two shall

[1] See Appendix 2, pp. 96f below.

become one flesh." The writer adds *to mustērion mega estin*, "this is a great mystery". These words were translated in the Vulgate, *sacramentum hoc magnum est* (this sacrament is great). Marriage is a sacrament, not in the later scholastic language of the Middle Ages, but in the sense in which it is described in the Epistle to the Ephesians. It is a sign of the relationship of Christ to his Church. As in marriage two people become one, so too Christ is permanently united to his Church. The two, although separable in thought, are so inseparably united that Christ loves the Church as his own body, of which Christians are actually members. The union within marriage is a mystery which is profound; yet even more profound is the relationship of Christ to his Church. The word translated as "mystery" in English, and as *sacramentum* in Latin, does not mean mystery or sacrament in the modern sense of either word. In the New Testament it normally signifies a secret which was formerly hidden but now has been revealed. The vocation of the married is to reveal a symbol or sign of the irrevocability, as well as the graciousness, of Christ's relationship to his Church. The one reality can illuminate the other; but both remain mysteries in the more ordinary sense that they can neither of them be fully comprehended or exhaustively defined.

75 If members of the Church of England are to continue to regard marriage as sacramental, it seems likely that they will use the phrase with the overtones of Eph. 5.32 rather than in the Tridentine sense; and in so doing they will be in line with Orthodox theology.[1] It is possible, however, that those who are unaccustomed to such a theological framework will prefer to use other terminology. It is to be noted that the documents of Vatican II have substituted the word *foedus*, covenant, for contract.[2] Marriage is much more than a contractual relationship. It is an "estate" or status of two people, and not only an agreement made between them. In English legal usage the two parties contract to marry, and marriage is the fulfilment of the contract, and not the contract itself. Part of the meaning of *sacramentum* was an oath or commitment, and the marriage service speaks in covenantal terms of "the vow and covenant betwixt them made". The word covenant is biblical, for the union between Yahweh and Israel in the Old Testament is depicted in terms of the marriage covenant, in which Yahweh remains faithful to Israel despite her unfaithfulness, and Israel continues to be subject to the demands as well as to the benefits of her divine partner.

[1] Cf. Appendix 2, pp. 96f below.   [2] *Gaudium et Spes*, section 48.

76 Whatever be the terminology, the essential meaning is the same. But the imagery of Ephesians 5, although it reveals profound insights into the nature of marriage, also contains elements which appear according to the common interpretation not to be essential to its fundamental meaning. Christ as the bridegroom is not only to "love" the Church, he gives himself for it, sanctifying and cleansing it. He nourishes and cleanses it. He is the head of the Church, as a husband is head of the bride. The bride is to "obey" him and to "fear" him. Wives are to be subject to their husbands "in everything".[1]

77 Nowadays in the West the conditions of women's lives are significantly different from those of the first century. Their social, economic, and educational subordination has been much alleviated. Contraception has set them free from unceasing child-bearing and child-rearing; and the process of emancipation continues. Yet, however far it goes or should go, there remains a real difference between masculinity and femininity. Does this difference imply a measure of subordination?

78 When St Paul affirmed that in Christ "there is neither male nor female" (Gal. 3.28) he was not abolishing natural distinctions, but rather he was testifying that gender is irrelevant to salvation. The Apostle seems to have realized that social conventions played a part as, for example, in the matter of women's hair. The question at issue now is whether the relationship between the sexes is purely a matter of convention and culture, or whether it has its basis in the nature of men and women: whether, for example, it is simply custom that decrees in our culture that a man shall normally invite a woman to marry him. According to Genesis, one of the results of the Fall is that a woman's "desire shall be to her husband" (Gen. 3.16); but even if it were clear what this phrase means, would it necessarily imply subordination?

79 Such questions are easier to pose than to answer. It is dangerous in these matters to generalize. Many women still wish to promise to "obey" their husbands, although by such a promise they seldom seem to imply an unconditional or literal obedience. Perhaps some are acknowledging a need for security which arises from their nature. Others, however, feel that difference of function in no way includes subordination and prefer to take the same vows as their husbands. In the Western world today there are such varieties of temperament and

[1] See Appendix 2, pp. 96f below.

differences of culture that it is difficult to distinguish in these matters what is contingent from what is essential. The mystery of Ephesians 5 is developed in terms of the relations between husband and wife as generally accepted within the social context in which the Epistle was written, and within the theological context of our all being subject to one another in Christ. What is certainly true in the argument is that the Church is subordinate to Christ. Whether subordination or complementarity belongs to the nature of the marital union remains an open question. It is in the fact of the union that the essence of the mystery lies—and about that there is no question at all.

The Single State

80 The use of the image of matrimony to illuminate the relationship between Christ and his Church could suggest that it is only through the experience of marriage that the mystery may be apprehended. This inference must be resisted. Marriage is, without question, the vocation of the great majority. But there are those who, for a wide variety of reasons, remain unmarried; and some do so voluntarily. In the Christian tradition there have always been men and women who have renounced the right to marriage in order to give themselves wholly to the service of the kingdom of God. This way of following Christ is rooted in sayings in the Gospels, and its value is assumed in other parts of the New Testament. Positively understood, it can be seen as a sign, however fragile, of man's final fulfilment beyond this world, pointing towards that universal relationship of love which is pictured in the parables of the Heavenly Kingdom and the Royal Banquet.

81 In Christian thought and experience there are close parallels between this way of dedicated single life and the way of marriage. In both cases it is affirmed that man's whole life can be consecrated to God in faithfulness and love. In both the value of permanent human relationships is underlined; for though the great majority of unmarried people do not take vows, the vows of religious life, where these are undertaken, also involve lifelong commitments. The religious community, which such vows safeguard, provides much of the continuity, reliability, and challenge, which are such an essential part of marriage. Without taking vows many other unmarried people find in the permanence of their dedication to their work, particularly work with

people, a similar element of continuity and reality. In the marriage of Christians the relationship of husband and wife is grounded in the relationship of both to God in Christ. In the religious community the primary relationship to God is worked out and made incarnate in the human relationships of the common life. And, whether living in community or not, the unmarried Christian finds, in his or her relationships with married friends and their families, a complementarity of role and function which seems to have a God-given quality about it. Although apparently opposed, the two ways in Christ support and illuminate one another.

Marriage in Church

82 Those who are aware that God calls them to marriage will wish their matrimony to be "holy", because they will want to offer to God their life in its wholeness, including their marriage. Many others, for less conscious and explicit reasons, will also want a church wedding in all sincerity. The occasion calls for an appropriate rite, a sacral occasion suited to the significance of the step that is being taken. The symbolism that forms part of the service has deep significance for those concerned. The wedding is celebrated in a building set apart for the worship of God, and this in itself signifies a further dimension to the marriage. It symbolizes the demands being made upon the couple, and the resources of grace which can assist and complement human effort. This aids the realization that more than human aid is required for the perfecting of persons, whether they be married or single. In church the bride and bridegroom receive the blessing of God, and they are surrounded usually by the prayer and good wishes of families and friends, and so marriage is set in its social as well as in its theological context. During the service they are reminded of Christ's presence at the wedding in Cana of Galilee, and they are thereby recalled to the unseen presence experienced in the married lives of all those who are "in Christ". A church wedding not only draws attention to the true nature of marriage but also makes explicit some of its distinctively Christian characteristics.

83 As has been said earlier, the ideal of marriage is often in violent contrast to the actual marriages of individuals. Christians suffer the same stresses and problems in their marriages as other people—problems often not the result of sin—but their faith will give them more

resources to overcome these and enable them to see their difficulties in a different perspective. Grace does not change nature, but it can perfect it. Pope Pius XI in *Casti connubii*, speaking of marriage in its wider sense as a complete and intimate life-partnership and association, regards as "the primary cause and reason of matrimony" what he calls "this mutual interior formation of husband and wife, this persevering endeavour to bring each other to the state of perfection".[1] Marriage is a process of character formation which prepares man for his final end, so that he may attain "to agreement in the faith and knowledge of God and to ripeness and perfectness of age in Christ", and finally share in heaven in the marriage feast of the Lamb. For those who are in Christ all life is lived in him, and he is their strength and inspiration whatever their vocation may be. In Christ all life is offered to God for his service and his glory, and all life enhanced through his blessing. "This spirit suffuses their whole lives with faith, hope, and charity. Thus they increasingly advance their own perfection, as well as their mutual sanctification, and hence contribute jointly to the glory of God."[2]

84 The state of matrimony is particularly apt for this end, not only because its proper foundation is itself love and hope, but also because it serves in so many ways as a model and mirror of divine realities. The mystery of marriage and the mystery of grace continually illuminate each other. Marriage becomes not only a model of grace but also a means of grace,[3] leading a partner towards that maturity which is his goal, so that he may attain to "the measure of the stature of the fullness of Christ".

85 As the couple share together in prayer for one another, in public worship and in the Holy Communion their marriage may not only be strengthened but also transfigured by the light of God. Christian partners have open to them through prayer the divine resources of grace. As the Homily on Matrimony puts it,

> Married persons must apply their minds in most earnest wise to concord, and must crave continually of God the help of his holy Spirit, so to rule their hearts and to knit their minds together, that they be not dissevered by any division or discord.[4]

God's grace does not only apply to "happy" or "successful" marriages. Christian marriage may be as much a school of unselfishness as a source of joy, as much a locus for pain and dereliction as a

---

[1] Section 24.   [2] *Gaudium et Spes*, section 48.
[3] See Appendix 4, pp. 126–8 below.   [4] *of the State of Matrimony*.

fountain of happiness and exaltation. For most people it is a relationship in which their inner inadequacies may be faced and overcome. In fact it is rare for any two people to share their lives without some degree of distress or suffering, through which the personality may be cleansed and purified in the journey towards perfection and maturity. But marriage may still be a means of grace, even in the darkest hour of helplessness, despair, and defeat, when a man or woman comes to a fresh realization of the meaning of the cross before passing through and beyond it to the experience of the "risen" life in Christ. It is not through some idealization of matrimony, but in the full day-to-day reality of two people's lives that Christian insight can bring fresh realization of what marriage is, and by so doing make available to the couple concerned the richness of God's grace.

3
The Institution of Marriage

86 In the previous chapter an attempt has been made to explore marriage in terms of a relationship experienced by the partners. It is hard, indeed impossible, to draw a line at which marriage becomes also an institution. Rather one must say that it is an institution in as much as the relationship is viewed from the social or public aspect. The marriage relationship itself creates other relationships, those between the couple and their children, and those between the couple and their families, neighbours, friends—even relationships (though of a different sort) between them and the public authorities such as H.M. Inspector of Taxes or the local Electoral Registration Officer who integrate them in various ways into public life. "Marriage in particular with its tendency to produce children becomes social not in spite of itself but characteristically";[1] and this characteristic "society" forms itself in a complex pattern of relationships as the married couple live as a "sociable" unit, taken and accepted as man and wife together, within their neighbourhood and circle of contacts. They acquire roles, in relation to one another, and in relation to those about them—husband or wife, father or mother, host or hostess, and so on. As such they create or accept—sometimes one, sometimes the other, in varying proportion—rituals, styles of living, which express both the personality of each partner and the duality of their marriage. Marriage, a "relationship", has imperceptibly but inevitably become an "institution". As such it is of significance to both Church and State.

87 On an historical view the distribution of interest between Church and State has varied in different ages. It was only after five to ten centuries of the Christian era that the Church "moved in" to marriage in an authoritative way, first liturgically, then juridically. In the high Middle Ages the Church and its canon law had control, as against the State and the royal law, over matrimonial and family life, except

[1] See "Marriage and Grace", an article by Helen Oppenheimer in *Theology* (December 1969).

over questions of land tenure and the inheritance of titles and property. In later times the balance has been redressed, leaving the Church with a mixed juridical and liturgical function in the solemnizing of matrimony, and with an undiminished pastoral responsibility and opportunity, both in the solemnization of marriage and towards those living the married life. Because this transfer of effective interest, which has taken place largely for social and economic reasons, has occurred during a century or so of a heightened Church self-consciousness, Christians sometimes speak resentfully of it, and of the State as an intruder into what is properly a "Church" sphere of influence. So, while there has been in the nation a mounting impatience with the Church and its attitude to divorce and to divorced persons, there has been little articulated opinion against the Church's concern with marriage as such. It is from the Church side, on the contrary, that such questions are asked as "Ought marriage to be independent of the State? What right has the State to intervene in marriage, for example, to limit the number of children?" An examination of these questions might serve as a model exercise in which the interrelation of the personal and the institutional factors in marriage may be more clearly demonstrated, and with it the interrelation of interests of the Church with those of the State.

Personal and Institutional Factors

88 The questions are in fact ambiguous. They may refer to the contracting of marriage or to the conduct of the matrimonial life, or to both. Both will therefore be treated in turn, but only after some preliminary reflections on the nature of marriage itself. The peculiar contribution of the Western, Judaeo-Christian, tradition has been to emphasize the personal character of the marital relationship. Canon law, which in turn influenced the common and statute law of England, insisted on freedom of personal consent. So strongly had this personal emphasis in marriage pervaded Christian thinking by the nineteenth century that strong conflicts arose when Christian missionaries, carrying this emphasis overseas, encountered cultures in which the emphasis was primarily corporate, where marriage was primarily an alliance of two families in the persons of two of their respective members. This corporate emphasis was symbolized in various ways in the traditional rites of marriage, and it had practical significance in the distribution of *lobola* or bride-wealth throughout the families, returnable in the event of ill-treatment or divorce, thus giving the families an interest in supporting or preserving the marriage-bond. This conflict continues to disturb Christian Churches in such societies, particularly when a sense of the worth of indigenous customs is being recovered.[1]

89 Another, though negative, expression of this personal emphasis in the West arose in the attitude to divorce. Many of the economic and social functions of the household and the family have now passed outside it, some few to the State, others to the network of economic, social, and educational systems of our developed society. Marriage has therefore come to be thought of, less in terms of its function, what it is for, than in terms of what it is. Thus many people have felt that, child-rearing apart, the only bond left to the married pair is their personal bond, the affection which they bear for one another and its modes of expression within marriage. If this bond fails, then there is "irretrievable breakdown" of the marriage; there is no reason why it should not be dissolved, for it is without social function either. The modern practice of divorce and legislation for it have arisen directly out of the development of this personal factor.

90 For all its richness, the personal factor cannot be the only consideration. Society, as well as the parties, has an interest in marriage. In simple terms, the day-to-day conduct of life in society, its ethics, rests on common expectations, and there must be some minimal certainties. It is necessary, for social purposes, to know who is to be accounted married to whom at any given time; without this knowledge intolerable personal and social conflicts could arise. The rearing of children rests now on a sort of partnership between the parents on the one side and the organs of political society on the other. The present debates on comprehensive education derive their vigour and their importance from the cultural power—to advance or to retard —exerted over children by the family milieu in which they are reared. In the days of extensive medical, educational, and social services, and of State-guaranteed insurance for provision in old age, the number of children born is of significance to the State; as is the knowledge of who are their parents, who share responsibility for them. This is manifestly true in the developed nations; its truth has yet to be realized, and translated into effective action, in the less

[1] See *Report of the All-Africa Seminar on The Christian Home and Family Life, Mindolo, 1963* (Geneva, 1963, World Council of Churches).

developed areas where the acceleration of population is not matched
by economic and social advance, and where, in some countries, there
is as yet no systematic registration of births.

91 It would follow that there is an important social interest in both the
contracting of marriage and in the conduct of matrimonial life. It is
the function of the State to give this interest adequate protection,
where necessary by legislation. Problems arise when legislation seeks
to do justice to this social interest without intruding too far upon the
personal interest of the spouses. When does State intervention
become a violation of essential personal relationships? Are there any
absolutes which are clearly inviolable? Such questions follow directly
from the nature of marriage and the nature of society; this generation
suffers no peculiar hardship in having to answer them.

The Role of the State

92 In our present plural society in Britain provision is already made for
valid marriages to take place within the context of the rites of
religions other than Christian. For such a marriage to be valid,
provided that the required notice or notices have been given and
authorities issued, it is only necessary that the parties to the marriage
should at some time in the ceremony speak the words of declaration
and contract laid down in section 44 of the Marriage Act of 1949 in
the presence of each other, of the witnesses, and of either a registrar
of marriages or an authorized person for the building, which must
itself be registered for marriages. In the United Kingdom, therefore,
one law of marriage applies to all, unlike certain countries of the
Middle East in which the laws of marriage differ according to the
religious community in which the marriage takes place. The State
has a duty to regulate the contracting of marriages. It must, as it
does, establish by legislation what society at a given time recognizes as a valid marriage, and what acts or ceremonies are held
to effect it. So the State sets an age below which marriage may
not be contracted, on the ground that child marriages lack full
personal consent and that they are, in general, personally and socially
harmful. Could this ground of harm be extended to include other
incapacities, for example, known dysgenic factors, known infection
with a communicable venereal disease, or supposedly incurable
diseases, for example, epilepsy, or alcoholism? Here care is needed
to distinguish, first between cases where there can be a certainty of

diagnosis and prognosis and cases where there cannot; and secondly between conditions of themselves inimical to a proper matrimonial life and conditions which can be borne, given the will. At present the law of England strikes a balance; it insists on a full disclosure of hostile factors as a condition of validity—a marriage can be nullified if there is concealment—without forbidding the marriage outright. This hesitation to go further probably rests on an assumption of the right of every adult person to marry if he so wishes and can—a position not reached in England for many centuries, until serfdom, with its restriction upon the right of marriage, disappeared.

93 Hitherto the right of marriage has carried with it the right of parenthood. But these rights are not inseparable. It is conceivable that, with the development of scientific methods of diagnosis and treatment, the right to marry could be upheld while denying the right to parenthood in cases where a serious dysgenic factor could be established with certainty; sterilization would then have to be required as a condition of marriage. At present such certainty does not exist; but probabilities can be calculated, and certainty may come.[1] Beyond this, it is difficult to see how far prescriptive legislation could go. The denial of the right to marry would bring more ill-consequence than the admitting of it. It may be socially desirable, for instance, that only those who are "mature", or "responsible", or economically self-sufficient, should marry; but such requirements can be met (where they can) only by education and diffused social influence, not by prohibitive legislation.

94 How far may the State intrude into the married life, and what are the acceptable ways of intrusion? English law, in its recognition of the married couple as "one person", reflects the Christian understanding of them as—in the biblical phrase—"one flesh"; the English legal phrase is, in many ways, a less misleading expression than our now accepted translation of the biblical one. The law is normally reluctant to intervene between spouses; one is not a compellable witness, for instance, against the other; a decree of nullity or of divorce may be sought only on the petition of either or both the spouses, and not by a third party or by an act of the State. English common lawyers, with general support, would almost certainly resist any prohibitive intervention of the State into marital sexual relationships, as, for instance,

---

[1] See *Sterilization, an Ethical Discussion* (Church Information Office 1962).

to set a minimum or maximum to the number of children in any one family or to enforce contraception, sterilization, or abortion for this purpose. Such legislation would be seen as an improper intrusion upon private rights and personal relationships; it could not be uniformly enforced, and the attempt to enforce it would occasion worse ills.

95 Nevertheless, the State has, and uses, intrusive power by other means. Family allowances were introduced when there was a falling birth-rate in the United Kingdom. If a financial inducement is admitted in principle to encourage a higher birth-rate in time of social need, there is nothing in principle to forbid the cutting off of these allowances if they were found to encourage the procreation of more children than were socially desirable. (In fact their relation to family size has yet to be demonstrated; it is by no means self-evident.) Practical difficulties which arose would be met by other means; provision from some other State purse would be made for necessitous large families; but in principle the State need not encourage more children when population growth appears to be reaching, or to have passed, an optimum.

96 As before, a distinction is to be drawn between persuasion and compulsion to achieve social goals in a way which does not violate the personal integrity of the spouses or their marriage. This is illustrated in the recent Divorce Reform Act 1969, in which the social interest in the reconciling rather than divorcing of estranged spouses is represented in the requirement that the petitioner for divorce on the ground of breakdown of marriage must furnish a legal certificate to the effect that his attention has been drawn to the existence of reconciliation agencies; though he is under no compulsion to avail himself of their services.

97 These considerations all seem to stem from what may loosely be called natural political philosophy, and not from elements peculiar to the Christian tradition. Even the emphasis on the personal character of marriage, and on the necessity for free consent in the contracting of it, though heightened by Christianity, is not peculiar to it, or to Western, Graeco-Roman civilization. In African marriage customs it is difficult to find a case in which the final *consent* of the parties to a marriage could be dispensed with, however strongly the family action in bringing them together and marrying them. Even where degrees of extramarital sexual relationship are permitted, rape, the enforcement of one will upon another, within the group, is universally reprobated. Christian theology, although it contains all the material for a strong emphasis on the social aspect of marriage, has in recent years concentrated on the personal element and the nature of the relationship between the spouses. This emphasis is understandable. Europe has lived through a century marked by aggression by the State against the individual and the small community. Modern science and technology offer the State, potentially, vast power to intrude still further through the mass media and the techniques of persuasion and conditioning. All this alarms the Christian as it must alarm the liberal humanist. Yet the whole pattern of truth, of the personal and of the corporate, has to be affirmed, and affirmed persuasively, in order that it may become embodied in the nation's culture, in its conventions for living. Conventions, grounded in true insights and socially accepted, are society's strongest preservative against intrusive legislation.

The Interests of the State in the Family

98 This analysis, which, so far, has been made in terms of the interest of the State in marriage, could also have been conducted in relation to the family. Many during the last two or three decades have tended to speak as if the family were being weakened in British society, if not by the deliberate intent of the State, at least indirectly through the extension of educational and social services which have been said to "undermine" family life by withdrawing from it its characteristic functions. Although this is not the place to rebut this sort of charge by detailed analysis, there is ample evidence against it.[1] The response, for instance, to the problem of juvenile delinquency and want of care has been, for many years, not the authoritarian attitude which this theory would have presupposed, but an attempt to keep a young offender out of the penal and corrective institutions of the State and to help him to grow up properly in his own social environment, and, where possible, in his own family environment, strengthened and supported by social workers trained for the purpose.

99 The argument has led, somewhat empirically and pragmatically, to a view of the State in some respects very near to that expounded by St

[1] Cf. *The Family is not Broken*, G. R. Dunstan (S.C.M. Press 1962); *The Family*, Mary Farmer (Longmans, Green 1970).

Paul. St Paul wrote of the temporal governor as a minister of God ordained for the upholding of the temporal or natural order within which God was to be worshipped, the brother to be loved, and the world to be served redemptively with the service of Christ. Christians, in so far as they were members of that temporal order, were to submit to it, to meet its obligations,[1] and to accept its benefits and protection—as St Paul himself did against the rabble at Corinth and in his appeal to Caesar against the accusations of the Jews. On the other hand, Christians were forbidden to use the instrument of the temporal order—behind which, in the last analysis, stands coercive power—to settle matters which, as a Christian community, they ought to be capable of settling for themselves; they were not to take their disputes for trial before a tribunal of unbelievers (1 Cor. 6).

100 Marriage and the family belong to the natural order. The State may rightly therefore be expected to have jurisdiction over them. It may rightly be expected to support and strengthen them where necessary, partly through the enactment of laws of various sorts, partly through the enabling and fostering of those conventions, voluntary associations, social rituals, and the like, which, in a healthy society, make intrusive law to a large extent unnecessary. The Law, with its provisions, commands, prohibitions, and penalties, is necessary in the temporal order as a safeguard of that order; but the less it is invoked, the better. The present position is rather delicate precisely because there is some impatience with, and suspicion of, conventions, which of their nature speak of the "old", the "traditional"; and, at the same time, there is a determination to restrict and even to reduce the influence of coercive law. From this experiment with freedom new conventions may emerge; but the experiment puts the Church itself to the test by facing it with a question: Is its own provision for the institution of marriage adequate? Are the conventions, the rituals, the symbols in word, association, and gesture, with which it articulates its understanding of marriage, adequate to convey that understanding, and to win the assent of people to it?

Pastoral and Liturgical Considerations

101 In the previous chapter a theology of marriage has been presented, not as handed down and imposed upon men and women from without, but as corresponding to their nature and to the nature of the

[1] Cf. Mark 12.13; Rom. 13.1–3; 1 Pet. 2.13–15.

relationship which they themselves seek in marriage and in which they find their highest earthly good; as a theology, indeed, in which they can find an instrumental symbol of their eternal good. On the occasion of a marriage the pastoral and the liturgical task are one; it is so to articulate this understanding of marriage that the parties themselves can see it, recognize it, take or apprehend it, and willingly form and declare their intention of making it their own, that is, of embodying it in their own marriage. These are the elements of the process called *consensus* (consent) which is expressed in the marriage vow.

102 The pastoral task is thus not mere instruction; it is more properly the bringing into focus of a vision, the enabling of two persons to see clearly, and to make their own, an image which is partly inside them —a creation of their own nascent love—and partly beyond them— something given from God who has from creation brought them as man and woman to be what they are, and to become the man and wife which they would wish to be. Some people need more help in this than others; some need more help than a priest can give; some, perhaps, need help not to marry, or not to make this marriage, at all. At all events, the Church cannot rest content unless it sees its clergy gaining more and more aptitude for this task, both alone and in collaboration with persons with other requisite skills. And the aptitude will not come except with gladness. A Church which would be effective in this ministry must not grudge it, must not succumb to the temptation to make a distinction between the "good church people" who are "within" and those others who are "without". The acceptance of a man and woman, who wish to express the pledging of their love with the ritual and with whatever setting of beauty that the Church has to offer, must be as generous and gracious as that of God himself; it must reflect to them the graciousness of God, his own primeval satisfaction, as it were, in the work of his hands, when he looked on his creation and saw that it was good. To feel rebuffed by the Church or its priests at the time of marriage may be an experience from which, humanly speaking, their confidence will not recover. They are accepted, first of all, as coming to marriage in the natural order, as the bread and the wine are first accepted from the natural order for the eucharistic offering.

103 The liturgical ministry follows upon this and it may be enhanced or prejudiced by the quality of the pastoral ministry as just described.

But a good marriage liturgy is an essential foundation for the pastoral ministry. It is a public document embodying the doctrine, the understanding, the intentions of marriage, which the man and the woman betrothed are to make their own. It has the status of a formulary; any inquiry as to "what the Church of England teaches about marriage", whether from a lay person interested, or from a theologian or lawyer, or from another Church, should be answerable by reference to the marriage liturgy. Yet the words and symbols used must be suited to their primary purpose, which is the celebration of marriage, more than the definition of it. The language must *sound* right, first of all. Upon a strict examination it must be found to carry ascertainable and acceptable meaning; but it cannot be required to make all this meaning plain to any and every casual hearer or reader. It must be the language of symbolism, of worship, not of flat description. It must embody the given truths, and convey them in a way which invites consent. Like everything else in marriage, its roots must remain deep in tradition, in the custom of the people; like the vesture of the minister, it links the action of today, for *this* man and *this* woman in the face of *this* congregation of their friends and neighbours, with those actions of a bygone day which have, by a long descent, brought them this grace and to this grace. It does not follow that the language, or the rite itself, is irreformable; it does follow that any reform must be organic, something evolved out of that which is given and not imposed upon it.

104 At the present time there are two liturgies for marriage authorized in the Church of England (1662 and First Series). In future it will probably be wise to continue this permission for the use of more than one form for the solemnization of matrimony. On the one hand, there is much to be said for a conservative revision, maintaining as far as possible the traditional style and structure of the rite, in order not to deprive people of the familiar elements in the service to which they are most attached. On the other hand, there will certainly be those who wish for more radical reforms, both in language and content. Their convictions should also be respected, and notice should be taken of experimental forms permitted in other Churches. The Book of Common Prayer has, in all its editions, made provision for a celebration of the Holy Communion in connection with the marriage. In future revisions it might be desirable to envisage a closer integration of the two rites, by permitting also the celebration of marriage within the framework of the Eucharist, for use on occasions when it is appropriate, and desired by the couple concerned.

105 The rite or order for the Solemnization of Matrimony (1662) mainly used in the Church of England must now be examined more closely. It has grown into what it is by a process of organic growth, adaptation, and revision, over the whole span of time which has seen the growth of the English Church and nation. It contains, probably, the oldest and longest sequence of middle English phrases and constructions ever occurring in the lives of most people and actually spoken by them. Only the coronation oath and some few oaths sworn upon admission to high judicial or administrative office go back so far in time as the affirmations and vows given to men and women to say at their marriage by the courtesy of their Church. They are not for that reason sacrosanct.[1] But their reform is to be enterprised and taken in hand, as marriage itself is, not unadvisedly, lightly, or wantonly, but reverently, discreetly, soberly, duly considering both the truths to be expressed and the most sensitive manner of their expression.

106 The rubric to the present service, and the priest's opening words, point to society's concern with marriage. It is a personal relationship in which the community has an interest, a part; therefore it must be celebrated, not only before God, but also before friends and neighbours, in the congregation. The assertion that marriage is "honourable", and the subsequent proofs, were necessary at the time of the Reformation, when both teaching and practice had tended rather to indicate the contrary—the teaching, by making of marriage only a second best;[2] the practice, by denying marriage to the clergy and so straining lay credulity and charity. Today the assertion is not less necessary, but for other reasons. The Church must be as the voice of God in saying what is true for all men to all men, that marriage *is* an "honourable estate", a state of life in which the simplest men and women, living in faithful love together into old age, "come to great honour", are "crowned with glory and worship"—a picture, and words, drawn from the Old Testament which has much to teach of covenanted love to those who will allow themselves to see.

---

[1] They contain within themselves evidences of variants and amendments: for example, "with my body I thee worship" (1662) follows the use of Salisbury; "with my body I thee honour" (1928) follows that of Hereford.

[2] John Colet gave that teaching clearly in his exposition of 1 Corinthians 7, *An Exposition of St Paul's First Epistle to the Corinthians*, ed. J. H. Lupton (1874).

107 To say that marriage was "instituted of God in the time of man's innocency" is a way to combat the thought—whether it arises merely from a distorted church tradition or from man's deep feelings of guilt—that marriage is God's afterthought as a remedy for sin. The sense in which marriage is God's gift of a new relationship in which grace may order and fructify our sexual nature has been touched on in an earlier chapter of this report. Perhaps a new form of words is necessary, to relieve those who find difficulty in accommodating the language of poetry to their understanding of man's evolution; perhaps "instituted of God in contemplation of man's innocency" might serve; the substance is important, so therefore is the choice of words.[1]

108 To recall Christ's "presence, and first miracle that he wrought" at the marriage in Cana of Galilee, was perhaps only to offer another proof that marriage is "honourable". But for the Church today it can be more. In other fields of interest much is made today of "the servant Church", meeting man, as Christ did, "in his secularity", at the point of his worldly need. In meeting a man and a woman at their marriage, placing them within the congregation, before the altar, the Church does precisely this. Christ, who by his resurrection became the first-born of the new creation, stands as a divine presence to bless this new union as, in the poetry of Genesis, God was present when Adam took Eve and knew her as his wife. In sacramental language, the man and the woman marrying are a means of grace to the Church as well as to themselves: they create an occasion of Christ's presence to his people, analogous to his presence at Holy Baptism and at the Supper of Holy Communion.

109 The section of the Preface on "the causes for which Matrimony was ordained" is clearly of importance as an expression of intention which the spouses are invited to make and declare to be their own. It requires, therefore, the closest scrutiny. It has been shown in the previous chapter how, biologically considered, procreation *is* the primary purpose of marriage. It was suggested there also that, psychologically considered, that is, looking outward from the mind of the persons coming to be married, their having children together is secondary, derived from their love, their desire to be together. Jesus, too, it was noted, placed this unity of love first, in his recalling the word of Genesis, that the twain shall become one flesh. The Greek

[1] See Chapter 2, p. 25 above.

Orthodox tradition of liturgy and theology[1] has kept the priority of this joyful affirmation of oneness to an extent which must now prompt the Western Church to look at its tradition afresh. Certainly the biological function, in its widest sense, actually requires a primacy of the unitive concept; children need, not simply to be begotten and born, but to be born into a home where the parental relationship is already deepening into that unity, that oneness, which is the primary theological characteristic of marriage. In this oneness, also, the sexual nature may find its full and ordered development—the achievement stated as the second cause of marriage in both the existing services.

110 It is at this point, therefore, that the marriage liturgy requires most serious revision, if it is to represent in words a true understanding of marriage. The language of "cause" may not be the best; it might be better to write in terms of the marks or characteristics of marriage, and to begin—as might well be expected in a Christian liturgy—with that goal or mark of oneness or unity which is both theologically given and psychologically most in accord with the uppermost desire of the spouses and the deepest needs of their children.

111 It has been suggested in Chapter 2 that it is not easy to reconcile the image of Christ and the Church—implying headship over a body— with the relationship of husband and wife conceived, as some now conceive it, as one of two equal persons between whom there is no superiority or subordination. To ask a modern wife to "obey" even a husband who is pledged to love her as Christ loved the Church— that is to die for it—is more than some sensitive priests can do; and certainly there are brides who prefer not to be asked to use the word; the liturgy of 1928 omitted it. Yet equally sensitive and intelligent people, brides as well as clergymen, see something in the old concept: they see that there is a sense in which, as there are occasions when the marriage and the next step for the family turn upon the decision of the husband, he has to take responsibility for the decision. Many believe that, granted this, "obey" is not the right word to express it. Any new word chosen should not attempt to be definitive or descriptive; it should "sound" right and match its context. "Acknowledge" is perhaps such a word.

112 Some people ask why today a bride should be "given away". The ceremony of the giving of the bride in marriage is as old as it is

[1] See Appendix 3, pp. 113f below, and Appendix 4, p. 130 below.

simple. It is one last vestige of the truth, symbolized universally in marriage customs, that marriage is a meeting or alliance of families, not simply of individuals. The symbol of "giving the bride in marriage" can betoken a graceful acknowledgement of this, a "go in peace" and with the family blessing, rather than a mere going away.

113 Christian theology has as much interest in mutuality as in equality; it is more concerned that people should accord together in charity, "high and low, rich and poor, one with another", than that all should be the same. Our marriage service needs a stronger symbol of this mutuality than the not-quite-identical forms of the vows contain. Provision could be made for the giving and receiving of two rings instead of one, a practice for which there is ample precedent in Orthodox and Lutheran Christian practice. It need not be insisted on as one of the declaratory ceremonies required by law; it might be allowed for by rubric for those who see the point and like it.

114 The note of spontaneous joy and gaiety in Orthodox marriage liturgies (and in the Jewish rite) has already been remarked. In the Church of England's authorized marriage services this note is muted or absent; and a remedy is often sought in additions such as hymns, anthems, or voluntaries. Future experimental forms for the Solemnization of Matrimony could also introduce such a note into the liturgy itself, either by borrowing from existing liturgies or by appropriate compilation; but self-conscious or forced compositions in order to promote gaiety would only be contra-suggestive in effect.

115 In the preface to the marriage service and in the prayers there are allusions to the complicated passage in Ephesians 5, in which the marriage of husband and wife and the marriage of Christ and the Church are interwoven. These allusions have a theological importance not immediately apparent to everyone hearing them. They are matched in most of the major Christian liturgies, Eastern and Western, holding them to a common theological anchorage. A disservice would be done to the wider unity of the Church if, for the sake of simplicity, this common ingredient were removed. But a revised form of words might make it more easily intelligible.

116 This chapter has been concerned with marriage as an institution, and with the witness to it, and support given to it, first in the State and then in the Church. The Church has a stewardship of this mystery of marriage, a custody of its truths. In this respect the Church is, so to

speak, the nation, or the village, or two groups of families and friends, acting Godwards; they come together for what is in its essence a natural act, the joining of two of their members in marriage, and enact it before God, assuming that their covenant together co-inheres with his covenant with them and desiring it to be blessed by him. The Church is, in a second sense, the community whose eyes have been opened to what is true for all men. It enshrines, therefore, in its liturgy certain truths about marriage—that it is lifelong, that it is exclusive, that it is a union having stated characteristics and to be accepted as such; and it declares these because it believes them to be true, because to accept them is to go along with the grain of human nature, and to reject them is to cross that grain and so to roughen it. In a third sense the Church has to be sometimes, as it has had to be in history, a voice of witness for these truths even against the nation, against forces, whether in the mind or in the exercise of political or other power, which imperil these truths, or make it excessively difficult for people to perceive them and to live by them. There is an inevitable tension between the Church and society, as well as a natural accord.

4

The Strengthening of Marriage

117 The first chapter of this report sets the context in which it was written. The second chapter studies the meaning of marriage, primarily as a relationship but also in some of its institutional aspects. It is an attempt to move towards a theology of marriage as a divine ordinance. In the third chapter there is an inquiry into its specifically institutional nature, and the part that liturgy plays in exhibiting its meaning.

118 Marriage in England has never been so popular as it is today; more people are marrying, more people are marrying younger, and more widowed and divorced persons are remarrying. If there is agreement with the arguments of the previous chapters, there will also be agreement that ways should be found for the strengthening of marriage. For marriages run into difficulties and there are breakdowns. As a result more and more divorces have been granted.[1] It may seem strange to include in a chapter on the strengthening of marriage a consideration of reliefs that have been afforded to those whose marriages have become intolerable. But in fact such unions, when unrelieved, do not strengthen the institution of marriage at all. On the contrary, they lower marriage in public estimation, and they give the impression that the now empty and outward forms of matrimony must be maintained at the expense of those who are imprisoned within them. Some people suppose that the provision of relief derives from a low view of marriage. Sometimes those who suggest this seem to have little acquaintance with the miseries suffered. The reports of the successive Royal Commissions which have examined the law of marriage and divorce over the past 120 years, and the report of the present Law Commission, which prepared the way for the Divorce Reform Act 1969, afford little evidence that a low view of marriage has prevailed.

119 The State, because family life is important to its citizens, has been active in its attempts to strengthen marriage. The High Court has

---

[1] See Appendix 6, pp. 142f below.

court welfare officers, and the Magistrates' Courts have probation officers, who may assist in marital reconciliation. Grants are given in aid of the work of marriage guidance agencies. Under the Divorce Reform Act 1969 it will not be possible for a petition to be tried until the partners have considered reconciliation and have been informed about the existence of persons qualified to help them. For those who have found the mutual obligations which are embodied in the institution of marriage in this country impossible to fulfil, the State affords relief, of which the new Divorce Reform Act is the latest instance. Contrary to common belief this relief has not altered the State's view of the nature of marriage, for it is made clear to those marrying in register offices that, according to the laws of this land, marriage is a lifelong monogamous union. To use legal language, it is not merely a contract, but a status conferred by contract.

120 The Christian community has its own contributions to make to the strengthening of marriage. This is done not only by teaching and by preaching, but also by the regular and public use of its marriage liturgy, in which the fullness of its doctrine is clearly expressed. It is also brought home through pastoral preparation of people for marriage by the clergy, increasingly carried out with lay assistance. It also requires an exemplary standard of marriage from its clergy who are exhorted at the time of ordination to the priesthood:

that ye may so endeavour yourselves, from time to time, to sanctify the lives of you and yours, and to fashion them after the rule and doctrine of Christ, that ye may be wholesome and godly examples and patterns for the people to follow.[1]

These are some of the positive ways in which the Christian community as a whole, and the Church of England in particular, has sought to strengthen marriage.

121 In the present circumstances more and better preparation is needed for marriage and family life. Attempts to do this, however, may be frustrated without more and deeper knowledge, more readily available, of the nature and causes (both personal and social) of marital and family problems and breakdown. Such knowledge requires research based on practical service.

122 Immigrant families coming to this country are bringing with them ideas, customs, and styles of marriage based on alien cultures and

---

[1] See Appendix 8, pp. 165f below.

non-Christian religions. More knowledge is needed about these. There is a natural tendency to mistrust what is new and alien, but there may be enrichment to be gained. Once more, however, problems are bound to arise, partly because of common marital difficulties, partly as a result of mixed marriages, and partly through the intermingling of differing cultures in a local community. What is needed again is knowledge based on practical work.

123 All this points to the need for an Institute for the Family.[1] There is good reason why the Christian community should undertake the foundation of such an institute in a fully ecumenical way, for the problems are common to all Christians. Such an institute, founded by church initiative, could attract secular co-operation and support, since it would be dealing with matters which concern all men in their family life and which affect the well-being of society. This task invites urgent consideration. It is as vital for the Church, if it is to be true to its theological nature, to be ready to minister to the world, as it is for it to provide a ministry for its own members.

The Medieval View of Indissolubility

124 For many centuries the Church in the West reinforced its doctrine of the permanence of marriage by the idea of a *vinculum* or bond, of its nature "indissoluble". The Roman Catholic Church maintains this position still. This concept calls for examination. At first sight it seems to express what Jesus implied. The most ready interpretation of some of his sayings would appear to imply a doctrine of indissolubility. But in fact a closer examination of the evidence shows that the matter is much more complex.[2] The "Pauline privilege" and the way in which the teaching of Jesus was interpreted in the tradition represented by St Matthew's Gospel form part of the evidence to be explained.

125 There have not been lacking those who have read back the notion of indissolubility into the writings of the early Fathers. On this point the distinguished Roman Catholic scholar, Fr Schillebeeckx, has this to say:

In the scholastic view of marriage which was elaborated in the twelfth and thirteenth centuries the *sacramentum* was not seen purely as a symbol, but as an effective symbol which brought something about—an objective bond

---

[1] See appended note to Appendix 6, pp. 150f below.
[2] See Appendix 1, pp. 79f below.

that could not be broken. According to the church Fathers the dissolution of marriage was not *permissible*; but according to the schoolmen its dissolution was not *possible*.[1]

This distinction is crucial for a right understanding and use of the term indissoluble. The notion of a metaphysical or ontological bond existing independently of any empirical features was satisfactory enough to philosophers and theologians in what is known as the Realist tradition. The difficulty today is to persuade ourselves of the existence of any such bond when everything observable in the relationship and dispositions of the persons concerned points to its non-existence. In other words, we can entertain and accept the idea of a complete breakdown of marriage, and when faced with this the Christian community is driven to determine its pastoral respónse.

126 In fact the medieval Church was forced to do just this. It escaped from the impasse of indissolubility by the use of the expedient of nullity, in conjunction with a flexibility in the definition of competence to marry. Prohibitive degrees of kindred and affinity were extended or narrowed, the validity of previous marriages was impugned, and after the Reformation even Holy Baptism as well, when celebrated in accordance with rites other than its own. Marriages were declared null on the basis of technical defects with at times no relation to the personal reality of the union. There are, of course, occasions where it must properly be said that no true marriage has ever existed, and the decree of nullity gives legal effect to this judgement. This is another matter altogether; and such cases are allowed for in the existing laws of England. But there are those who look for further relief from present difficulties of marriage breakdown by an extension of the use of nullity today. Some would do this on the ground of an alleged defect in the intention to marry. Others deduce from a failure to grow in matrimonial union an incapacity to do so from the beginning; this is an extension from the notion of physical incapacity to consummate into the psychological. Reluctantly, this Commission is unable to see a way forward in either expedient. The whole case was thoroughly examined in *The Church and the Law of Nullity* (1955), the report of a commission appointed in 1949 by the Archbishops of Canterbury and York at the request of the Convocations. The parties to a marriage are and must be presumed to intend the natural interpretation and consequences of their

[1] E. Schillebeeckx, o.p., *Marriage: Secular Reality and Saving Mystery* (Sheed & Ward 1965), II, p. 70.

words and acts. We therefore agree with the conclusion of the Commission:

We are opposed to any extension which could leave the validity of a marriage dependent upon the private stipulations or mental reservations of the parties.[1]

As for psychological non-consummation, two things need to be said. The clergy, in the exercise of their canonical duty to prepare people for marriage (Canon B 30 3), and those who assist them in this task, should do their best to bring such psychological incapacity to light before the marriage has taken place, so that the two people concerned may realize their unsuitability for this union. If, however, the marriage has taken place, the area of uncertainty is too wide to permit the possibility of framing a just and practicable law of nullity on this basis.[2] It would appear that people could never in this life be absolutely certain whether they were married or not. Uncertainty, also, whether their marriage was in law void or merely voidable would leave the legitimate status of their children seriously in question. We are faced, therefore, with the need to find some response to the fact of breakdown, other than the extension of the laws of nullity.

Present Practice in the Church of England

127 Over the last twenty or thirty years there has grown up a practice, authorized by the resolutions of the Convocations,[3] whereby divorced persons, who have been refused a second marriage solemnized in church, but who have subsequently remarried in a register office, are invited in suitable cases to church for prayers in church shortly after their marriage. They are also advised to resume the communicant life, sometimes after a period of voluntary abstention. The resolutions enjoined that reference in such cases should be made by the parish priest to the bishop, although these resolutions do not possess the force of law. Under the Matrimonial Causes Act 1937 the incumbent has discretionary power to admit divorced persons to remarriage in church, and in law the responsibility for this decision remains his. Legally also a person who makes use of the permission given to remarry, which the law affords, is not thereby brought within

---

[1] Op. cit., p. 29.
[2] Further, such a policy would apparently give a clear right to be remarried in church to some of those who, while deeply needing Christian compassion, are least capable of forming permanent unions. See Appendix 6, pp. 144f below.
[3] *Acts of the Convocations of Canterbury and York* (S.P.C.K. 1961), pp. 90–5.

the canonical grounds for exclusion from Holy Communion.[1] It seems a theologically questionable practice to use a request for abstention from Holy Communion for a period as a means of discipline for those who have remarried. First, moral pressure is used to bring about a self-imposed excommunication which seems to many people more like an official exclusion from the Holy Communion. Secondly, the practice suggests an equivocal attitude to the status of the persons who have remarried. They can hardly be regarded as honourably married in the eyes of the Church, for it is because of their marriage that they have been requested to abstain for a period from the Holy Communion, and that at a time when they are particularly in need of the means of grace. Yet they can hardly be regarded as "living in sin", for they are asked to abstain only for a period. They are not required to separate from each other before returning to the Holy Communion. They are not asked to repent of their action in remarrying before the period of their abstention is ended. Indeed it may be asked what repentance could mean in this context. An essential part of repentance is the forsaking, or the genuine intention to forsake, the sin disowned. But a person who has undertaken new responsibilities in a second marriage cannot responsibly disown them; and this is what separation would require him to do. There are many times in life, in which we find ourselves in situations into which sin has entered, and from which we cannot extricate ourselves without still greater sin. While we may repent of what is sinful in such a situation and seek to repair it, we cannot simply step out of the situation, as if it did not exist. Part of repentance, indeed, may be in facing the continual tensions of an apparently irresolvable dilemma.

128 So far as the teaching of our Lord himself about marriage is concerned, it is beyond question that it was vigorous and demanding. Nevertheless

it is not possible to ground the judgement that all divorce and remarriage is forbidden on the fact that Jesus definitely forbade it. He may not have done so—some would say he most probably did not. Some criterion other than the clear teaching of Jesus must be found if the Christian Church is to hold that all marriages are indissoluble and that all remarriages are contrary to God's will.[2]

That criterion cannot properly be found either in the New Testament

---

[1] Canon B 16 1.
[2] Appendix 1, p. 95 below.

as a whole or in the tradition of the universal Church. It must be
found elsewhere with the aid of moral reasoning.

The Eastern Orthodox Church

129 Among these traditions is the practice of the Orthodox Church,
explained by the principle loosely called *oikonomia*. This can be
traced back to a period earlier than that in which the indissolubility
tradition of the Western Church was formed.

> In the Eastern tradition both a second and third marriage after divorce are
> permitted by the canons, but only under strict conditions. There is indeed
> a good deal of evidence to suggest that the Eastern practice reflects an
> attitude which was common both in the East and West in the first mil-
> lennium of Christian history.[1]

At first sight it might seem that the permissibility of divorce involves
a low view of marriage. But this is not the case:

> This permission for divorce in no way denies the tragic and sinful nature of
> every marriage breakdown. Even at a purely human level such a break-
> down implies the disappointment of hopes, the betrayal of faith, the defeat
> of love. In the case of the marriage of Christians, within the family of the
> Church, where the couple have before them the words of Christ in the
> Gospels, the tragic character of the situation is underlined. There is no
> question of the Church's belief that lifelong fidelity is the goal of the
> married couple.[2]

There is undoubtedly in every marriage breakdown a deep element of
tragedy. There is also always an element of sin, in the sense that the
union exhibits more of the disorder of the fallen world than of the
glory of God. Sin is also often present in the sense that one or both
partners may be culpable. There are some who mistake their misery
for a sense of sin, and there are others who rightly feel a burden of
sin. For both there is a ministry to be sought from the Church.

130 It would have been negligent of the Commission not to have considered the Orthodox tradition as a way for the Church of England,[3]
since it has been held for so many centuries by a group of Churches
of such antiquity, orthodoxy, and extent, and it has something in
common with the teaching and practice of many Protestant Churches.
The permission to remarry in the Orthodox tradition has sometimes
been criticized as merely a concession to the dictates of an authori-

---

[1] Appendix 3, p. 122 below.
[2] Ibid., p. 121.
[3] Cf. *The Church and Marriage* (1935), pp. 55ff.

tarian State. Modern scholars of Orthodoxy question this suggestion; they maintain that there is a genuine theological tradition here.

131 Eastern theology has always insisted on the freedom and transcendence of God, and has done so more consistently than that of the West. It is this very freedom and transcendence which make possible the presence and activity of God throughout the whole of his creation. God, in his revelation of himself to man, reveals himself as a God of order and of faithfulness. But he is not bound by our understanding of his activity. He is also a God of many plans never defeated by man's sin, always drawing good out of evil. The death and resurrection of Christ establishes the righteousness of God, but establishes it as a mystery in which life and love are triumphant over hatred and death. In the light of the cross the Christian can never belittle the seriousness of sin, or of its deadly consequences. But in the light of the same cross he sees that "new possibilities open up in the tragic areas of man's life", which in relationship to marriage must mean new hope "for reconciliation and restoration in marriages which seem to have broken down . . . possibilities of a new beginning where the first relationship has gone beyond repair".[1]

132 If a practice similar to that of the Orthodox East were to be adopted by the Church of England, there would be no question of direct pressure from the State, because the State has legislated already for civil dissolution and new marriages by civil registration. The Church of England is therefore free to make pastoral provision in the case of marital breakdown wholly in accordance with Christian principle and to take such steps as will best serve the Christian interests of those to whom it ministers.

Some Unacceptable Proposals

133 One expedient not yet examined in this report but continually pressed upon the Christian community is to accept universal civil registration, leaving the State to devise what sort of marriage contract it will. Christian people would register their contract in these terms like everyone else, but they would then go to church to solemnize holy matrimony in accordance with the doctrine and discipline of

[1] Appendix 3, p. 123 below.

the Church. The union contracted in the civil ceremony would be dissoluble: that solemnized in church would be indissoluble. The Church would, in the exercise of its undoubted canonical power, legislate that for its purposes a valid marriage must be solemnized with the Church's rite. In other words, there would be a decree for the Church of England similar to the *Tametsi* decree of the Roman Catholic Church at the Council of Trent, which was later applied universally by the decree *Ne temere*.

134 Such an expedient invites serious objections.[1] It would incur grave practical difficulties. In the first place, it would follow that the Church would have to regard a large number of persons who used the register office as living, if not in sin, then in some form of respectable concubinage; and this would be offensive to the moral sense of very many committed Christian people, both clerical and lay. Engaged couples could put very unfortunate pressures upon one another to have a church wedding as a safeguard from desertion, or to have a register office wedding to leave a loophole for escape. Contact might be lost with large numbers of young people, whose rudimentary or eclipsed Christian faith would miss the chance of renewal which a wedding in church can give. Nor would there be any ground for refusing a marriage in church to persons who, having contracted a union in a register office which was later followed by a divorce, then wished to contract a fresh union with another partner. This too would be morally offensive, recalling the least satisfactory features of the practice of granting ecclesiastical decrees of nullity.

135 A further expedient would be to persuade the State to legislate for two kinds of marriages: one to be obtained by civil process and dissoluble, and the other solemnized by the rites of the Church and indissoluble. This would not only be open to the same formidable practical objections to which the former expedient is exposed, but to another as well, namely that "it is very doubtful whether the State would sanction legislation, whether by Act or by Measure to bring this about".[2]

136 However serious these practical objections may be, the theological

---

[1] This suggestion has in fact been examined already in *The Church and Marriage: Evidence laid before the Royal Commission on Marriage* (Church Information Office 1952), p. 19.
[2] Memorandum of the Worshipful Chancellor the Reverend E. Garth Moore.

objections seem insuperable. Far from strengthening marriage, these measures would actually weaken it. Marriage is effected by the exchange of consent and vows. In the case of marriage by universal registration, followed by solemnization in church, the exchange would have to be made twice, once in the register office and again in church. In the nature of the case this would belittle the civil form in the eyes of Christian people. In the event of the State legislating for two kinds of marriage, civil and ecclesiastical, the one dissoluble and the other not, a lesser and more restricted intention would be imputed to those marrying by civil process than to those whose weddings would be solemnized in church. It would presuppose that non-church people, when they marry, desire or design a terminable contract. But in the present situation, and with the form at present used in the register office, it must still be presumed, in the absence of evidence to the contrary, that a permanent marriage is being made. The words used in the register office are as explicit on this point as the service in the Book of Common Prayer.[1] The new Divorce Reform Act 1969 alters the law of *divorce* and not of marriage, and so does not invalidate the nature of *marriage*. There is no reason to assume that people who marry in a register office do not intend a lifelong union.

137 If it came about that marriage by civil process were reduced to a merely contractual relationship, then it would be needful for the Church to renounce its present association with the State in the matter of marriage. But to do so when no essential difference can be established would be for the Church to give up its ministry in that field to which it is sent, and indeed in one of the few areas of ministry remaining where the Church is brought into contact, liturgically and pastorally, with the world. To do this would show the Church to be more concerned with ministering to its own members than with its duty to all men, exhibiting the true nature of marriage and assisting them towards its realization. Moreover, to withdraw needlessly would have wide and regrettable consequences. Withdrawal along a wide front might follow, further restricting the Church in its pastoral ministry. Compulsory expulsion, if it ever happened, would be quite another matter: it is voluntary withdrawal that is under discussion.

[1] The Registrar General states that "no change is contemplated in the wording of the notice concerning the nature of marriage which is displayed in Register Offices or in that appearing on the forms of notice of marriage".

The Promises

138 If these expedients are found lacking, should we then continue as we are? In the past those who, when they were faced with the breakdown of their marriage, felt bound to witness to the lifelong obligation of their vows, could do so by refusing to initiate divorce proceedings. Under the new Act, when initiative may come from either side, they can still maintain their witness unimpaired by remaining unmarried after their marriage has been legally dissolved. In fact such people are relieved of an interior conflict of motive. In the former situation charity on the one hand might have required the release of a spouse by initiating divorce proceedings, while on the other hand fidelity to lifelong vows might have forbidden that course. Under the new Act witness to the permanent nature of marriage may be borne without such conflict. Fidelity in either circumstance may be entangled with less worthy motives.

139 There are those who have bravely borne this witness with personal self-sacrifice. For this they are held in honour and respect and the Church has a special pastoral duty towards them. It does not, however, follow that it is necessarily right for the Church, in Christ's name, to impose this course upon divorced Christians generally, with all its inherent dangers of legalism. There are those who do not feel called to this way, or able to follow it. What way forward is there for them? Solemn vows, taken in marriage, help to effect that which they signify and herein may be found their sacramental quality. The Church has not claimed to release from marriage vows. But it can recognize when they can no longer be fulfilled. It cannot alter the past, but it can assure men of the power of God's forgiveness, and it has an efficacious ministry of absolution for those who are burdened with guilt. When a marriage has irretrievably broken down, and has been dissolved by the process of law, in what sense, if any, are marriage vows still binding on either partner?[1] Those vows which can never again be honoured obviously cannot be binding. What of those which can, such as "forsaking all other", "for better for worse"? These vows refer to married life. If the marriage is dead, are these vows without further effect? For a Christian there remains his loyalty to Christ and his teaching with all its hard sayings on divorce. But what does loyalty to Christ entail for a Christian in this

---

[1] Appendix 5, pp. 131f below.

situation? Some will feel bound to witness to the permanent nature of marriage by not marrying again. Others find that loyalty to Christ does not forbid them to remarry. And there is an increasing number of responsible church people, clerical and lay, who in conscience find themselves unable to deny that remarriage can be the will of God. Others again are uncertain and perplexed. This Commission believes that the Church should not universally require the first course, and indeed that the Church's loyalty to Christ requires it to allow this liberty of choice to Christian men and women.

The Question of Moral Consensus

140 There are, as we have seen, ecclesiastical regulations which discourage a second marriage of divorced persons from being solemnized in church. Unquestionably such regulations should remain in being if the moral consensus of Christian people in the Church of England requires it. But the question must be asked whether there is this moral consensus. It is not for the Commission to attempt to determine the answer to this question; but there is sufficient evidence to oblige us to raise this question and others which follow from it.[1] Is there a growing consensus among Christian people, both clerical and lay, first, that some marriages, however well-intentioned, do break down; secondly, that some divorced partners enter into new unions in good faith and that some of these new unions show such evident features of stability, complementarity, fruitfulness, and growth as to make them comparable with satisfactory first marriages; and thirdly, that Christian congregations are not scandalized, in the theological sense of the word, by the presence of such persons in their midst or by their participation in the Holy Communion? If an affirmative answer is given to these questions, then we are bound to raise the question that naturally follows from such an answer. Is there also a growing moral consensus that such persons, with due safeguards, may properly have their marriages solemnized according to the rites of the Church? Indeed, it may well turn out on inquiry that a moral judgement on this matter has already formed itself within the Church of England, as it has in some other Churches of the Anglican Communion, in the belief that remarriage in church would be not a weakening but a strengthening of marriage. It is

---

[1] The changes in the legislation of a number of provinces of the Anglican Communion are noted in Appendix 7, pp. 152f below.

possible that those who say that to remarry in church would cause offence to the Christian conscience may find that failure to do so causes greater offence.

141 This leads us to recall what happened to the Anglican Communion on another matter and on a previous occasion, at the Lambeth Conference of 1958. The question at issue was the use of contraception in family planning. It has been said by the Bishop of Durham,[1] that the report on this matter prepared for this conference[2] marked a watershed in the Anglican approach to moral problems. In the course of this article he writes of the recognition "that the status of the theology used in the argument was subordinate to the moral claim which in one way or another it was endeavouring to articulate". In other words, at times the Church may have moral insight prior to and at least as fundamental as the theological insight necessary to explain it. The bishops at the Lambeth Conference were called upon to ratify a decision made in Christian consciences and acted upon for many years before. We feel bound to ask whether a similar process is at work in the matter of remarriage in church. If so, the General Synod of the Church could be called upon to make provision for remarriage in the light of a moral judgement which has already formed itself, or is in the process of formation, within the Christian community of the Church of England. The Synod could presumably attempt to determine this question by making inquiry among its lay, presbyteral, and episcopal members at parochial, deanery, diocesan, and national level.

142 If it were to be found that a moral consensus in favour of remarriage in church (with due safeguards) does exist, then it would be the duty of the Bishops-in-Synod to determine whether this consensus is theologically well founded. *It is the unanimous conviction of this Commission that this is the case.* Such a moral judgement would not be inconsistent with the witness and teaching of the New Testament as a whole, nor with the traditions of the Orthodox and Protestant Churches;[3] nor would it be inconsistent with the Western Church, if account be taken of the wide gulf between the developed theory of indissolubility and the divergent practice based on the use of nullity decrees. These considerations, however, are neutral. They may permit theological validation; they do not construct it. Positively speak-

---

[1] *The Church Quarterly* (January 1970), p. 221.
[2] *The Family in Contemporary Society.* S.P.C.K. 1958.
[3] Cf. Chapter 1, p. 11 above.

ing, it is necessary, as so often in difficult matters of theology, to go behind the doctrine of the Church and even the doctrine of man, to the doctrine of God and the doctrine of grace. An adequate doctrine of grace can loose as well as bind, forgive as well as bless, create again as well as create at the first; an adequate doctrine of God reveals him as over and in his creation and able to turn even the wrath of man to his praise.[1]

A Possible Course of Action

143 If this theology be true, as we believe it to be, and if there were to exist a moral consensus on the matter of remarriage in church, then competent authority in the Church of England would have to decide how best to give effect to it by establishing procedures for remarriage in church. It would be necessary to do justice to competing claims. The claim of the integrity of vows taken in the original marriage service[2], and of the intention of those taking vows in the future, must be upheld; indeed, since we believe that the vows simply affirm what marriage is, then to tamper with the vows would be treason to lovers, poets, and visionaries everywhere. The claim of the integrity of the spouses undertaking the second marriage must also be upheld. The first claim would be imperilled if, with no other action, parties to the second marriage after divorce simply repeated the service used for first marriages. The second claim would be imperilled by the resort of introducing what is loosely called "a penitential note" into the second marriage service. The time for penitence is not then. The white robes of those called to the marriage supper of the Lamb (Rev. 19.9) were the robes not of the innocent but of the forgiven; they were washed before they came. This would be the time to strengthen the new union and make it permanent. It would be theologically as well as psychologically unsatisfactory to cloud the life beginning with the shadow of the life that has passed. Further thought is therefore needed in order to do justice to both competing claims and not to confuse them.

144 Before the marriage could be solemnized, discreet but adequate inquiry by the competent authority would have to be made in three respects. First, there would have to be inquiry into the discharge of all possible obligations remaining from the first marriage (for

---

[1] See Appendix 3, pp. 113f below.
[2] See Appendix 5, pp. 131f below.

example, social and economic responsibilities to the former spouse and to any children of the first marriage). In the second place, there would have to be inquiry into the character and dispositions of the two persons seeking solemnization of their marriage in church. This would involve investigation into the circumstances of the previous divorce, and also an assurance that they are both the kind of people who are capable of the stable and permanent relationship of marriage and who have a genuine desire for the blessing of God in marriage according to the Church's rites. Thirdly, assurance would be required of the same intention of lifelong fidelity that is required of any two persons who come to be married in this country, whether in church or register office. This inquiry would need to be not so remote from the parties as to be technical and juridical only, nor so dependent upon unsupported local judgement as to make consistency within one diocese impossible. Various procedures are adopted in different Churches of the Anglican Communion.[1] Means, suited to the requirements and circumstances of this country, could be devised. Reference would be made to the bishop, who might well want to associate suitably qualified clerical and lay advisers with his decisions. Such procedure, while respecting the statutory right of an incumbent to remarry a couple in church if he so decides, would rely on the same courtesy, good will, and respect for spiritual authority, which is already deployed in the Church's matrimonial affairs.

145 Satisfaction on these counts having been given by the competent church authority, the parties to the second marriage would be invited, before the wedding, to a private occasion of prayer with the parish priest; this might well take place in church. In it they would give expression, first, of penitence for past faults; secondly, of their intention to meet those obligations which still remained; thirdly, of a right intention in the new marriage; and fourthly, of desire for God's renewing and recreative grace within which to live. Such prayer would be theologically appropriate for such an occasion; but the composition of any such forms of prayer would have to be sufficiently sensitive and skilled to match the spiritual realities of the occasion. Great care would be needed not to make of it a stumbling block in people's way, in deference, not to levity or presumption, but simply to shyness. The form would need to be plain, dignified, and straightforward; it could be sincere without being embarrassingly

---

[1] See Appendix 7, pp. 152f below, for further details.

emotional. There might be something to be said for using familiar and traditional words for the penitential part, rather than risk this becoming unduly subjective.

146 So far the procedure would be private. Marriage, however, has a public aspect touching society and the Christian community. The integrity of the marriage must not only be unimpugned, it must also be seen not to be impugned. The congregation must know that the second marriage is not being lightly undertaken, and they will want to know that the assurances noted above have been given.[1] This knowledge would be conveyed not in any interference in the marriage service itself, but in a preliminary declaration to be read at the beginning of the service. In order to show what we have in mind, we suggest as examples the following possible forms:

147 A PRELIMINARY DECLARATION

To be made by the Priest before the Congregation
in the presence of the man and woman to be married

I AM TO DECLARE THAT OF the two persons now coming to be married, one has (*or* both have) had a previous marriage dissolved by due process of law. Accordingly, acting under the authority of a resolution of the General Synod of the Church of England, I declare further that the competent Church authority has been satisfied that he (she) has (they have) discharged, or bound himself (herself) (themselves), to discharge, such obligations as remained from the former marriage as fully as possible, and that this proposed marriage may now properly be solemnized in church. They have accordingly, on a recent day and in my presence, expressed in words before God penitence for such elements of the past as call for penitence, submitting themselves to his liberating grace, and have prayed to him for renewal in the common life which they intend together now.

I HAVE TO DECLARE BEFORE proceeding to solemnize this marriage, that one partner has (both partners have) previously entered upon a marriage which has later been dissolved by due process of civil law. Acting under a Measure of the General Synod of our Church, I have further to declare that the Church authorities, after due inquiry, have been satisfied that he (she) has (they have) fulfilled all such responsibilities as remain from the former marriage(s), or have solemnly undertaken to do so.

ACCORDINGLY these two persons in the recent past have, in my presence, addressed themselves in prayer to Almighty God, as part of their preparation for a fresh start in the new marriage which they both intend to make now in Christ.

I SHALL THEREFORE proceed now, under ecclesiastical licence, to solemnize this marriage in church.

[1] The need for some such procedure is integral to our proposal of remarriage in church, not just a helpful suggestion towards its greater seemliness.

148 If the General Synod, after due inquiry and consultation, decided to give effect to remarriage in church, this would not be a mere accommodation to secular pressure; it would be an acknowledgment of human weakness and a declaration of faith in God's forgiveness and recreative power. We believe that the grace which God may bestow in a first marriage he may also bestow in a subsequent marriage. Certainly such a second marriage could not be a witness to the permanent nature of marriage in the same way as an unbroken first marriage can be, but it could become a permanent union, and it could bear eloquent witness to the true nature of marriage in other ways. Solemnization in church would bear witness to the belief that God does bless such marriages with the riches of his grace, whereas the denial of solemnization seems to witness to the contrary, and to deny grace to some who might need it most.

149 This report has not been easy to write. The conclusion to which it argues has required a number of difficult decisions, involving the exegesis of Scripture, the interpretation of tradition, and the discernment of a right policy for today. The Commission has been aware throughout of the ecumenical significance of what it has been doing. Its double task is one for all Christians, namely to maintain a faithful witness to their understanding of marriage, and to strengthen all that helps towards its expression in the lives of married people. Inevitably there are in the report elements which are new and untried, and these may make hard reading for people in whose minds the major questions have already been settled. In the life of the Church there must always be a tension between the settled way and the exploratory way. Only from a basis of stable security is it possible validly to explore; only by exploration can stability retain the pulse of life.

APPENDICES

1

Jesus on Divorce and Remarriage

by Hugh Montefiore

THE BACKGROUND OF THE GOSPELS

What is the teaching of the New Testament on marriage and divorce? In particular, what did Jesus teach on this subject? In this, as in other matters, the teaching of the New Testament can only be understood in the light of the Old Testament and its current interpretation.

Among the early Hebrews matrimony had taken differing forms. Polygamy, which is occasionally found even down and into the Christian era, was not forbidden. Various forms of marriage and concubinage were practised. However much love the wife might inspire in her husband, and however great was the respect in which she was held in her family, she remained in many respects the property of her husband. To divorce her was easy; but she was protected by the Deuteronomic legislation in that the husband had to give his wife a bill of dismissal for divorce to take effect. The woman was further protected in that, if her husband had committed an offence against her before he married her, or if he had brought à false accusation of adultery against her after he had married her, he could not divorce her; such marriages were indissoluble (Deut. 22.13ff, 28ff). Elaborate laws and traditions by the end of the second century A.D. grew up concerning the bill of divorce, as may be seen in the tractate of the Mishnah on the subject (Gittim). (The Mishnah was reduced to writing by the end of the second century A.D. but contains much earlier material.) The husband had to return the marriage dowry (as laid down in the marriage contract) and he had to declare that his wife was henceforth free to marry anyone she chose. Once, however, she had remarried she was not able, after a further divorce, to return to her first husband (Deut. 24.4).

According to Jewish law, a woman was not able to divorce her husband, although the rabbis of the first century A.D. held that in certain circumstances (for example, cruelty, denial of conjugal rights, etc.) she could make her husband divorce her. In the Jewish list of priorities, procreation was more important than marriage, so that, if a marriage had lasted for ten years without issue being born, the husband had either to divorce his wife and take another, or to take a second wife in addition to the first (M. Gitt. 4.8).

These Jewish laws may be contrasted with Roman laws of that time. According to the latter, either partner could divorce the other. Neither partner had to give a reason or ground for complaint. Originally there had been among the Romans a solemn form of matrimony (*confarreatio*) which was quasi-sacramental in character and indissoluble; but, perhaps for that very reason, it was practically obsolete by New Testament times. Divorce among the Romans was not subject to any kind of stigma— Pompey was married five times, Caesar four, and Cicero three. By contrast, although marriage was not considered indissoluble among the Jews and divorce was freely permitted, nevertheless the rabbis did not look on it with favour, as may be seen from the saying of R. Eleazar, based on Mal. 2.16, that "the very altar weeps when a man divorces the wife of his youth" (Gitt. 90b). In Zadokite Fragment 7.1, probably connected with Essene circles, divorce seems actually to have been forbidden.

According to Deut. 22.22 the penalty for adultery is death when the parties are found *in flagrante delicto* (in the very act). (According to Jewish law, only a wife could commit adultery, so that a man could only be found guilty of adultery for an offence with a married woman.) It seems probable that, in New Testament times, the Jews did not have power to carry out a death sentence. In John 8.3ff a case of adultery seems to have already been proved against a woman "taken in the very act", and yet she had not been put to death, for Jesus is asked whether or not she should be stoned. The incident is of the greatest importance because Jesus' pronouncement "Neither do I condemn thee" (John 8.11) to the woman taken in adultery shows that he believed that adultery could be forgiven. According to the Talmud, however, a husband, if adultery was proved or confessed, was under an obligation to divorce his wife (M. Yeb. 2.8). (The ordeal by bitter waters (Num. 5.11–31) was applied to suspected cases simply as a test, with a view to eliciting a confession.)

It is plain that in the time of Jesus, controversy did not centre on the possibility of divorce, since in certain circumstances this was mandatory, but rather on the circumstances in which divorce was possible. The ground stated in Deut. 24.1 is translated in the A.V. "because he hath found some uncleanness in her". This is undoubtedly what the Hebrew phrase came to mean, and indeed it is thus that the phrase is rendered in the Septuagint; but literally translated it means "for the exposure of a thing", and it seems probable that originally this phrase was a euphemism for some kind of indecent exposure.

Argument in Jesus' day centred on the meaning that should be given to the uncleanness. Rabbi Shammai believed that Deut. 24.1 referred to immodest behaviour by a wife, such as going into the street with her hair undone, whereas Rabbi Hillel interpreted the biblical phrase to mean that any cause for the husband's displeasure sufficed. It was during the period A.D. 70–90 that controversy about this flared between the opposing disciples of the two rabbis. The school of Hillel prevailed.

THE EVIDENCE OF ST MARK

What did Jesus himself teach? It is generally agreed that St Mark is the earliest Gospel, and although this does not necessarily mean that its contents are more authentic than that of the other Gospels, there is a certain presumption that this might be the case. In Mark 10.2–12 the following passage is found:

And the Pharisees came to him, and asked him, Is it lawful for a man to put away his wife? tempting him. And he answered and said unto them, What did Moses command you? And they said, Moses suffered to write a bill of divorcement, and to put her away. And Jesus answered and said unto them, For the hardness of your heart he wrote you this precept. But from the beginning of the creation God made them male and female. For this cause shall a man leave his father and mother, and cleave to his wife; and they twain shall be one flesh: so then they are no more twain but one flesh. What therefore God hath joined together, let not man put asunder. And in the house his disciples asked him again of the same matter. And he saith unto them, Whosoever shall put away his wife, and marry another, committeth adultery against her. And if a woman shall put away her husband, and be married to another, she committeth adultery.

The following points on this passage are noteworthy:

1. Jesus is not asked about the grounds for divorce (the current rabbinical controversy) but about the permissibility of divorce at all. It must have been well known that Jesus held unusual views about the permanence of the marriage bond, and his opponents, by a test question, tried to make him incriminate himself against the Mosiac law. As elsewhere, Jesus met their question with one of his own. He asked what the Law demanded about divorce.

2. The Pharisees replied by making a distinction between the mandatory and permissive parts of the Law. The Mosaic law permitted divorce by means of the *get*, or bill of divorce.

3. Jesus replied that this permission was a concession to human weakness. It was God's intention that marriage should be lifelong. Jesus attested this view by means of two proof texts, both of which are taken from a Mosaic book, but both of which come from the Book of Genesis and so precede Moses. Jesus went behind Mosaic legislation about marriage to God's purpose in his original institution of marriage, the same method as he used concerning the Jewish Sabbath (Mark 2.27).

4. The first text (from Gen. 1.27) showed that sexual differentiation was part of God's original purpose in creation. The second text (from Gen. 2.24) proved that the purpose of distinguishing the sexes was to join them together in marriage. It has been suggested that behind this text lies a conception of Adam as androgynous, but it seems improbable that Jesus was alluding to this somewhat obscure rabbinic speculation. Most probably, the phrase "one flesh", although it contained undoubtedly a sexual connotation, referred to the new family unit which is created when a woman leaves her family home to join her bridegroom. She becomes as it were "flesh of his flesh" and he in turn "cleaves" to her. The Hebrew word here is not sexual in meaning; it signifies to "cling on to, to stick to" someone, when it is used of persons. It is this word which proves from Scripture the permanence of marriage.

5. "What God hath joined together" (i.e. marriage) is not quite identical in meaning with the phrase in the Book of Common Prayer, "Those whom God hath joined together". The Gospel saying is concerned not with individual spouses but with the institution of marriage itself. "Let not man put asunder" does not, as has been suggested, mark a contrast between man and woman. On the contrary, the contrast is between the divine purpose of permanence in marriage and human action which can thwart this. Deliberately to cause the breakdown of marriage is to frustrate the purpose of God in instituting it. God intended marriage to be enduring. This saying is not legislative in form. It deals in sweeping terms with the pure will of God in instituting marriage. It does not define "what God hath joined together". It does not differentiate between true marriage and those unions (e.g. John 4.18) which are not in accordance with God's will. It simply draws the corollary of God's intention that marriage should be permanent: what God has instituted no one should destroy.

Thus the saying gives a warning against anyone who brings a marriage to an end; but it does not necessarily conflict with a formal pronouncement that a marriage has already come to an end. It certainly does not assert the indissolubility of marriage.

6. So far the incident as recounted has progressed in typical rabbinic style, as befits the occasion, with question and counter-question, text and counter-text. There follows a private session with the disciples. Elsewhere in St Mark's Gospel private explanations seem suspect (4.10ff; 7.17ff; 13.3ff). They are most easily understood as opportunities for introducing the interpretation by the early Church of the teaching of Jesus. This suggests that what follows may not be so much Jesus' teaching on divorce as the way in which the early Church interpreted his teaching.

7. This suspicion is deepened when Mark 10.11ff is examined. The two verses seem to reflect a non-Jewish environment.
(a) A divorced man who remarries is said to commit adultery "against" his wife. According to Jewish law, however, a man could not commit adultery, save as the co-respondent of a married woman.
(b) A woman who remarries after divorce is said to commit adultery. The phrase "if she shall put away her husband" suggests a Gentile environment where it was possible for a woman to initiate divorce, such as Rome, for which St Mark's Gospel was probably written. Some scholars have tried to show that it was possible in Judea for a woman to initiate divorce in the time of Jesus, on the basis of the Elephantine papyri, and Samaritan and Karaitic sources. Josephus, however, writing in the first century A.D., makes it clear that this custom was unusual and illegal (*Ant.* 15.7.10). Other scholars prefer the alternative reading "if she be divorced from her husband"; but the principle of *difficilior lectio potior* (the more difficult reading is to be preferred) seems to apply here, and for this reason this alternative reading is to be resisted.

It has been suggested that vv. 11 and 12 are genuine sayings of Jesus; that the uniqueness of his teaching on marriage and divorce consists in the equality he accorded to the sexes, or that Jesus gave this teaching for the benefit of his non-Jewish hearers. Elsewhere, however, Jesus addresses his teaching to Jews, on the basis of the Jewish law, as one who was "not sent but unto the lost sheep of the house of Israel" (Matt. 15.24); and so it seems more probable that vv. 11 and 12 represent the teaching of the Gentile Church at Rome where St Mark's Gospel was written. These two verses, then, are either an adaptation from an unknown original, or (more probably) the authentic teaching of Jesus ends at v. 9 with the words "What God hath joined together, let not man put asunder". Indeed, it could be argued that the whole incident in Mark 10.11ff has been built up around this original pronouncement of Jesus.

Such a saying was revolutionary to Jewish ways of thought. So far as we know, Jesus was alone among Jewish teachers when he asserted that marriage was intended by God to be lasting and permanent, and that to cause a marriage to break up was to act contrary to the will of God. It is inconceivable that this hard saying does not go back to Jesus himself. As elsewhere, Jesus formally based his teaching on the Jewish scriptures, but in fact it sprang from his own inspired insights and creative thinking. "He knew what was in man", and so he saw clearly into the nature of matrimony. The teaching of Jesus is not authoritative simply because it is "revealed teaching" but because it reveals what is true.

ST MATTHEW AND ST MARK

The same incident as Mark 10.2-9 is reported in Matt. 19.3-8:

The Pharisees also came unto him, tempting him, and saying unto him, Is it lawful for a man to put away his wife for every cause? And he answered and said unto them, Have ye not read that he which made them at the beginning made them male and female, and said, For this cause shall a man leave father and mother, and shall cleave to his wife: and they twain shall be one flesh? Wherefore they are no more twain, but one flesh. What therefore God hath joined together, let not man put asunder. They say unto him, Why did Moses then command to give a writing of divorcement, and to put her away? He saith unto them, Moses because of the hardness of your hearts suffered you to put away your wives: but from the beginning it was not so.

There are important differences from Mark here, the most important of which are noted below.

1. St Matthew frames differently the question which Jesus was asked. "Is it lawful for a man to put away his wife for every cause?" (v. 3). The context of this question lies in the Jewish controversy about the proper grounds of divorce. Jesus was not asked whether divorce was ever permissible, but whether he stood with R. Hillel (that a man can divorce his wife for every cause) or whether he stood with the stricter interpretation of R. Shammai (that divorce can only have as its ground an immodest or indecent action by his wife).

2. The distinction between the mandatory and the permissive clauses of Mosaic law is made not by Jesus' opponents but by Jesus himself, showing him to be well conversant with rabbinic interpretation of the Law.

D

3. St Matthew does not give a private explanation to the disciples, as in St Mark, immediately after the saying "What God hath joined together. . . ". Instead, there is a saying markedly different from that of St Mark, prefaced by the words "I say unto you".

And I say unto you, Whosoever shall put away his wife, except it be for fornication, and shall marry another, committeth adultery; and whoso marrieth her which is put away doth commit adultery.

Whereas the Marcan pronouncement suggests a belief in the indissolubility of marriage, this Matthaean saying shows Jesus taking up a position within the current Jewish controversy over divorce, permitting it for one sole reason, *porneia*, translated "fornication" above. Attempts to translate the exceptive clause here (and in Matt. 5.32) so as to remove the exception (i.e. "least of all for *porneia*") are grammatically untenable.

4. The Matthaean form of the saying on adultery does not state (as in Mark) that a man can commit adultery "against his wife", nor is the possibility mentioned of a woman divorcing her husband. To this extent, St Matthew does not conflict with contemporary Jewish law and custom, although his saying still allows a husband to commit adultery, in contrast to Jewish law.

5. It is after the pronouncement on divorce, not before it, that a private explanation is given to the disciples in Matt. 19.10–12:

His disciples say unto him, If the case of the man be so with his wife, it is not good to marry. But he said unto them, All men cannot receive this saying, save they to whom it is given. For there are some eunuchs, which were so born from their mother's womb: and there are some eunuchs, which were made eunuchs of men: and there be eunuchs, which have made themselves eunuchs for the kingdom of heaven's sake. He that is able to receive it, let him receive it.

It is not clear whether "this saying" refers backwards to the saying on the permanence of marriage or forwards to the saying on eunuchs. If it refers to the former, it suggests that Jesus' teaching on divorce was so rigorous that not all men could hope to keep to it (cf. the not dissimilar type of saying on riches in Matt. 19.25ff). In any case, the remark of the disciples that it might be expedient not to marry suggests a very rigorous pronouncement about marriage.

It is hardly possible to imagine that the Matthaean version is the original version, and that the Marcan version is the result of editorial alterations to make it more rigorous. The priority of St Mark over St Matthew is not in doubt. The question arises whether the differences between the two Gospels here are the result of St Matthew's editorial activity, or whether they are due to the possession by St Matthew of an alternative and possibly more trustworthy tradition.

It is possible that the differences here between St Mark and St Matthew are due to the fact that Jesus taught differently at different times; that he changed his mind, or that there was an interior inconsistency in his teaching. Such an explanation could never be completely disproved or discounted; but it can be shown to be a very remote possibility. The critic cannot avoid here a value judgement about the character of Jesus. He must ask himself what must have been the quality of person and what must have been the kind of teaching that gave rise to the Gospels. It seems unlikely that Jesus taught systematically. But it does not seem credible that the Person who gave rise to the Gospels did not know his own mind, or would have been content to give teaching which suffered from interior inconsistency, or, during the brief period of his public ministry, made important changes in his ethical principles of conduct.

The conclusion that the differences between St Mark and St Matthew are not due to interior inconsistency in the teaching of Jesus is confirmed by a study of the relevant texts.

The Matthaean version of the incident is far more Jewish than that of Mark, and more suited to a Jewish Christian Church, compared with Mark's cosmopolitan Church of Rome. Some have held that St Matthew gives the more authentic version because his is the more Jewish, but this seems most improbable. The teaching of Jesus in St Matthew is adapted to the controversy about divorce which agitated the Jewish rabbis in the years A.D. 70–96, when St Matthew's Gospel was written. The astonishment of the disciples at the rigorousness of his teaching is perfectly natural if we regard St Mark as giving the authentic version, but St Matthew's faulty editing makes it inappropriate in its Matthaean setting, where Jesus makes an exception to the ruling on divorce.

But what does *porneia* mean here, and why is the exceptive clause found in St Matthew and not in St Mark?

THE MEANING OF PORNEIA

The Greek word *porneia* has a sexual meaning, and refers either to an act of, or an attitude resulting in, sexual immorality. It has a wide variety of meanings in various contexts, and it has been given a large number of different interpretations in Matt. 19.9 (and in Matt. 5.32).

1. In 1 Cor. 5.1 *porneia* is used of an incestuous union, and so some would interpret it here. (It has been alleged that the word has the same meaning in the apostolic decree of Acts 15.29; but this seems extremely doubtful.) But marriages which transgressed the biblical laws of incest did not need a bill of divorce. Such marriages were null and void, and simply needed to be annulled, so that to make divorce allowable for such unions would seem to be contrary to Jewish principles, although a *get* might be useful if the "wife" wished to "remarry". But it is not credible that such incestuous unions were sufficiently common to warrant a special exceptive clause about them.

2. *Porneia* can mean prostitution, but this meaning should not be given unless the context demands it. Once again, it is not credible that so many Christian wives were whores that a special exceptive clause permitting their divorce had to be inserted in St Matthew's Gospel.

3. *Porneia* usually means fornication, and some scholars believe that this is its meaning in the exceptive clauses of St Matthew's Gospel. According to Deut. 22.20, if a man finds on his wedding night that his wife is not a virgin, she is to be stoned to death. This death sentence probably could not be carried out in first-century Palestine, but (in contrast to modern attitudes) premarital intercourse was regarded as a very grave sin. In such circumstances, a husband was under obligation to divorce his wife (Ket. 5a). It seems to have been to avoid such publicity that Joseph, according to St Matthew, "was minded to put her away privily" (Matt. 1.19) when Mary was found with child. Such a divorce was really an annulment: since the wedding contract had not been honoured, no real marriage had taken place. It follows, therefore, that if *porneia* in these clauses refers to premarital intercourse, the exception is only an apparent one. If a wife was found at her marriage not to be a virgin, the marriage should be terminated forthwith. On such a view, St Matthew does not provide a less rigorous ruling on divorce than St Mark. The editorial insertion of the former merely articulates what is implicit in the latter. Such an explanation may seem at first sight to be attractive, but on examination grave difficulties remain. In the first place this explanation of the exceptive clause seems over-subtle in its context; and in the second place it is incredible that, in the Jewish Christian milieu in which St Matthew's Gospel was written, so many Christian wives were found to have engaged in fornication that a special interpretative gloss on the divorce pronouncement was necessary. In a Gentile Church this might be understandable; but in a Jewish Christian milieu it would have been impossible.

4. Some scholars believe that *porneia* in these exceptive clauses means adultery. It is held that the exception of adultery would bring a Church in close contact with Judaism closer in its marriage discipline to Jewish practice. A Jewish husband had to divorce his wife if she was found guilty of adultery. The difficulty about this meaning is primarily linguistic. Although in certain contexts *porneia* can refer to adultery, this is not its real meaning. Moreover, in the New Testament there is a distinction between fornication and adultery, *porneia* and *moicheia*. Furthermore, this very distinction is made only a few chapters further back in Matt. 15.19. It is impossible to believe that, in what is evidently intended to be a legal regulation about divorce for the Church for which St Matthew wrote, the word *porneia* should be employed with a connotation unknown elsewhere in St Matthew, or in the New Testament as a whole.

5. It has already been noted that *porneia*, while it can be used in particular contexts to denote a particular form of sexual misconduct, normally has a more general meaning of sexual immorality. This general meaning is best understood in these exceptive clauses. It has been noted above that in St Matthew's version of the incident Jesus is asked where he stands in the controversy between the Hillelites and the Shammaites. The Hillelites permitted divorce for "every reason"; the Shammaites permitted it only for some reason of indecency. It cannot be supposed that, if the Church for which St Matthew wrote had adapted its discipline of marriage to Jewish

practice, it would have agreed to the laxer ruling of the Hillelites. On the other hand, if it did not hold to the indissolubility of marriage, it would be unlikely to take up a third position unlike that of either the Hillelites or the Shammaites. Therefore, if any adaptation was made to Jewish practice, St Matthew would be more likely to follow the Shammaites. If our suggestion be accepted that *porneia* be understood as sexual immorality, the saying can then be understood as adapting Jesus' teaching to the rule of the Shammaites: no divorce, except for some sexual indecency or immorality (including of course adultery and premarital fornication).

IN THE SERMON ON THE MOUNT

A further ruling on marriage and divorce is found in the Sermon on the Mount at Matt. 5.31–2:

It hath been said, Whosoever shall put away his wife, let him give her a writing of divorcement: but I say unto you, That whosoever shall put away his wife saving for the cause of fornication, causeth her to commit adultery: and whosoever shall marry her that is divorced committeth adultery.

This saying has points of similarity with the saying in Matt. 19.9, but there are also important points of difference.

1. Instead of the Greek phrase *me epi porneia* (except for *porneia*) there is the unusual phrase *parektos logou porneias* (saving for the cause of *porneia*). The latter sounds very much as though it were a literal translation of the Hebrew words *'erwath dabar* in Deut. 24.1 or their Aramaic equivalent; but whatever be the origin of the phrase, *porneia* must mean the same here as in Matt. 19.9—sexual immorality. Jesus is again made to side with the Shammaites against the school of Hillel.

The saying here occurs in a list of antitheses in which Jesus contrasts his own teaching with that of the Jewish law, "It was said by them of old time . . . but I say unto you". Thus the sense requires a contrast between the Mosaic law of divorce and Jesus' teaching against divorce. But in fact we do not get this; instead, there is a contrast between the Mosaic ordinance and a rabbinic interpretation of it; not a real contrast at all. If, however the phrase *parektos logou porneias* be removed, the required contrast is obtained. It therefore seems most probable that this phrase has been inserted by St Matthew in order to adapt the Church's law to that of the Jewish community where the Gospel was written.

2. In this form of the saying the man who initiates the divorce is disregarded. The saying is concerned only with the effect on his wife and her second husband in the event of her divorce and remarriage. It seems very improbable that Jesus himself would have omitted to say anything about the status of the first husband. But, as the saying stands, it accords completely with the Jewish law according to which a man cannot be an adulterer unless he commits misconduct with a married woman. If divorce is immoral, then an "ex-wife" on her remarriage is really an adulteress and her new husband an adulterer. (The status of women at the time made it

very likely that any "ex-wife" would have to remarry.) Thus St Matthew, in this form of the saying, conforms completely to Jewish law and practice.

3. Some exegetes hold that *porneia* here means adultery, and therefore the exceptive clause does not mark a ground for divorce, but merely qualifies the predicate, "causeth her to commit adultery". Since his wife is an adulteress already, no action by her husband could make her what she already is! This explanation, however, must be resisted for two reasons. In the first place the addition of the phrase *parektos logou porneias* must have more point than a statement of the obvious; and secondly, *porneia* here must mean the same as in Matt. 19.9. The meaning of *porneia* has already been examined, and the sense of "sexual immorality" has been preferred.

4. What is the source of Matt. 5.32? Matt. 19.9 was thought to be an edited version of Mark 10.11. But it would be strange if Matt. 5.32 were the result of further editorial activity from the same source, since it appears in St Matthew's Gospel before Matt. 19.9. We cannot say more about this source than that it was probably derived from the Jewish Christian environment in which St Matthew's Gospel was composed.

THE EVIDENCE OF ST LUKE

A saying of Jesus about divorce and remarriage is also found in Luke 16.18:

Whosoever putteth away his wife, and marrieth another, committeth adultery: and whosoever marrieth her that is put away from her husband committeth adultery.

The second half of this saying, "Whosoever marrieth her that is put away . . .", is very similar to the second half of the Matthaean saying in Matt. 5.32b. This has led many critics to attribute both sayings to Q (a hypothetical written source common to both St Matthew and St Luke). Since Q is thought to have been written earlier than St Mark's Gospel, the attribution is important. But the first half of this Lucan saying, "Whosoever putteth away . . ." is not like Matt. 5.32a; on the contrary, it is very like Mark 10.11. This similarity to the early St Mark has led critics to infer that the Lucan form of the Q saying, Luke 16.18, represents its earlier or more original form.

However, this attribution of Matt. 5.32 and Luke 16.18 to Q is very doubtful. After examination of Matt. 5.32 we found reason to attribute it to Matthew's special material circulating in the Church where he wrote his Gospel. Similarly Luke 16.18 seems likely to come from Luke's special material, for the following reasons. Firstly, Luke 16.18 (like Matt. 5.32) is not placed in a "Q Passage" among other Q material. Although attempts have been made to integrate it into its Lucan context, it appears to be an isolated saying. In the second place, it has a most odd context in St Luke's Gospel. The previous verse reads: "It is easier for heaven and earth to pass, than for one tittle of the law to fail." This may originally have been meant ironically; but, as it stands, it states the permanence and irrevocable nature of the Law. It is incongruous that it should be followed by a saying about divorce and remarriage which, far from attesting the irrevocable nature of the Law, appears to go against one of its important provisions. The passage is puzzling; but it seems best to assume that St Luke found this isolated saying in his source and qualified it by putting it next to the saying about the irrevocable nature of the Law, preferring it to the Marcan incident which he does not reproduce.

JESUS AND ST PAUL

The letters of St Paul were written before any of the Gospels, so that St Paul is the earliest witness in the New Testament to Jesus' teaching on marriage and divorce, and therefore of very great importance. St Paul too believed in the permanence of Christian marriage. Writing as early as A.D. 51 to the Corinthians, he declared in 1 Cor. 7.39:

The wife is bound by the law as long as her husband liveth; but if her husband be dead, she is at liberty to be married to whom she will; only in the Lord.

On a later occasion, when writing to the Romans, he seems to assert that this is the teaching too of the Jewish Law (or even conceivably Roman law). "The woman which hath an husband is bound by the law to her husband so long as he liveth . . . but if her husband be dead, she is free from that law; so that she is no adulteress though she be married to another man" (Rom. 7.2–3). It seems likely, however, that St Paul here disregarded the possibility of divorce according to Jewish (or Roman) law in order to make his analogy more cogent for the purpose of his argument; but it may have been because of the Christian teaching on the permanence of marriage that he felt able to do this.

St Paul in his teaching on sex distinguished between his own teaching and the teaching of "the Lord". He told the Corinthians that the Lord not merely forbade remarriage, but also divorce. But Paul was a realist, and in 1 Cor. 7.10ff he added his own teaching in cases where, notwithstanding the Lord, a woman was divorced from her husband:

Unto the married I command, yet not I, but the Lord, Let not the wife depart from her husband: But and if she depart, let her remain unmarried or be reconciled to her husband: and let not the husband put away his wife.

It has been suggested that in this passage St Paul was not writing about divorce, but separation *a mensa et thoro*; but the latter was unknown in the early Church, except for a period and that by mutual consent (1 Cor. 7.5). Plainly St Paul had inherited a tradition "from the Lord" about the permanence of marriage; and a few verses earlier he had just cited, in a way that suggests that it was received teaching, the very same text of Gen. 2.24 on which Jesus had hung the lasting nature of marriage.

While St Paul makes clear what was the teaching of the Lord, he does not hesitate to use his apostolic authority to mitigate this teaching immediately after he has stated it. In 1 Cor. 7.12–15 he wrote:

But to the rest speak I, not the Lord: If any brother hath a wife that believeth not, and she be pleased to dwell with him, let him not put her away. And the woman

which hath an husband that believeth not, and if he be pleased to dwell with her,
let her not leave him. For the unbelieving husband is sanctified by the wife, and
the unbelieving wife is sanctified by the husband: else were your children unclean;
but now are they holy. But if the unbelieving depart, let him depart. A brother or
a sister is not under bondage in such cases: but God hath called us to peace.

This "Pauline privilege" of divorce and remarriage is only permitted in the
extreme case of a "mixed marriage" when one of the two partners becomes
a Christian and the other refuses to continue the marriage. Some scholars
have held that St Paul was speaking here of separation and not divorce;
but, as explained above, the former was unknown in the early Church, and
in any case the language of "bondage" and "freedom" makes it clear that
St Paul was thinking of divorce. It has been suggested that the reason for
this exception is that spiritual regeneration made all things new and therefore annulled a previous pagan union. But this is to misunderstand the
practice of the early Church, which accepted marriage as it was, and then
applied to it Christian standards and Christian interpretation. In any case
St Paul stated here the principle he had in mind—"God hath called us to
peace". Assuming that v. 15b is taken with v. 15a (and not with v. 16) we
may take it that St Paul believed that evangelical peace was more important
than matrimonial legality. So despite the Lord's clear teaching, Paul was
prepared on occasion to sanction divorce.

SCHOLARSHIP AND CHURCHMANSHIP

Jesus asserted the permanence of marriage in the purposes of God. He
made revolutionary statements about the divine intention in the institution
of marriage which cut across all the matrimonial controversies of his day.
There can be no doubt that the New Testament teaching on marriage
stemmed from the new and creative teaching of Jesus himself. Since
marriage was intended to be permanent, Jesus taught that "what God hath
joined together let not man put asunder".

The questions at issue are whether Jesus asserted the absolute indissolubility of marriage, so that any other teaching (for example in St
Matthew and St Paul) marks a declension from this; or whether Jesus
asserted the indissolubility of marriage with one single exception (as in St
Matthew); or whether Jesus gave, not binding laws governing each and
every marriage whatever its circumstances might be, but inspired teaching
about the true nature of marriage as it is intended by God.

The case may be clarified by a consideration of the development of
Gospel criticism. There was a time when interest was centred on the recovery
of the actual words spoken by the historical Jesus. People argued that, if it
could be shown that Jesus had asserted the permanence of marriage, there
was an end to the matter; marriage was indissoluble, except perhaps for
porneia. But the development of form criticism has resulted in people
asking themselves how the early Church understood Jesus' teaching. The
interest shifted from "What did he say?" to "What did he mean?", or at
least to "What did the early Church understand him to mean?". After all,
meaning matters most.

When the question is put in this way, a view different from the "indissolubilist position" can be held. Jesus asserted the permanence of marriage in the intention of God, and he may have included words similar to those found in Luke 16.18. But the fact that St Luke places this saying immediately after a blunt assertion of the indissolubility of the Jewish law shows that St Luke, at any rate, did not regard these words of Jesus as legislative rules. As for St Matthew, with his tendency to lay down the laws of the eschatological age, when he turned Jesus' pronouncement about the nature of marriage into legislation about marriage, he felt bound to insert the exception of *porneia*. Similarly St Paul, in the different circumstances of the Corinthian church, made another exception to deal with a broken mixed marriage. St Paul regarded the principle of peace as overriding the law of no divorce. As for St Mark, his matrimonial legislation had to be adapted to the circumstances of the Gentile world where a woman could divorce her husband (but for St Mark this adaptation did not involve sanctioning divorce).

The question at issue may be framed in a different way. In Jesus' day, Jewish rabbis taught in two ways: by *halakah*, that is, rules governing conduct, such as sabbath laws or food laws, and by *haggadah*, that is, teaching by edification, often expressed in a vivid or exaggerated way, appealing to the heart by way of the imagination. It is clear from the Gospels that Jesus on occasion used both *halakah* and *haggadah*. Into which category does his teaching on the permanence of marriage fall? Or does it not fall neatly into either?

It is at this point that scholars so often part company. It cannot be coincidence that their academic conclusions are here often in agreement with the discipline of the Church to which they belong. Thus Roman Catholic scholars usually assert (on the basis of the New Testament evidence) that Jesus gave a ruling that marriage is indissoluble (cf. Dupont, Bonsirven);[1] whereas Protestant or Reformed scholars (whose Churches usually permit marriage after divorce at the discretion of the minister) tend to infer from the same evidence a very different conclusion (cf. Bornkamm, T. W. Manson).[2]

Anglican scholarship is often divided at this point (and it is worth noting that Anglican discipline too has differed). Anglo-Catholic scholars tended to infer from the New Testament that Jesus pronounced marriage to be indissoluble. Charles Gore wrote that "Our Lord formally and decisively declared marriage indissoluble" (*The Question of Divorce* (London 1911), p. 24). Replying, with Box, to R. H. Charles (*The Teaching of the New Testament on Divorce* (London 1921)), he wrote, "One must

[1] But cf. P. Hoffmann, "Jesus' Saying about Divorce and its Interpretation in the New Testament Tradition", *Concilium* (May 1970). He concludes: "In his teaching on divorce Jesus does *not* lay down a *law*, but rather reveals the *reality* of marriage and does so precisely in opposition to any legal narrowing of the issues" (op. cit. p. 64).

[2] J. J. von Allmen, however, is a Reformed scholar who believes marriage to be "indissoluble according to New Testament teaching" (*Pauline Teaching on Marriage* (ET 1963)). W. Manson also believed that Jesus' veto on divorce and remarriage was unconditional (cf. "The Interpretation of Christ's Teaching on Marriage and Divorce", Appendix III in *Church of Scotland Report of Special Committee on Remarriage of Divorced Persons* (1957) with which may be contrasted the view of M. Black, "Marriage and Divorce in the New Testament", Appendix II of the same report).

recognise Christ as a legislator for his Church in the matter of divorce"
(G. H. Box and C. Gore, *Divorce in the New Testament* (London 1921),
p. 49). The same viewpoint is echoed by K. E. Kirk: "Our Lord's teaching
has the same value, authority and application today as it ever had. . . . In
this matter more than any other our Lord surrounds his teaching most
firmly and definitely with the atmosphere of 'rule' or 'legislation' "
(*Marriage and Divorce* (London 1948), pp. 74ff). Some Anglican scholars,
while agreeing that Jesus "legislated", inclined to believe that he made an
exception of adultery (F. H. Chase, H. B. Swete); while R. H. Charles
thought that the exceptive clause added by St Matthew correctly explained
Jesus' own teaching. Others believed that Jesus' saying asserted not law
but a principle (A. W. F. Blunt, A. H. McNeile). Many sat on the fence,
contenting themselves with the statement that the exceptive clause in St
Matthew is an interpolation.

A recent treatment of the subject by Anglican scholars[1] is to be found in
Five Essays on Marriage (Louisville 1946), written at the request of the
Joint Commission on Holy Matrimony of the Protestant Episcopal
Church of U.S.A. The three scholars who dealt with the biblical evidence
all agreed that Jesus did not enunciate principles of law. According to
B. S. Easton, "What Christ actually taught was: A man and his wife are
no longer two but one flesh: what, therefore, God has joined together, let
not man put asunder. This, and no more" ("Divorce and the New Testament", p. 8). S. E. Johnson concluded that "to take a rigoristic attitude and
to refuse to consider cases on their merits, is to do precisely what our Lord
condemned: it is to deify a legal provision rather than to serve God by
helping human beings in their need" ("Jesus' Teaching on Divorce",
p. 60). F. C. Grant wrote that "there is no use trying to soften Jesus' pro-
phetic pronouncements on this subject. They were not enunciated as
principles of law, but as proclamations of the pure will of God" ("The
Mind of Christ on Marriage", p. 39).

What are the arguments which led scholars to take these very different
views?

DID JESUS LEGISLATE?

Dr Sherman Johnson in the essay already quoted above distinguishes
halakah and *haggadah* thus (op. cit., pp. 36ff):

The term halakah is applied to prescriptions for conduct drawn from the traditional law; everything else, all that side of Jewish teaching that attracts and
inspires the Jewish and Christian reader, is haggadah: "religious truths, moral
lessons, discourse on just reward and punishment, inculcation of the laws in
which the nationality of Israel is manifested, pictures of the past and future

[1] Among recent non-Anglican writing:
H. Preisker, *Christentum und Ehe in den ersten drei Jahrhunderten* (1927).
G. Delling, *Paulus' Stellung zu Frau und Ehe* (1931).
K. H. Rengstorf, *Mann und Frau im Urchristentum* (1954).
E. Kähler, *Die Frau in den Paulinischen Briefen* (1960).
Abel Isaksson, *Marriage and Ministry in the New Testament* (1965).
H. Baltensweiler, *Die Ehe im Neuen Testament* (1967).
D. W. Shaner, *A New Testament View of Divorce* (1969).
D. H. Greeren, "Ehe nach Neuen Testament", *N.T.S.* (1969).

greatness of Israel, scenes and stories from Jewish history, parallels between the divine institutions and those of Israel, encomiums on the Holy Land, inspiring narratives, and manifold consolation" (G. F. Moore, *Judaism*, Cambridge, Mass. 1927, I, p. 161ff). One who undertakes to classify Jesus' teaching in this way finds that it is predominantly haggadic. Such are all the parables; the exhortations to prayer, almsgiving and generosity; the Beatitudes; the rebukes against hypocrisy and cruelty; the eschatological teaching, etc. Jesus is much more the synagogue preacher and Sabbath school teacher than the rabbi.

The question is: Given this distinction between *halakah* and *haggadah*, should the saying on divorce be classed among the haggadic material? Or was it even *halakah*? Or does it fit precisely into neither category? First, in his ethics Jesus stressed the overriding importance of the inward attitude. Thus in the very same passage as that about remarriage we have in Matt. 5.28: "Whosoever looketh on a woman to lust after her hath committed adultery with her already in his heart." This does not mean that Jesus made no distinction between lust and adultery, but that he stressed the priority of the inward attitude. Secondly, Jesus made impossible demands which drive men to penitence and a fresh start; the same saying in Matt. 5.29 is a good illustration of this point. Thirdly, Jesus' choice of concrete situations bring home to us the absolute demand of God in whatever situation we may be. For example, the saying "If thy right eye offend thee, pluck it out" appears in the Sermon on the Mount sandwiched between Matt. 5.28 and the saying on remarriage and adultery; and so it seems to have a sexual reference. But the Church has never taken this teaching literally, whether or not it has in St Matthew any sexual reference. It is a striking saying bringing home the absolute demand of God for purity, but not a piece of legislation to be obeyed literally at all times of sexual temptation. Then, again, Jesus demanded practical action in accordance with his principles. If we ask what these basic principles are, he gives us the answer himself: they are love of God and love of our neighbour as ourselves, on which two principles "hang all the law and the prophets" (Matt. 22.40). Jesus again and again emphasized that these principles must be shown in action (cf. Matt. 7.21, etc.). Finally, the ethics of Jesus are the ethics of the Kingdom. This does not mean that they can only be put into practice in the fulfilled Kingdom of God; indeed Jesus expressly said that there there will be no marriage or giving in marriage (Mark 12.25); it means rather that his ethics are signposts to right action which can only be fulfilled by those who are already being strengthened by grace within his inaugurated Kingdom. The New Testament as a whole bears eloquent witness to the way in which grace transforms human behaviour and opens new possibilities of relationships.

If we examine the contexts in which the sayings of Jesus about remarriage appear in the Gospels, we shall find that they are neither pure *haggadah* nor pure *halakah* (in the sense in which these terms have been defined); they show the pure will of God by reference to extreme and vivid circumstances. This is clearest in Matt. 5.32. The other sayings in this passage are not generally understood to be taken literally. "If thy right eye offend thee pluck it out" (Matt. 5.29) is not to be literally obeyed. Similarly, "Swear not at all" (Matt. 5.34) has not been taken by the Church down the ages as a veto on all oaths. "Resist not evil" (Matt. 5.39) has not been generally understood to mean that all Christians must always be pacifists; and similarly "Give to him that asketh thee" (Matt. 5.42) has not been taken as an absolute command to Christians to give away whatever is asked regardless of their own commitments and responsibilities. Matt. 5.32 is the only saying in this whole passage that is taken as *halakah*. Why do not those who say that Jesus was legislating about the indissolubility of marriage in these Gospel sayings take absolutely literally such other sayings as "Call no man your father" (Matt. 23.9) or "Let not thy left hand know what thy right hand doeth" (Matt. 6.3)—the latter being a superb piece of teaching about secrecy in almsgiving but which if taken literally conflicts with every known principle of stewardship! Seen as inspired teaching, Jesus' sayings on the permanence of marriage give superb insights into the true nature of matrimony as God intends it. But if they are applied without thought to the circumstances of the individual, they can degenerate into the heartless legalism which Jesus so condemned.

But, even so, might not these sayings after all be *halakah*? Perhaps Jesus taught as we would rather he had not! Such a view would have behind it the consensus of the primitive Church and the preponderance of Christian tradition thereafter. And Jesus did at times teach *halakah*; not new teaching for a new Church, but reinterpretation of the Mosaic Law in the light of the kingdom of God. He gave definite instructions about the propriety of healing on the Jewish Sabbath (Mark 3.4, etc.). He seems to have given a ruling about Corban which the Pharisees themselves followed soon afterwards (Mark 7.10ff); and he seems to have given rulings too about ritual ablutions (Mark 7.5) and possibly kosher foods as well (Mark 7.19). All these pronouncements seem to have been made for humanitarian and anti-legalist reasons. Might it not be argued that, if Jesus gave a pronouncement about the indissolubility of marriage, this too was for humanitarian reasons, for it protected a wife and it protected the young children of a family? Yet the counter-argument might equally easily be made that there are occasions when divorce could bring blessed relief from intolerable conditions for both wife and children.

No certainty about the interpretation of Jesus' sayings on remarriage can be attained. Either view might be right. All will agree that Jesus taught that in the purposes of God marriage was meant to be permanent. Deliberately to cause or to contribute to the breakdown of a marriage is, in Jesus' teaching, to go against the known will of God.

Beyond this point certainty ends. Gospel criticism, by its nature, is concerned with the balancing of probabilities. Some scholars say that marriage of its nature is indissoluble, so that remarriage during the lifetime of a partner is always adultery; so Jesus taught because such is the nature of the case. Other scholars believe that Jesus, in asserting the permanence of marriage, broke out of the sphere of law, as he did in the other antitheses of the Sermon on the Mount. It was his opponents who equated God's will with the Jewish law and so made the law into the supreme authority. But Jesus presented men, not with law, but with the pure will of

God. This was not a mere ideal or a counsel of perfection to which comparatively few can attain. Failure to reach an ideal may evoke only mild nostalgia
or regret. But Jesus, in presenting men with the pure will of God, laid upon
them extreme demands, requiring their utmost fidelity.[1] Every effort must
be made to avoid the breakdown of a marriage. To acquiesce in or to
promote marital breakdown is grave disloyalty to the teaching of Christ,
and irretrievable breakdown of marriage is a mark of grave human failure.
The pure will of God makes no compromise with frailty, sin, and error;
and it may not be set aside lightly or without moral distress. In an actual
human situation, however, where marriage has already broken down,
people have to go on from where they are. It may be that in the circumstances in which they now find themselves, divorce and remarriage are the
least unsatisfactory and therefore the best way forward in God's sight.
Such a decision can only properly be made after a deep searching of conscience and an acknowledgement of human weakness, error, and sin.
Nevertheless, in specific situations divorce and remarriage cannot be ruled
out as an authentic response to God's will for particular people, the way in
which they can best know and experience the recreative and healing grace
of God. Those scholars who hold this view (among whom the writer of
this note must class himself) would say that, when Jesus asserted the
permanence of marriage, he did not thereby rule out of court the propriety
of all divorce and remarriage.

All that can be said here is that either view *may* be right. And from this
there follows a point of the utmost importance. It is not possible to ground
the judgement that all divorce and remarriage is forbidden on the fact that
Jesus definitely forbade it. He may not have done so—many, perhaps most,
would say he most probably did not. Some criterion other than the clear
teaching of Jesus must be found if the Christian Church is to hold that all
marriages are indissoluble and that all remarriages during a partner's lifetime are contrary to God's will. The solution to our problem must be
found by an evaluation of factors other than purely biblical considerations.
This is attempted in Chapter 4 of the report.

---

[1] These demands can only be met by way of response, as "fruit of the Spirit", not
by way of setting oneself to keep them.

An additional note to this appendix appears on p. 169.

2

The Correlation of Theological and Empirical Meaning

by J. W. Bowker

1

In paragraph 73 it was pointed out that, although theological understanding is necessarily informed from the New Testament, the actual "return to the New Testament" is not a simple procedure. In the case of passages which have a bearing on marriage, it is possible for there to be "genuine uncertainty and disagreement". This is so, because Scripture is not a timeless abstraction, nor is it the insertion into the world of immutably definitive legislation. The fact that there can be disagreement, and that consequently there must be an unceasing quest for meaning in the Church, is of profound theological importance: it is a necessary consequence of the way in which God is believed to have revealed himself. It is fundamental to a *Christian* knowledge of God that an access to this knowledge is given to us in the particularities of a life bounded by space and time. From the one particularity of being flow the other particularities of words and meaning. Equally—and this is of paramount importance—it is through an unremitting attention to the meaning of the particular words of Scripture—making use of all the constant extension of knowledge which this involves—that our understanding of the nature of God in Christ is itself established and built. This is manifestly one of the means through which the Spirit gives life to the Churches, from one generation to another. This is why the impossibility of arriving at a final and definitive understanding of the words of Jesus on marriage and divorce—and hence also the impossibility of constructing immutable legislation—is not a disturbing conclusion; and this is why, equally, any claim that such an understanding has in fact been universally obtained is simply, as a matter of fact, false.

But it does *not* follow from this that the Church has nothing to say about marriage at all. On the contrary, Christian theological meaning arises, in part, in the very process of relating (or of endeavouring to correlate) what is given in the revelation of God to the circumstances and lives which subsequently occur. In this process of correlation Christian theology has a great deal to say, but equally it has a great deal to learn, simply because lives and circumstances change.

It follows that when this report offers itself as a contribution to the forming of thought and action in the Church and to the testing of consensus (see Chapter 4), it does so, *not* because the members of the Commission are themselves undecided (which would be irrelevant), still less because the members are agreed on every syllable (which is improbable), but because it would be theologically improper to do anything else. This appendix will argue that theologically the Church is committed, from its inception in the person of Christ, to exactly this kind of procedure—to a constant relating of the mind and spirit of Christ to circumstances which themselves change and vary from one generation to another but which *already* belong to him as risen Lord. The ways of knowing and of understanding the nature of marriage have been vastly extended in recent generations; the social and economic circumstances in which many marriages are now lived have changed. For this reason there cannot be a report on "Marriage". There can and must be an attempt to bring theological insight to bear on the actual conditions (in this case of marriage) in which, as Augustine put it, men and women set out across the sea of this world. The purpose of the Church is not to produce statements on marriage, but to be instrumental of the salvation, the final and true belonging, which is already in being in Christ, and which is to be extended to all men. But this means that the Church cannot attend to marriage without attending to the breakdown of marriages—nor can this be done in the abstract. The facts of human joy do indeed invade us with splendour; but the facts of human frailty are those which give meaning to redemption. The gift of God to the world through the Church is not a statement on marriage but a real attention to facts, to *both* sets of facts, those of joy and those of desolation; and the gift of God is their reconciliation in Christ. The great danger, therefore, which confronts the Church is that of putting its faith, not in God, but in an abstraction: if marriage is abstracted from its context in life *or* from its context in the redemptive purpose of God, we shall end up talking of an abstraction of our own invention which has little to do with either God or man. This is not an idle warning. It has happened in the past (when, in Maitland's view, the Church's marriage laws became "a maze of flighty fancies and misapplied logic")[1] and it is entirely possible for it to happen again. But if these two contexts, in which an understanding of marriage arises, are held together—and are held in precisely that correlation of the human and the divine which is manifested incarnationally in Christ—then Christian doctrine becomes an inspiration, a breaking into life of a new spirit, a new hope, and a new resource of love.

This means that, although a universally agreed statement on marriage, or on divorce, or on remarriage after divorce, cannot be "read off" from the New Testament, nor even, *simpliciter*, from the traditions of the Church, it does not follow that no statements can be made at all; still less does it mean that Christian decisions are without authority. On the contrary, the resources of principle and decision are profoundly rooted in the Church. But the fact remains that these are always brought to bear on situations which may themselves contribute a totally new dimension of meaning and of consequent action. It is here that correlation can be seen, not as an abstract word, but as a means through which the Spirit works. The purpose of this appendix is to give (though necessarily in a highly

[1] See D. M. Stenton, *The English Woman in History* (London 1957), p. 45.

abbreviated form) some illustration in the case of marriage of how and why this occurs.

2

Any attempt to reflect on the meaning of marriage must begin with the fact of marriage itself, with the fact that human beings marry. Although this may appear to be pointing out the obvious, it is a necessary reminder that marriage is not approached as an abstraction, but as a means through which, as a matter of actuality, human beings have recognized and safeguarded fundamental needs of their own nature. In particular, it is a means through which they have come to realize what is involved in the creation of relationship. It is, of course, obvious that the human organism exists in many states of association with its environment, which are temporally or functionally limited, and which do not require any great degree of reflective or widely consequential commitment. The question raised by marriage is the question of transition, the question of how the transition is in fact made from association in the restricted sense to relationship which *does* call for greater degrees of commitment. The simplest degree of association may perhaps need to be extended on pragmatic grounds (at least until other arrangements can be made) for the procreation and nurture of children; this is relatively straightforward:

> What we had in common was enough
> To rear four children. . . .[1]

What really needs to concern us is what lies behind that sufficiency, that "enough", in the transition to relationship (in the sense defined above), which in reverse contributes to the adequacy of nurture in terms of care and love.

A great deal is now known, both of the physiological base of these (as of other) aspects of behaviour, and of the extent to which its particular forms are a social product, and no doubt more will be known in the future; but this does not in itself affect the distinction in experience between association and relationship, an experience which the human brain is able to interpret to itself:

> Just so may love, although 'tis understood
> The mere commingling of passionate breath,
> Produce more than our searching witnesseth. . . .[2]

If marriage is explored in this way, as a context in which particular, experienced, realities of relationship are able to come into being, the question inevitably arises to what extent marriage is a *necessary* context, a context without which certain characteristics of relationship would be difficult to attain, and for some people might be impossible to attain. This at once raises the further question of what characterizes marriage— what, in other words, are the characterizing features which make it, at least for some, indispensable for the full meaning of relationship to

---

[1] C. Ashby, *In the Vulgar Tongue* (London 1968), p. 35.
[2] See n. 1 on p. 112 below.

emerge. To ask this is not, suddenly, to slide away into an abstraction, marriage. On the contrary, by asking what has and does characterize particular marriages, one can attend, much more seriously and without feeling vulnerably defensive, to the many variations on the theme of marriage—to recognize, for example, that relationship is not exclusive to marriage; or to recognize that some marriages fail to achieve relationship; or that the failure of marriages makes serious, for some people, the question whether, in their case, marriage may hinder, rather than help, relationship; or that for some people a homosexual rather than a heterosexual relationship arises within their own nature; or that the institutional forms of marriage and of marriage custom vary greatly in different parts of the world. In this report an attempt has been made to consider some of these (and similar) questions which arise from the relativity of human situations. But what, nevertheless, remains a point of focus is the fact that marriages exist, in which and through which men and women are able to realize in their own case the meaning of relationship. Furthermore, they have created a language with which to point to its significance and worth, not the somewhat academic language of relationship, but the language of love. Few people would doubt the biological and physiological base of this language; but few people who have experienced their being in this way, even if for a moment only, would doubt that they need this language:

> Love is not love
> Which alters when it alteration finds,
> Or bends with the remover to remove:
> O, no! It is an ever fixed mark,
> That looks on tempests and is never shaken. . . .
> Love's not Time's fool, though rosy lips and cheeks
> Within his bending sickle's compass come;
> Love alters not with his brief hours and weeks,
> But bears it out even to the edge of doom.
> If this be error, and upon me prov'd,
> I never writ, nor no man ever lov'd.[1]

This particular sonnet has been deliberately chosen as an illustration because of its obvious neutrality and because of the indeterminacy of its object. It is a reminder that the language of love can and does arise within the many varieties of particular natures, and that the word itself can have many possible meanings and points of reference. Consequently, there can never be a defence of marriage, in the sense of its being a necessary condition of love for all people; there can only be an affirmation of marriage as the actual circumstance of love for some people, the condition in which the word ceases, so to speak, to be verbal, and receives a meaning in their case. Furthermore, it is a meaning which could not occur similarly apart from marriage, because marriage, in a particularly formal way, involves in this definition the consequentiality of time. It is true that a single image can pass into the soul for ever, as it did for Stephen Daedalus on the sea-harvest

---

[1] W. Shakespeare, Sonnet 116.

shore; what seemed to him to be "the wonder of that mortal beauty" made the moment seem as though time had ceased. From this momentary encounter love may indeed arise, and one may begin to know why it is a necessary word. But prosaically time is *not* destroyed—even Stephen had to halt suddenly and hear his heart in silence and wonder how far he had walked and what hour it was.[1] For this reason it belongs to the understanding of marriage to realize the sense in which it is a response to the irreversibility of time, a way of extending the momentary awakenings of love into the long accumulations of consequence which are a human life. Love may apparently be a single moment of intensity, a brief encounter; certainly the word is claimed for such encounters. It *may* be rightly so claimed, but in another sense it cannot be, because love always has within itself the capacity to transcend whatever it has so far been or become. And for this, time is required.

3

It is at this point of focus that theological and empirical reflection on the meaning of marriage have much to offer to each other—indeed, at this level they are indispensable to each other: the empirical study of human behaviour emphasizes the physiological and neurological base of human consciousness in its social contexts, but it is equally aware that a function of brain behaviour is to represent to itself the meaning, or the interpretation, of its own states of consciousness—however illusory or pretentious some of these interpretations may be; theology points to the transfiguration of consciousness in its recognition and acceptance of the reality of God as of effect within it. Clearly, there are those who believe that this interpretation *is* illusory and pretentious; but even so, those who are engaged in empirical and theological reflection *can* be in agreement, not only that interpretation arises from the external cues of the universe, but also that interpretation itself exemplifies what the sociologist Luckmann has called "the transcendance of biological nature by the human organism".[2]

This means that theology is constantly committed to indicating the grounds on which it believes that God can, in effect, be known; and if it accepts the adequacy of these grounds, then the explication of theological meaning is necessarily an assertion of the particular meaningfulness of all things in relation to God.

This is of fundamental importance in the Jewish and Christian tradition, which is particularly clear that, if there *is* any genuine knowledge of God, it must be knowledge of God; that is to say, God must precede or pre-exist our knowledge of him; he is not created simply by our attempts to know. How this understanding was arrived at in the Hebrew and Jewish tradition is a matter of biblical history. In effect, it meant that instead of things giving meaning to God (as in tendencies towards animism), still less of things being identified with God (as in some forms of idolatry), God was believed to give meaning to things—to all things and all lives, including,

---

[1] James Joyce, *Portrait of the Artist as a Young Man*, ch. IV.
[2] T. Luckmann, *The Invisible Religion* (1967), p. 49.

eventually, time and space. This reversal of significance was by no means easily achieved. Although it was founded on the necessity (for the Jews) of recognizing the reality in effect of God in such events as the Exodus, there were many people in many generations for whom the implications were too demanding to be borne; equally there were many events in which the reality of God in effect was difficult to discern. It was this conflict which gave to the development of the Jewish people and tradition an almost ruthlessly astringent honesty, as one can see in such people as Jeremiah, or in such books as that of Job; and although in one sense it was perfectly true that God *was* created by the Exodus—in the sense that before the Exodus God was not known to be "like that" in his own name and nature (Exod. 6.2)—yet it was very rapidly recognized that, if God is known in effect in this, or in any other, event, he must precede the knowledge of that effect, in order to give rise to it. In traditional terms this led directly back to the original creative act, *bereshith bara elohim*, "in the beginning God created . . ." (Gen. 1.1). This is an intentional act, not an accidental consequence of conflict with chaos, and hence it is in itself the first act of self-revelation on the part of God.

It is in the context of a created order, distinct and other, that the conditions of knowledge and relationship arise. Hence, although Genesis represents a way of describing what it may be in the nature of men and women to become, in relation to God and to each other, it was quite clearly recognized that the reality of relationship all too frequently does not exist. But the fact that we are able to *know* the gaps between what is naturally or originally possible and what in fact occurs produces a supremely important biblical insight, that God now reveals himself to men within the process of revealing men to themselves, by calling them, constantly, to a new character. Men lose life, but gain knowledge (Gen. 2.16f; 3.1–7, 19, 22–4), and it is in their faithfulness to the conditions of knowledge (refusing to yield to any degree of pretence or self-deceit about their real possibilities for good or for evil, for splendour or for despair) that they discover that they are being faithful to God—indeed one might say that they *rediscover* God, not in abstraction but in life. The choice of knowing creates a consciousness of subject and object, a "gap" which requires attention to the means and condition of its healing; the biblical narrative (particularly up to the call of Abraham) exemplifies the wide and ever-extending effects of this alienation, but equally (particularly up to the giving of Torah) it exemplifies the means of healing. This explains the extreme emphasis in Scripture on categories of relationships as the point at which the meaning of God is learned, perhaps most obviously in the basic category of the covenant, but also, and insistently, in marriage. Hence in Genesis the verb *yada'*; "he knew" (Adam knew Eve his wife (Gen. 4.1)), although it is frequently referred to as a euphemism, may mean exactly what it says. Adam *knew* his alienation from God (Gen. 3.8) and from Eve (Gen. 3.7, 12) and in a sense from the whole created order (Gen. 3.17ff); but in *knowing* his wife in the concentrated form of sexual relationship the long but real return to the intended (in a later sense, paradisal) state was begun. "And Adam knew Eve his wife" (Gen. 4.1); this is the first action—the first verb[1]—after the expulsion from Eden. There is, therefore, one highly important sense in which the Fall is, so to speak, a fall upwards, a move into new structures and new opportunities of knowing and of relationship; but structures now attendant with pain:

Her image had passed into his soul for ever and no word had broken the holy silence of his ecstasy. Her eyes had called him and his soul had leaped at the call. To live, to err, to fall, to triumph, to recreate life out of life! A wild angel had appeared to him, the angel of mortal youth and beauty, an envoy from the fair courts of life, to throw open before him in an instant of ecstasy the gates of all the ways of error and glory. On and on and on and on . . .[2]

4

This background is of extreme importance in any attempt to interpret the attitudes of Jesus to marriage and divorce; for what underlies the words, through which his answers to questions about the nature of marriage are constructed, is not an existing theory about marriage, but an assertion of the way in which God is present to all circumstances and of the way in which all circumstances can potentially represent the natural and intended state of men in relation to God, even though this potentiality is not necessarily, nor always, realized. In the case of Jesus, the appeal to the natural was inevitably an appeal to the original, because the creation narratives in Genesis concentrate this fundamental insight into the way in which the natural and the theological give meaning to each other. What is said of Adam and Eve, in their relation to God and to each other, can be said of marriage; no matter how great the disintegrations may be which drive a man to hide himself from God and to conceal himself from his wife (Gen. 3.7f) (that is, to withold himself from commitment to whatever an unconcealed, spontaneously loving relationship might be) any marriage potentially points towards the recovery of the natural or "paradisal" state, the total bonding of a man and a woman, and of both with God. "Male and female created he them" (Gen. 1.27 and 5.2). It is to this focus of the natural and the theological, not to arguments about marriage and divorce in his own time, that Jesus appealed (Matt. 19.4; Mark 10.6); and in some of the versions of Genesis current at the time of Jesus the text (in Gen. 5.2) is even more emphatic—and this, significantly, is one of the very few variants which the rabbis accepted from the Greek Bible as correcting the Hebrew text: "Male and female created he *him*".[3] This gave rise to extravagant theories about the original form and appearance of Adam, but in essence the change in number from plural to singular emphasizes the total, creative, harmony of relationship in the original intention of God. This *is* the natural state of man, the state which marriages endeavour to recover;

---

[1] The possibility of a different underlying Semitic root cannot altogether be discounted (for example, "to be reconciled with", Arab. *wāda‘a*), but even so the play on words would make the point.

[2] James Joyce, op. cit.

[3] For details see my *Targums and Rabbinic Literature* (Cambridge 1969), Appendix III "The Recognised Variants in the Septuagint"; the original variant probably arose from the second half of the verse, where the name Adam is given to *both* Adam and Eve, to "them".

it is in part the reason why there cannot be "marriage in heaven" (Matt. 22.23ff; Mark 12.18ff; Luke 20.27ff) because, when marriage has regained the paradisal state, it has transcended its own institutional necessity. The deliberate reconstruction of relationship which initiaties a marriage is no longer necessary; the bridge exists because it is entirely built.

When we turn to the specific questions on divorce in the Gospels (Mark 10.1ff; Matt. 19.3ff), we find that in effect the replies of Jesus transfer the issues put to him, so that they become a single issue of discrepancy between two parts of Torah. By appealing to Genesis Jesus implies that divorce would not have arisen except as a consequence of human hardness of heart. From this point of view Jesus' response becomes a statement, not so much about *divorce* as about *marriage*. Both for Jesus and for those who questioned him Genesis offered a means of knowing the original and creative intention of God, what he intended for men and women. Where this intention of God is in being, to separate the "one flesh" and to attempt to create a new union is to commit adultery. But here the exceptive clause in Matthew becomes critical (unless, of course, it is eliminated on the grounds that it is not original to Jesus, or, equally, that it does not represent a faithful interpretation in the early Church of Jesus' intention); for the effect of this clause (no matter what *porneia* may mean) is to argue that where the intention of God is frustrated and marriage is not becoming that which it should be, an entirely different situation obtains. The passages in Matthew and Mark do not particularly consider that situation. They record an instance in which Jesus resists a primary discussion of divorce as though it is a subject *in itself,* by going back to the positive foundations of marriage; if that intention is being realized, divorce cannot come into the matter. What is *not* considered here is the whole range of quite different questions about, for example, the position of those who, as a consequence of human "hardness of heart"—or as a consequence of *porneia*—are in a state of having divorced, or of having been divorced (the latter being a position in which, at the time of Jesus, women, often through no fault of their own, were more likely to find themselves than men). What Jesus might have said to those in this condition is not known, and can only be inferred; and it must, therefore, be inferred from more than the particular passages under discussion. It is here that Jesus' attitudes, so far as they are recorded, to the sinner and the outcast become immediately relevant.

This means that Jesus' particular responses must be understood in the whole context of what Jesus was claiming about the relation of the intention of God to men, of which Torah and its interpretation represents only a part. That a divorce signifies an instance of disintegration of the natural (i.e. original) state of man is obvious; in that sense it must be contrary to what God intended, and on this point Jesus is adamant. But this does not *in itself* answer the quite different question, how are all individuals, whether married or unmarried, divorced or undivorced, to be helped to realize the fundamental truth of all lives, that they are able to know and realize the reality of God in the kind of relationship prefigured in Adam and Eve—how, in other words, the lost condition, or Garden of Eden, can be reattained? This question cannot be answered by confining attention to the texts about marriage and divorce, but only by setting those texts in the whole context of Jesus' claim to disclose the way in which God can and does become totally of effect—a claim which led to the later response that the effect of God in his case was so great and so dramatic that it required the language of incarnation to describe it with any degree of adequacy.

From this point of view it is indispensable to grasp how and why Jesus came to make so startling an assertion—not a theoretical assertion, but an embodied, enacted claim that God can be known in effect. It arises, in part, from a dilemma of many Jews at the time when Jesus was alive: if God has indeed been known to be of effect in such events as creation, or the Exodus, or the inspiration of prophets, or the restoration of the temple under Judas—and if, further, he could not be known to be if he had not been of these effects—then where is his effect to be seen now? How might one legitimately continue to be expectant of his effect, without which claims to knowledge are abstract? Jewish movements and individuals at the time of Jesus gave many different answers to these questions, some rival, some interlocking—apocalyptic, messianic, ritualistic, sectarian, sacrificial, social; the mosaic is brilliant with urgency. What is essentially clear is that Jesus offered his own self as a solution to the dilemma—a dilemma, not of the transcendence of God (which was no problem) but of the immanence of God. Jesus claimed that God can be known to be, simply and directly, by lives that look for his effect and are created, or recreated, by it. This claim would scarcely be of enduring value (no matter how brilliant the parables which taught it or the miracles which exemplified it) if it had not also been carried through in an actual life to the point of death; for if God is of no effect there, he is in effect nowhere. It was a desperate agony in Gethsemane and in the crucifixion to know how, since rescue comes neither by angels (Matt. 26.53) nor by evasion (Matt. 26.39; Mark 14.36; Luke 22.42), the sense of the reality of God could continue—how, in other words, even this would be given meaning by God. Hence, as Luke so acutely observed, the highest point of manifest transfiguration in the life of Jesus is inextricably involved in the lowest point of degradation and defeat (Luke 9.31); for if his embodied claim to the truth and total possibility of God for all men does not endure in the latter, it is nothing more than a curiosity in the former.

Yet it is *not* simply a curiosity, at least for some people, precisely because the death of God did not occur; God did not die in and with the death of Jesus. The continuity of effect is precisely what the resurrection of Jesus meant; a continuity of effect, not simply in his own case, but immediately and actually in his disciples; nor even in their case alone, but in an extension through time and space in which, in many lives, the prayer of Jesus, that what he had known of the effect of God might be known by others (Matt. 11.25ff; John. 17.20–6), has been realized to be true. If Jesus had not made this claim, and if this claim had not so variously and so extensively been known for truth, it is doubtful whether anyone would be much concerned, two thousand years later, with his opinions about marriage and divorce. But precisely because what he said about marriage and divorce is set in the context of a claim about the way in which God can be known, no matter how dark the existing circumstances of disaster or of deprivation may be, our own consideration of divorce must be set in the same context. In his sayings about divorce Jesus affirmed the natural state of relationship from which marriage derives and to which marriages can lead. But it is an understanding of relationship which includes relationship with God. It is the return, not to a part of the paradisal state (man and woman), but to the whole of the paradisal state (the reality of God to every creature and to every part of his creation) which Jesus ceaselessly affirms and practises. There can be no limit to the creative power of God, even in dealing with the most intransigent material; faith can be seen as much in a Roman centurion as in a Jew—perhaps more; as much in a Samaritan—perhaps more; can one continue, as much in one who in the past has been divorced as in the unbrokenly married—perhaps more, because it is the ill who have need of the physician? Jesus affirms the reality of marriage, but he does not deny the repair of its destruction in the condition of repentance and faith. Still less does he specify that healing cannot, in *any* circumstances, be mediated through a new marriage, even though there *are* circumstances in which a second "marriage" is adultery. In some circumstances a new marriage may in fact conceivably be necessary, if marriage is indeed that means of foreshadowing the unity of God and men, as Genesis speaks of it, and as Ephesians also insists on it (Eph. 5.21ff) as the place of learning—the place where the meaning of all relationship, in Christ, with God, and in the world, can be most clearly learned.

None of this creates a casual attitude either to marriage or to divorce. It is precisely because marriage is a focal image of the splendours of all relationship gathered up in God that divorce is both the shattering of all that God creatively intended and yet is an example of the broken condition in which the very redemption which Jesus embodied—the restoring of God to men and men to God—can really *work*, not as a matter of verbal recognition alone, but of actual healing, of rebuilding, of the renewing of life in the image of God. To regain the lost image of God; there is nothing here which, in a recognized condition of existing failure and disorder, prohibits the possibility of subsequent marriage as a means of grace to that end—precisely that means of grace which it represents in Genesis. Both Jesus and Paul recognized that the restoration of a real and effective atonement between God and men cannot usually (or perhaps ever) obtain without a conscious recognition on the part of men of the existing fact of failure, and hence of need; nor can it obtain without a deliberate redirecting of life towards the truthfulness of God in the faith and hope that his promises will hold. Knowledge, in both senses, is once again required: to know that one is naked, vulnerable, alone, and capable of great and destructive evil; yet also to know, in the hard facts of a relived and a recreated life, that God still searches in the garden and comes to our frightened condition to be once more of real effect within it. The apparent conflict between the intention of marriage and remarriage after divorce reflects the contrast between the fact of failure and the fact of redemption. No one doubts the reality of failure which divorce necessarily represents. Without a recognition of this reality another marriage is likely to be a casual self-indulgence, as much an adultery as is sexual relation on the part of a married person with someone outside the marriage. But where this failure is recognized without pretence, a *metanoia*, a change of direction, a new possibility can be created. To say that in this new creation the fact of the previous failure runs on, and that there cannot in any circumstances be another marriage after divorce while a previous partner is living, prejudges to what extent a marriage existed previously in anything more than a legal or nominal sense (in the *Genesis* sense marriage is created, not by proximity alone, nor, for that matter, by vows; it is created by becoming what it should be and by being what it is, in recreating the paradisal state); furthermore, it imposes the one condition in which human beings can never be absolved, except in a verbal sense. To say that forgiveness requires reparation and that in this most sensitive area of relationship it requires the silent witness of no subsequent marriage (until the death of the previous partner) is another matter; but it certainly does not arise from these texts.

5

This long (though in fact over-brief) discussion of remote texts and of pre-Freudian mentality may perhaps, for some people, confirm the former Prime Minister's use of the word "theological" as meaning "obscure and unnecessary". In fact it has been an attempt to show that Christian theological meaning does not arise simply from the quotation of texts in isolation, but from the whole context of Jesus' embodied and enacted claim that God is, and that he is of real effect—not necessarily the effects which we would like, but the effects which we need to give us life and hope. In the case of marriage and divorce, as elsewhere, the texts contribute to the understanding of the whole context, but the context is a part of the meaning of the texts. There is nothing surprising or novel in this; this process of interaction is already visible in the New Testament itself. Furthermore, the New Testament already exemplifies the correlation of theological and empirical understanding, not least in the case of marriage. This can be seen very clearly, both in 1 Corinthians and in Ephesians; for what is observable in 1 Corinthians is a pressure to establish the implications of Christ for particular and contingent circumstances. How are these implications understood? How are they arrived at? They are certainly not arrived at by the application of an already existing circumstantial legislation. So far as Paul is concerned, the answer lies fundamentally in the basic fact of *ecclēsia* (1 Cor. 1.2); it lies in the fact that there *is* a Church, a body (1 Cor. 12) of those who are "called unto the fellowship (to share in the life—*eis koinōnian*) of his Son Jesus Christ our Lord" (1 Cor. 1.9). Without Christ (to point out the obvious) there would be no Church, nor any Christian decisions to be made. But *with* Christ, as a consequence of Christ, a totally different resource of wisdom, of righteousness, of sanctification, of redemption, is in being—and is in being for *us* (1 Cor. 1.30). It is the *fact* of Christ—"Christ nailed to the cross" (1 Cor. 1.22; 2.2)—which is the new reality, and consequently the only conceivable foundation on which Christian lives are to be built (1 Cor. 2.2; 3.11). On this foundation a new spirit of judgement and decision is "freely given" (1 Cor. 2.9–16), through which the mind of Christ continues to work its effect (1 Cor. 2.16). Part of the problem of the Christian communities at Corinth lay in the fact, as Paul observed, that they were not yet *pneumatikoi*, possessed of the Spirit in this sense (1 Cor. 3.1ff). But Paul insisted emphatically that the Corinthian Christians would never arrive at the spiritual interpretation of the mind of Christ by going to the law courts of the *adikoi* (NEB, "pagan") and hoping to get decisions there (1 Cor. 6.1ff). In such cases as the one raised in 1 Cor. 5.1, the Christian body ought to be able, collectively, to decide what is, and what is not, in accord with the mind of Christ—and Paul, in his own view, can be involved in this collective decision (even though he is physically absent), because he too has the Spirit of God (1 Cor. 7.40).

What, then, informs this collective judgement? The answer to this becomes clear in 1 Cor. 7ff, where Paul attends to specific questions raised by the Corinthians; in these chapters a primary source of decision is "the word of the Lord" (1 Cor. 7.10) and the example of Christ, including the extension of that example through lives already transformed by him (1 Cor. 11.1); in one case (1 Cor. 11.23) Paul hands on that which he "received from the Lord". But it is manifestly clear that there is not, so to speak, a "word of the Lord" for all the contingencies raised. Paul, therefore, applies his own spiritual understanding (1 Cor. 7.40) and forms his own judgement (for example 1 Cor. 7.12, 25). In the case of *some* questions to do with marriage Paul has a "word of the Lord": "Let not the wife depart from her husband: but and if she depart, let her remain unmarried, or be reconciled to her husband: and let not the husband put away his wife" (Cor. 7.10). This is clearly in accord with what is recorded of Jesus' teaching about marriage and divorce in the Gospels. But Paul immediately goes on to deal with a situation, or circumstance, for which there is not a "word of the Lord" of immediate applicability: "But to the rest speak I, not the Lord" (Cor. 7.12). In the particular circumstance then discussed, the ideal is upheld (much as Jesus upheld it by appealing to Genesis), but a possibility of separation is nevertheless allowed, because the persistence of one partner as *apistos* (1 Cor. 7.15, NEB "heathen") should not be allowed to enslave the other.

It follows, therefore, that Jesus was not understood by Paul to have legislated for all circumstances in every detail, but to have made possible the creation of a body in which a quite different quality of life is learned and expressed—the quality of love, of *agape* (1 Cor. 13). The purpose of the body of Christ is always to be seeking the meaning and the expression of that "more excellent way" (1 Cor. 12.31). This remains the case as much for us as for Paul. Obviously there are resources from which we, in our turn, can inform our attempts to arrive at the meaning and expression of *agape*, and they are much the same as they were for Paul: the words and actions of Jesus (as far as they have been recorded; and in this is included the preparation for those words and actions in what became for Christians the Old Testament); and the collective appropriation of these in the continuing generations of the Church (of which the first generations have an obviously distinct importance). But these resources do not in all cases *dictate* our judgements; they are the materials of judgement. What is required is a relating of these resources to the situations which now occur for us, of which some will, at least in part, be unprecedented—just as they were for Paul; however much we may be guided—and often may be very strongly advised—from the past, the past cannot be relied on to supply invariable judgements on all circumstances. The claim of the Church to be the Church—to be the body of Christ—is tested by its willingness to relate the mind and the spirit of Christ to that which contingently occurs. This would be hopelessly vague if it were said in any context other than that of the Church; appeals to the spirit of ——, or to the mind of ——, might well be rhetorical, if it were not for the fact that the fundamental materials of this appeal are embodied in space and time—in Christ and in the consequences of Christ which constitute his body.

It is on this basis, and on this basis alone, that the work of the Church in applying theological insight can be redeemed from the destructive "scissors" relationship of a Raglan and a Cardigan: "Snip, snip, snip, and God help the poor devil that comes between them"; though it is salutary to remember that Christian theological argument frequently *has* resembled this, and that the various protagonists have usually been able to appeal to the *same* source (the New Testament) to justify their positions. This has been possible precisely because the New Testament is *not* a dictation of decisions, not even in the case of a question like that of remarriage after divorce; for this question is not the *same* question from one generation to another. On the other hand, the New Testament compels us to decisiveness, and it has the power to transform our approach to all decisions and to all people, because here, uniquely, is a characterizing of the nature of God as love. The theological work of the Church is the translation of that love, "l'amor che move il sole e l'altre stelle".

The implication of all this is very precisely articulated in Ephesians 4. The only unity which can exist in the Church is that which already exists in Christ; it exists, not to be created, but to be entered into and received. The facts of distinction, or of disagreement, or of variety, are not the contradiction of love, but the opportunity of learning the painful costliness, *meta makrothumias*, of *agape*, of "forbearing one another in love" (Eph. 4.2). This does *not* mean that for Christians disagreement is trivial; *agape* does not mean that all things have to be regarded as equally true, nor, conversely, that nothing can ever be known to be true. It is entirely possible to be "carried about with every wind of doctrine, by the sleight of men" (Eph. 4.14). But the responsibility of those who are "sparing no effort to make fast with bonds of peace the unity which the Spirit gives" (Eph. 4.3, NEB) is to relate the saving gifts of God to the circumstances of men (Eph. 4.11ff); and this involves "speaking the truth in love" that we may "grow up into him in all things, which is the head, even Christ" (Eph. 4.15). There is one primary objective here, one test of its truth: that the whole body should be built up to be an expression of that quality of love (Eph.

4.12). Either this is practical and visible, or else the crying of "Lord, Lord" is a sound in the air (Eph. 4.17–24). Hence the remaining chapters of Ephesians exemplify, in entirely practical terms, what this transfiguration of life should mean—this consequence of the Spirit which is offered to us as an armour and defence against destruction (Eph. 6.10ff). There is only one criterion of judgement: the Christ-given, God-given, Spirit of love, of *agape*. But is this entirely vague? Not in the least. *Agape* is tested for worth by reference to its focal, archetypal expression, *kathōs ho Christos*: "Walk in love, as Christ also hath loved us, and hath given himself for us an offering and a sacrifice to God for a sweetsmelling savour" (Eph. 5.2). Hence the statement above about *agape* as the criterion of judgement can easily be stated in another way: *agape* is the word which summarizes the quality of life which Christ alone makes possible for us, precisely because his own life was an embodiment of it, and because he extended that quality of life through his own person into the world—particularly into the lives of those who catch a glimpse of its splendour and who receive into themselves the possibility of being made "new men" (Eph. 4.24). Christ cannot, therefore, be described simply as the man for others; he is the man for God through whom others can enter into that same inheritance (Eph. 5.2, 5).

It is in this whole context that Ephesians considers the many circumstances in which men and women have to learn the meaning of Christ's example, "making sure what would have the Lord's approval" (Eph. 5.10), "trying to understand what the will of the Lord is" (Eph. 5.17). It follows that different circumstances offer different means of learning, and that all of them point beyond themselves to that which, apart from Christ, could not be known, "the mystery of the gospel" (Eph. 6.19). This is true of the situation of children, of fathers, of servants, of masters (Eph. 6.1ff); but it is luminously and intricately true of husbands and wives: in Eph. 4.1—5.21 it is argued that the body of Christ cannot learn the meaning of Christ without a basic willingness on the part of each member to admit that it *needs* to learn—not least because this learning is constantly threatened by the works of darkness. But there is no possibility of our learning from one another unless we are prepared to allow that others may have something to offer us, much though such a recognition may go against the grain: "Be subject to one another out of reverence for Christ" (Eph. 5.21). Subjection and reverence (not as abstract principles but in the sense of the context just given) are equally necessary in marriage, because in marriage there is much learning to be done—much offering of the one to the other if the two are indeed to become one body (Eph. 5.31f). In the relationship of husband and wife there is a chance of learning and practising in a particular setting that which in general should always be true of the Church. Hence repeatedly in 5.22ff fundamental words from the previous chapters are picked up and exemplified in this relationship of marriage. Verses 22–33 are not an independent homily on marriage—grammatically alone this should be obvious, since the datives in verse 22 depend on the participle in the previous verse. But equally these verses are as clear an illustration as one could have of the way in which theological understanding raises the stature of an empirical circumstance by pointing to the significance it obtains in relation to Christ, yet in which it is itself formed by that circumstance through which the meaning of Christ is discerned.

We return, therefore, in full circle. The New Testament does not contain definitive rulings on every circumstance of marriage or of breakdown which are so unequivocal and so simple of interpretation that the Church has nothing to do but apply them. If this were so, it would be so; but in fact Corinthians and Ephesians are not constructed in this way, nor is the recorded teaching of Jesus. On the other hand, the letters to the Corinthians and the Ephesians *do* face up to situations as they occurred, and the New Testament *does* contain teaching on marriage, which contributes to marriage a stature far beyond even that high syndyastic quality which Aristotle offered to the Greeks;[1] for Christianity has other things to say about the transfiguration of nature, of *phusis*, particularly in marriage, in which a man and a woman can become a means of grace and healing to each other:

> Let us go deeper
> you and I
> for we belong together
> and love's image dwells within
> God's you and I
> we must explore
> in prayer
> and find the real each other
> awareness growing all the time
> for each is for the other
> in the likeness of Christ's mind.[2]

The purpose of Christian exegesis is not to impose legislation on the world, but to relate the word spoken in Christ to all words, and through all words to all lives. By one way or another all men, whether married or unmarried, in one circumstance or another, whether strong or weak, even if broken by catastrophe or by folly or by the casualties of their own particular history, *all* are able to be recovered by God into his own life; but in his own way. This is his action, not ours; and if we, as the Church, are to be instrumental of that action, it can only be by real attention to the truth of circumstances, never by defining in advance what God can or cannot do. There is only one responsibility of the Church: to be the Church, to be the body of Christ, to venture where he would venture, to heal where he would heal, to be angry where he would be angry, to love where he loves:

I would fain, therefore, wind this into your hearts, brethren; that if you would live godly and Christianly, you must cleave to Christ, such as he became for us,

---

[1] "*anthrōpos gar tē phusei sunduastikon mallon ē politikon*" (*Nich. Ethics* viii. 12.7). Unfortunately Aristotle did not adequately explore the visionary possibilities of this brief and single word in relation to his much longer reflections on *phusis*—with unhappy consequences, not least for medieval biology; see, for example, A. Mitterer, "Mann und Weib nach dem biologischen Weltbild des hl. Thomas und dem der Gegenwart" (*ZKT* 1933) pp. 491–556—a reminder that even Aquinas' theology did not—and could not—escape its own context.

[2] *Exploration into Love* (Malling Abbey 1970), p. 25.

to the intent you may attain to him, such as he is, and such as he was. . . . For us he became that, whereon the weak may be borne, and may cross the world's sea, and reach their own land. There, a ship will no longer be needed, for there is no sea to cross. It is better, therefore, not to discern *that which Is*, and yet not depart from the cross of Christ, than to discern it, and yet despise the cross of Christ. Better beyond this, and best of all, if it may be, is it for a man both to discern whither he is to go, and to hold fast that on which he is to be borne. . . . But "the little ones", who cannot understand this, so they depart not from the Cross, and Passion, and Resurrection of Christ, are brought safely to that which they see not, in the very same ship in which they also arrive who see.[1]

6

What men make, for good and for evil, of all that Christ offers to us is a matter of church history and of the existential history of our own lives. In the area of sexuality it is clear that great fears and hesitations have been in operation. *In part* this arose from a feeling that the revelation of God in Christ is so clear and so demanding that the proper focus of human attention is on God, not on the world, despite the fact that incarnation must, virtually by definition, confirm the Jewish discovery that the meaning of God is only to be learned in and through the realities of human living. A great danger lies in asserting that the object of what is being learned in empirical situations is so much more important than the situations through which the reality of the object begins to be discerned, that an *ascēsis* which detaches itself from situations is the highest state of faith—in other words, that it is more important to attain the vision of God than to attend to the conditions in which that vision can be begun to be realized here and now; hence arises the danger of regarding sexuality, or even marriage, as a threat or an impediment to the knowledge of God, as opposed to the Pauline view that it is an illuminating model of that knowledge. Empirical studies of what belongs to the nature of the human organism are thus able to do theology a great service in refusing this "by-pass" approach, the approach that hopes to arrive at God without having to go through the human city. But conversely theology has much to contribute *to* the human city by providing real grounds on which any tendency to degrade it or to turn it into a waste land can be resisted; for if Christian theological meaning arises from the *actual* transfiguration of life, both in and beyond Christ, and if also it constantly attends to the conditions of that dimension of direction and healing and hope, it gives to us all a way of justifying and recreating the words through which we interpret to ourselves the most hopeful aspects of our empirical condition: it grounds the language of love in an actual exemplification of wide effect and of very high demand.[2] Theological meaning thus arises from the world, but it recreates the world in hope, because it shows the way in which a proper and necessary connection can be established between the objective, empirical study of behaviour and the subjective experience of what is

---

[1] Augustine, *Homilies on John*, ii.3.
[2] The extreme importance of the high demands of Christ I have attempted to discuss elsewhere, and I have not repeated the discussion in this appendix; see *Making Moral Decisions*, ed. D. M. MacKinnon (London 1969).

being described; and it establishes a reason why that experience is neither illusory nor empty:

> Just so may love, although 'tis understood
> The mere commingling of passionate breath,
> Produce more than our searching witnesseth:
> What I know not: but who, of men, can tell
> That flowers would bloom, or that green fruit would swell
> To melting pulp, that fish would have bright mail,
> The earth its dower of river, wood, and vale,
> The meadows runnels, runnels pebble-stones,
> The seed its harvest, or the lute its tones,
> Tones ravishment, or ravishment its sweet
> If human souls did never kiss and greet?
>
> Look not so wilder'd; for these things are true,
> And never can be born of atomies
> That buzz about our slumber like brain flies,
> Leaving us fancy sick. No, no, I'm sure,
> My restless spirit never could endure
> To brood so long upon one luxury,
> Unless it did, though fearfully, espy
> A hope beyond the shadow of a dream.[1]

In those last lines Endymion looks for a love *beyond* "the steady splendour" of human friendship and love—the love of a goddess unaffected by mortality:

>   My higher hope
> Is of too wide, too rainbow-large a scope,
> To fret at myriads of earthly wrecks.[2]

In contrast the theological understanding which arises in and around the person of Christ, turns us back to human life, not to evade the myriads of earthly wrecks, but to bring to them precisely that healing and renewal which he himself extended into the world; the *consequences* of that healing cannot be wholly dictated by us, because they are a continuation of that new effect. Thus, the contribution of theological meaning is that it knows the grounds on which we also, in turn, can *know* that hope is not a matter of dreams and shadows, but of a life which overcomes death. Theology is bound to hesitate a long time before it denies the gift of hope, and of the new life which it brings, to any particular condition of men.

---

[1] J. Keats, *Endymion* I, 832–42, 850–7.   [2] Ibid., 774ff.

3

The Sacrament of Marriage in Eastern Christianity

by A. M. Allchin

As in many other fields of Christian thought and practice, so in relation to the subject of marriage, the position of the Eastern Churches is not very well known in the West. Too often it is assumed that there is little essential difference between Eastern Orthodox and Western Catholic positions, except that on this or that point the Eastern Church has deviated from the catholic norm. In the case of marriage it would be easy enough to suppose that the one outstanding difference in discipline, the permission given in certain cases to remarry after divorce, is simply an inconsistency on the part of the Eastern Churches, always too prone to be influenced by the State in matters where a conflict arises between the Church and civil society. In fact, further reflection and a closer examination of the topic yields a very different picture. The practice and the theory of the Eastern Churches knew its greatest development in the period before the schism between East and West, and since that time has, for a variety of reasons, remained remarkably constant. If there are marked divergencies between East and West they are more likely to be due to changes which have taken place in the West since the Hildebrandine reform in the eleventh century. Indeed, if we are to understand the position of the Eastern Churches on this matter, we need to remember that we are dealing with a tradition which has known neither the influence of St Augustine, nor the particular developments of scholastic theology and canon law during the Western Middle Ages.

In this appendix we shall begin with an examination of the understanding of marriage current in the Orthodox Church today. We shall then look at the rites used in the Eastern Churches (Orthodox and other) to see what they can tell us of the meaning of this mystery. Finally we shall consider briefly the difference of development of East and West since the period of the schism, and the difficult questions raised by the Eastern permission for divorce. It may be well, at least at the outset, to reflect that the existence over hundreds of years of Churches which have upheld our Lord's teaching about marriage in a great variety of social and cultural contexts, while employing a theology and discipline of marriage somewhat different from our own, should lead us to a certain humility which has not always characterized Western theologians. There is evidently more than one way of bearing witness to that fullness of human life together, which the Christian understanding of marriage seeks to express.

In approaching this subject we may begin with the question of the first and primary end of marriage. Here already the Eastern Orthodox view seems clear, and distinct from the Western tradition. In an article published in *The Listener* in 1957, Lady Namier (Julia de Beausobre) wrote:

> Whatever worldly reasons men and women have for setting up house together, and whatever dynastic or proprietary needs may be served by the birth of heirs, neither can be a cause for marriage in the eyes of the Eastern Church. Mutual devotion is the only adequate cause. Children and accrued property, prosperity and universal regard, may well follow—God willing—but can not be the cause, and should not be the excuse for marriage.[1]

An outstanding authority on this subject among Russian theologians, Professor Paul Evdokimov, made the same point.

> In face of *prolis est essentialium in matrimonio* [offspring is of the essentials in marriage], and *Matrimonii finis primarius est procreatio atque educatio prolis* [the primary end of marriage is the procreation and education of offspring], Orthodox doctrine affirms that the first purpose and final end of marriage is to be found in conjugal love, in the fullness of the unity of husband and wife, which makes of them a home church. Marriage may be useful in society, but its own autonomous value remains royally in itself.[2]

If we turn to one of the senior theologians of Greece, Professor Panagiotis Trembelas, we find the same thing, and the accord is the more interesting because in general approach and method he differs much from Evdokimov.

> It is then as a couple that the partners in marriage become helpers of one another throughout life, exercising mutual forbearance, encouraging one another, so as to bring their different characters into harmony, so as to love and serve one another, experiencing together the same joys and sorrows, supporting one another in their weaknesses, giving a helping hand in the time of need, spending themselves wholly for one another, together carrying the burden of life and the responsibility of a family.[3]

Trembelas defines the second end of marriage as remedial or therapeutic: the redirection and control of the human desires. The procreation of children is the third end, the longed for crown upon the married union, but not itself essential to it.

Such a view of the purpose of marriage implies a different and more positive assessment both of human love and of the sexual act within marriage, than was for a long time current in Western theology; and this despite the fact that many of the Greek Fathers, like their Western counterparts, seem to have taken a heavily pessimistic view of human sexuality. We may perhaps discern two basic reasons for this more positive evaluation of the married state, one of which relates to the understanding of men, the

---

[1] *The Listener* (12 December 1957), pp. 991–3.
[2] P. Evdokimov, *L'Orthodoxie* (Paris 1959), p. 296.
[3] P. Trembelas, *Dogmatique de L'Eglise Orthodoxe Catholique*, vol. iii, p. 351.

other to the understanding of the action of God. In the first place, it must be said that in large parts of the Orthodox tradition a more biblical and Pauline view of the nature of man as a psychosomatic unity has been maintained than in the West. This can be seen in the emphatic teaching about the part played by the body in man's spiritual life, that is, in his approach to God. It underlies, for instance, the whole theology of icons, and leads to the view that the bodily senses as well as the moral and intellectual faculties of man have some share in the perception of divine things, even in this life. It can also be seen in the way in which in marriage the purely physical aspect is regarded as something which can be fully integrated into the relationship of love between the two persons concerned. In the second place, as regards the activity of God, we can see in the East that there is no tendency to make of grace and nature, God and man, mutually exclusive entities, having only external relationships with one another. It is only in God that man becomes truly man. Nature is truly nature when it is open to, and receptive of, the activity of grace. In such a view, while we must distinguish what is human from what is divine, we must never separate them. It is in and through the love of man that the love of God is at work. In many cases the Greek Fathers are not afraid to use the term *eros* both for man's love for God, and for God's love for man. Nor do they hesitate to speak of the folly and "ecstasy" of the divine love. It is a love which carries man beyond himself. It is love which causes God to break the bounds of his own nature and descend into the world which he has made. It is in such a context as this that we can begin to sense the full force of the parallel between husband and wife, and Christ and the Church; and it is this which is at the root of the Orthodox understanding of marriage as a sacrament.

Such a definition of mutual love as the end of marriage has very important consequences for our understanding of the relationship of marriage to the calling to a single life. Even when, as in Anglicanism, the view that celibacy is a higher way than marriage is repudiated, the rather negative definition of the end and purpose of marriage current in the West, in itself tends to suggest that there should be some higher or nobler way. (For instance, "It is the will of God that men should find in marriage the remedy against sin which they need the more, as they are morally weak. . . . The sacrament of marriage cannot be safely withheld from those who need it . . . for the generality of men and women, marriage is the way of safety."[1]) But once maturity, integrity of love is defined as the end of marriage, then its relation to the call to celibacy at once becomes clearer. It is in love that we become persons; love for God and love for one another. The fullness of that love is the goal of both ways. A contemporary Greek writer accuses Western Christendom of having misused the true meaning of both vocations, by making extrinsic, utilitarian purposes primary in marriage and monasticism alike; in the one case the procreation of children, in the other apostolic activity. Both these things may well follow from these vocations, but in neither are they primary.

[1] T. A. Lacey, *Marriage in Church and State*, revised edn by R. C. Mortimer (London 1947), p. 51.

E

The way which leads to the life of celibacy is the way which leads to marriage, a way of devotion in love. The tradition of the Eastern Church does not know that kind of "devotion" which aims at an undistracted life with the purpose of producing results, the maximum availability for a spiritual mission. The content of a life of virginity cannot be either a work or a mission, even the highest, but only a love; the love which has as its object the beauty of the divine person. Marriage and virginity in Christ are therefore two parallel ways towards the healing and restoration of affective desire. Sexual relations, or sexual abstinence, taken in themselves, relate only to biological *individuals*. Marriage and virginity relate to *persons*. If marriage were only a religious legitimation of sexual relations, then it would be unacceptable to honest people. It is impossible to understand Christian marriage without understanding the way of Christian celibacy, just as it is impossible to approach the reality of celibacy without knowing Christian marriage.[1]

We see here two things which are vital for our inquiry: first, the personalist nature of Orthodox thought, and secondly, the understanding of the inner harmony which exists between the contrasted vocations of celibacy and marriage. On the first point one must say that for most Orthodox writers in contact with the West the distinction between individual and person is of vital importance. *Individual*, in this perspective, is a way of speaking of a human being as a unit, separate from others, but strictly comparable with them, a replaceable part of a much larger whole. *Person*, on the other hand, speaks of the human being in relationship with his fellows but sees him as unique and irreplaceble, regards him not as part of a larger whole, but as one in whom the whole is mysteriously present. As we shall see, the marriage rites themselves presuppose that the couple who have come together in some way recapitulate the history of man, and in their union give expression to a reality of universal significance. This understanding of human persons is in Orthodox theology directly dependent on the understanding of the persons within the Trinity. In God there are three persons, totally distinct, completely united, in each one of whom the whole divinity is present. So in mankind, made in God's image and likeness, there is a common nature and many persons, distinct yet not separate, united yet not confused, who find themselves as free, unique, responsible beings, "persons", as they learn to recognize their unity with all their fellow men, and thus come "to love their neighbours as themselves". This is true at every level in human society, not least in marriage, where the two become one, not by devouring one another, or merging into a confused amalgam, but by finding their true selves in mutual self giving.

Mankind [writes Yannaras], made in the image of the God who is one in nature and three in persons, mankind itself is one nature and many persons. Then only does man fulfil his destiny and calling to become a person when he finds himself in a communion of love with other persons, in the image of the Triune God.

These words could be paralleled amongst many contemporary Orthodox writers, Russian and Greek alike.

But, and this is the second point, it is not only in marriage that man can find this fulfilment. He can also find it in virginity. In the one case he will be called to love God in and through his fellow men, in the other to find his

[1] Christos Yannaras, *Honest to Orthodoxy* (in Greek: Athens 1967), p. 74.

fellow men in and through the love of God. The fact that in the Eastern Church the parish clergy have always been married, so that the distinction of married and celibate does not coincide with the distinction between lay and ordained, has probably had something to do with the close relationship between the two ways of marriage and celibacy. Another factor is probably to be found in the way in which there has been no sharp separation between monastic and lay spirituality. The monasteries have always been open to the faithful, and the great majority of monks have not been ordained. But there is also a more theological reason, a deep conviction about the complementary nature of the two ways of life which only seem to be opposed. For in Christianity the command to love God and the command to love our neighbour cannot be separated. The transformation of a merely selfish relationship of passion between two individuals into a free, responsible relationship of love between two persons becomes possible as man's perverse and wayward loves are redirected and purified through the love of a crucified and risen God. Man's desire, whether in marriage or in celibacy, must pass through death in order to come to fullness of life.

It takes years of living soul-to-soul (as a Russian saying has it) for the whole of matrimonial love in its Christian aspect to be followed through—the fullness of it requires a lifetime of joy and sorrow, compassion and discipline. For in the East marriage and the whole of family life are seen as a discipline often likened to that of monasticism. Both rub away the sharp edginess of personality, as pebbles tossed together by sea-waves rub each other smooth in the long run.[1]

In both ways the integrity of love is not something easily achieved. Chastity or virginity are things to be sought and fought for. In so far as virginity is understood not in terms of a merely physical abstinence, but of an integrity of life and singleness of aspiration (purity of heart is to will one thing), virginity no less than chastity may be said to characterize married life no less than single, when it approaches its goal.

Viewed empirically, it would seem that monasticism and marriage deny one another. More profoundly understood, at the level where our life comes together in the life of the Spirit, they are seen to be intimately complementary. . . . Two aspects of the same mystery, they converge in the virginity of the human spirit, a supreme and universal value.[2]

It is in such a view of things that we may find the meaning of the constant parallel made between Christ and the bridegroom, and the Church or Mary and the bride, which occurs in the Eastern marriage rites.

Thus we see that the Eastern Churches develop very fully the thought that the union of man and wife in marriage is a union which reflects, and in some way partakes in, the union of man with God in Christ. As we shall see in the marriage rites themselves, the love of the bride and bridegroom is thought of as founded in the love of God himself. In the union of two persons in a relationship of one flesh we see something of the nature of God, reflected in man, made in his image and likeness. This is the teaching not only of contemporary Orthodox writers, but of a Father such as John Chrysostom. It is the faith which the marriage rites at times express, at

[1] Lady Namier, art. cit.   [2] Evdokimov, op. cit., p. 292.

times presuppose. It is a teaching which is based on the concluding verses of the fifth chapter of the Epistle to the Ephesians.[1] "Thus it is that (in the words of scripture) 'a man shall leave his father and mother and shall be joined to his wife and two shall become one flesh'. It is a great truth that is hidden here. I for my part refer it to Christ and to the Church, but it applies also individually."

The "great" and "hidden truth" is in Greek a great *musterion*, and it is this word *musterion* which in Latin is translated *sacramentum*. It is Christ himself who is *the* great *musterion*, the place in which the hidden counsel of God is made known, in which we come to meet God. The Church too, which is his body, is also a great *musterion*, and all the particular *musteria*, sacraments, of the Church, pre-eminent among them Baptism and the Eucharist, are articulations of this great and primal sacrament of Christ and the Church. Marriage may be seen as a sacrament in two principal ways: first, as an image and reflection of the great sacrament of Christ and the Church; then as one of the gifts and callings within the Church which goes to make up the life of the whole community. It is true that in the later Middle Ages and particularly in the sixteenth and seventeenth centuries, the Orthodox Church adopted the theory of the seven sacraments. But this enumeration has never aquired in Eastern Orthodoxy the status or the importance that it has had in the West. Alivisatos, for instance, says of marriage, "It is a sacrament and one of the seven." But he adds at once

Of course the number *seven* of the sacraments does not consist an official doctrine of the Orthodox Church, formulated, exposed and finally accepted by an Oecumenical Synod as is the case with the Roman Catholic Church, through the Tridentinum. . . . Fathers and teachers of the authority of St John Damascenus speak about two sacraments, and some about three, five or even more than seven. It is probable that the number seven was accepted by Orthodox theology later, possibly through some Roman Catholic influence.[2]

Thus in Orthodox theology the line between sacraments and other rites has not been sharply drawn as it has been in the West, so that monastic profession, for instance, is frequently regarded as a sacrament. More recent writers furthermore have increasingly seen the unsuitability of regarding the Eucharist simply as one among six other rites, all equally regarded as "sacraments". For all the other sacraments centre in the Eucharist. Baptism and chrismation introduce us to it, confession and unction of the sick restore us to it, ordination provides the ministry which presides at it. Marriage establishes the unit of the family, the "little Church" as Chrysostom calls it, on the basis of which the great Church is built up. Out of the love of the partners for one another, love for their children overflows, and this again extends itself to the world around. Neither the family nor the Church should be a closed or self-regarding unit. Both should be open to the world's need, places where the peace and presence of Christ may be made known. There is a special petition in the Byzantine marriage rite for the prosperity of the newly married couple, so

[1] Eph. 5.30–3, NEB.
[2] H. S. Alivisatos, *Marriage and Divorce in Accordance with the Canon Law of the Orthodox Church* (London 1948), p. 7.

that they may have to give to the help of those in need. In all this we see an understanding of the sacramental nature of marriage which is common to all the Eastern Churches, Byzantine and oriental alike, and which antedates the Western medieval development of thought about marriage as a sacrament, with the particular understanding of the *vinculum* which goes with it. Even if, as many Anglicans have done since the Reformation, we prefer not to speak of marriage as a sacrament, at least we may recognize that to do so need not necessarily involve us in the theology of the Latin Middle Ages.

To illustrate the character of the Eastern understanding of marriage, we shall now turn to the rites themselves as used in the Eastern Churches.[1] If, as Schillebeeckx argues, the Byzantine rite was influenced by the practice of the Syrian and Armenian Churches,[2] we may see here an indication of the possibility that the Eastern Christian understanding of marriage has Semitic, more than Hellenistic, roots. It may be that it is the Syrian Churches, which both in language and culture stood nearer to the world of the Bible than did either Greece or Rome, which are responsible for giving to the Eastern wedding rites such amplitude and such magnificence. For there can be no question either of the complexity or of the exuberance of these services. In all there is a variety of actions involved: a blessing of rings, a blessing of a common cup, from which bride and bridegroom drink, sometimes a laying on of hands, always, except in the Chaldean rite, a coronation or garlanding, which in practice has come to be the most memorable and impressive part of the ceremony. As Schillebeeckx points out,[3] in contrast to the Western emphasis on the contract, both in the ceremony and in theory, in the East the stress is laid on the union of bride and bridegroom, in the image of Christ and the Church. The services are carried forward by a luxuriant and often repetitive poetry which expresses the happiness of the bridal pair and those who are gathered together with them.

If as we have stressed, the central theme is that of Christ and the Church, the fact that marriage is a universal human institution, "instituted by God in the time of man's innocency" is not lost to sight. The marriage is seen as the expression of something ordained by God in creation, no less than in redemption. Two prayers from the Coptic rite for the espousals express this well. The first is a blessing of the wedding garments.

Master and Lord, Jesus Christ our God, you have adorned the sky with stars, you have enriched the earth with the beauty of flowers and the fruitfulness of plants, you have granted to man your heavenly gifts, and given him the earth to rejoice in; we pray to you, who are good and the lover of man, bless these clothes here prepared, and in your goodness and loving-kindness grant that they may be for your servants who will wear them, garments of glory and salvation, clothes of joy and gladness. . . .

The second is a thanksgiving:

[1] I am quoting here from A. Raes, S.J., *Le Marriage dans les Eglises d'Orient* (Chevetogne 1959).
[2] *Marriage: Secular Reality and Saving Mystery*, II, pp. 163–4.
[3] Ibid., p. 149.

We give thanks to you, Lord God, master of all things, existing before all ages, master of the universe, who by your word adorned the heavens and established the earth and all that is in it, who brought together the scattered elements and created the two (man and woman) that they might become one. . . . May the love without flaw which they have for one another establish and make sure their union. Build them up upon the foundation of your holy Church so that they may go forward together in a concord and union sealed by the promise which they have exchanged. For you are yourself the bond of love, and the law which will guide their union. According to your word, may they be one in the union of their two persons. May they accomplish, Lord, the precept which your only Son, Jesus Christ our Lord, brought to its perfection.[1]

In the first of these prayers, we have the impression that something of cosmic significance is taking place in this wedding. The moon and the stars, the trees and the hills have their part to play. In the second we see how the love which unites the bridal pair is both their own love and the love of God. Their faith is made sure in his faith. In their two persons a universal mystery is expressed, an age-old history is recapitulated. Time and again, and at almost interminable length, the prayers and hymns remind us of Adam and Eve, of Abraham and Sarah, of generation after generation of the marriages of the Old Testament, in all their diversity and ambiguity. In the union of man and wife is to be found the great mystery, the sacrament of Israel, indeed of all mankind.

In services which take as their basic pattern for the union of husband and wife the story of Adam and Eve and the relationship of Christ to the Church, there can be no question about the priority of the man in the marriage relationship. But what is striking to the reader who is accustomed to our ceremony of "giving away" the bride, is the great stress on reciprocity which marks them. Most of the ceremonial acts are mutual or shared; (for example, the rings are exchanged, both drink from the common cup, both are crowned, "for" the other). A blessing from the Syrian rite may well illustrate this characteristic.

May God by whose will the world and all creation have their being, and who wills the life of all men—may Christ, the true Bridegroom, seal your marriage in the truth of his love. As he finds joy in his Church, so may you find your happiness in one another; that your union may abound in love and your coming together in purity. May his angel guide you, may his peace reign between you, that in all things you may be guarded and guided, so that you may give thanks to the Father who will bless you, the Son who will rejoice in you, and the Spirit who will protect you, now and for ever and world without end.[2]

There is no doubt here as to the primary end of marriage.

All this expression of the joy of marriage, speaks to us of unfallen man, of Adam and paradise, of a kind of nostalgia for Eden.

The early phase of marriage [writes Lady Namier], is thought to give a young couple the clearest possible inkling of heavenly love; because they are discovering a new joy in each other and a new selflessness in themselves. Without the healthy amazement of these discoveries, no marriage is thought to have a propitious start.[3]

---

[1] A Raes, op. cit., pp. 30 and 31.   [2] Ibid., p. 129.
[3] Op. cit.

But the rites of the Church do not neglect the fact of sin, nor the reality of the cross. How could they, when it is on the cross that the Saviour has given the example of that love on which the very possibility of fully and truly human love is based? It is from the cross that the power comes by which the love of the bridal pair may be healed and purified.

Lord we worship your holy Cross. By it salvation has come to the race of man. . . . It is the holy Cross for which the saints have shed their blood. . . . It is the Holy Cross by which the faithfulness of bride and bridegroom is confirmed. It is the holy Cross which we worship in love and concord. It is by the holy Cross that the fidelity of your servants is sealed.[1]

We remember the striking phrase in the Coptic prayer which speaks of the couple as being "built up upon the foundation of the Church", their love made firm in the divine love which goes through death to life; the "little Church" of the family, like the great Church itself, built up upon the faithfulness of God.

In the Byzantine rite this juxtaposition, or better this blending of the notes of joy and suffering, finds vivid expression. Immediately after the bridal pair have drunk three times from a common cup, they process three times round the table set up in the middle of the church, and the choir sings a number of short verses. One of these reads, "Holy martyrs who have fought valiantly and have received the crown, intercede to the Lord for us that he may have mercy on our souls."[2] The crowns which are crowns of joy are also crowns of martyrdom. Marriage no less than martyrdom, no less than monastic life, is an exploit, a struggle, a combat in faithfulness, and hope, and love. This interpretation of the crowns which, at least in the Russian Church is still part of the popular lore of marriage, goes back to St John Chrysostom in the fourth century.[3]

How if such is the Eastern Churches' understanding of marriage is it possible that they permit both divorce and remarriage after divorce? First, it must be said that this permission for divorce in no way denies the tragic and sinful nature of every marriage breakdown. Even at a purely human level such a breakdown implies the disappointment of hopes, the betrayal of faith, the defeat of love. In the case of marriage between Christians, within the family of the Church, where the couple have before them the words of Christ in the Gospels, the tragic character of the situation is underlined. There is no question of the Church's belief that lifelong fidelity is the goal of the married couple. Indeed, in the Eastern Church this fidelity is believed ideally to go even beyond death. For there is a certain prejudice against a second marriage after the death of the partner, and in most Orthodox Churches such a second marriage is not permitted to the clergy.

On the other hand, there is a clear recognition that marriages do break down.

Human relations are open to catastrophe. Yesterday's lovers do turn almost overnight into haters and tormentors. If all efforts at reconciliation have broken

---

[1] A. Raes, p. 173.   [2] Ibid., p. 67.   [3] See Schillebeeckx, op. cit., p. 153.

down, if the very basis of marriage is seen to have crumbled, if there can be no hope, no thought of rekindling true, vigorous, mutual love, untarrying forbearance and unwavering compassion for one another—then it is compassion, together with a lack of illusion about life and sex, that opens the eyes of clergy and laity on the healing possibilities of a new and different marriage. Different it will of necessity be. Even a rugged landscape is altered by a cataclysm; men and women are more vulnerable than the most delicate landscape can be.[1]

Thus in the Eastern tradition both a second and a third marriage after divorce are permitted by the canons, but only under strict conditions; and a different and more penitential form of service is provided in the service books for use on such occasions. This is a practice which goes back into the period long before the schism of East and West.

There is indeed a good deal of evidence to suggest that the Eastern practice reflects an attitude which was common both in East and West in the first milennium of Christian history, and which is summed up by Schillebeeckx in the words "According to the Church Fathers the dissolution of marriage was not *permissible*; but according to the schoolmen its dissolution was not *possible*",[2] and by Smith and Cheetham, that "the general sentiment of the early Church was in favour of the legality and against the propriety of a second marriage".[3] A second marriage is *possible*, and, however undesirable in principle, may in a particular case be the best solution *possible*. In certain circumstances permission for such marriages was given not only in the East, but also in the Western Church during the first ten centuries. One outstanding case of such regulations can be seen in the penitential of Theodore of Tarsus, Archbishop of Canterbury.[4] Permissions of this kind do not of themselves seem to have been taken to undermine the sanctity of the marriage bond.

It must be admitted that neither the theory nor the practice of the Eastern Orthodox Churches is altogether clear and consistent on this point. The grounds for which divorce is permitted vary from one Church to another. The different form of service provided for a second marriage is certainly not always used; in some instances the first service is used again. In Greece, for instance, the penitential form is normally used only when both partners are being remarried. But an Orthodox theologian would reply that the fact that both the theory and practice of remarriage after divorce are to some extent untidy and unsatisfactory is altogether what one would expect. The situation is one in which the Church cannot act by strict rule, but is bound to act by "economy", that pastoral concern which recognizes the fragility of human life and the infinite forgiveness of God, and which also recognizes that what is best in a given situation may not always be what is absolutely best.

What is it that accounts for the difference between East and West at this point? I believe it is a deep but not easily expressed difference about the nature of the activity of God. Both traditions are agreed in their thinking

[1] Lady Namier, op. cit.   [2] Op. cit., p. 70.
[3] Smith and Cheetham, *Dictionary of Christian Antiquities* (John Murray 1908), p. 1103.
[4] For this and other examples see T. A. Lacey, op. cit., pp. 109–10.

that God is active in the first marriage. Is it then possible to believe that he could also give his blessing to a second? Eastern theology has always insisted on maintaining the freedom and transcendence of God who goes beyond all our concepts and can never be limited by them. This freedom and transcendence is indeed the very condition of his presence and activity throughout the world which he has made. Vladimir Lossky, one of the outstanding theologians of the Russian diaspora, constantly maintained that there was much greater danger in a philosophical anthropomorphism than in the more naïve anthropomorphism of the Old Testament. We are not liable to think that God is a rock. We are liable to think of him as just, and to think that we know what this means without sufficiently reflecting on the way in which all such concepts fall short when applied to the living God.

God, as he reveals himself in the history of man's salvation and in the history of the Church, in the history of the life of each man, is a God of order and of faithfulness. But he is also a God of many plans, of infinite possibilities, who is not defeated by man's sin, nor bound even by laws which express his will. His wisdom is many-sided, and we do not comprehend it. In his dealings with men he constantly reveals himself as redeemer and life-giver, and it is forgiveness and redemption which lie at the heart of his relationship with man. It is this God that the Church serves, his love and forgiveness which it is to make present in the world. One might quote St Isaac of Syria, one of the most influential of Eastern spiritual writers. "Compared with the mercy and loving-kindness of God, all the sins of all mankind are like a handful of dust thrown in the sea"; or again, "Tears of repentance are able to restore lost virginity." A Christian cannot say these things lightly; to do so would be to do justice neither to the seriousness of life, not to the price of the cross. But if the gospel is really *good* news, can he possibly say less? On the basis of such a faith in the recreative power of the triune God, who is able to bring good out of evil, new possibilities open up in the tragic areas of man's life, possibilities of reconciliation and restoration in marriages which seem to have broken down, but also possibilities of a new beginning where the first relationship has gone beyond any repair.

DIVORCE IN THE ORTHODOX CHURCHES
CANONICAL PROCEDURES

The present Archbishop of Thyateira (Dr Athenagoras Kokkinakis) in his book *Parents and Priests as Servants of Redemption* (New York 1958) has a chapter on the subject of divorce entitled "Moral and Physical Death break the Marriage Bond". In this chapter he considers the Orthodox practice about divorce, which, he argues, though not free from abuses, is "rather more realistic and sincere", than that of those Churches which allow release from the marriage bond only through nullification. He sees divorce as a concession to the hardness of men's hearts, as the lesser of two evils. "In the case of broken families the lesser evil is divorce, which the Church, following the example of Moses, grants, not easily and gladly, but hesitantly and sorrowfully, to those who . . . feel unable to continue living their married life 'in two bodies as in one' ".[1]

The book was written at a time when the Archbishop was Dean of the Greek Orthodox Theological School in Boston, Massachusetts, and reflects the practice and pastoral teaching of the Greek Orthodox Church in the United States of America. The reasons which are considered by the Church before granting divorce and permitting remarriage are the following

1. Adultery, fornication, all other immoral actions committed by either of the spouses.
2. Treacherous actions and threats against the life by either of the spouses.
3. Abortion without the consent of the husband.
4. Impotence existing prior to marriage and continuing two years after.
5. Either of the spouses abandoning the other for more than two years.
6. Apostasy and fall into heresy.
7. Incurable insanity, lasting four years after the marriage, or leprosy (op. cit., p. 54).

The Archbishop adds an important paragraph to this list of causes for divorce.

Divorces granted by civil courts are not binding in the eyes of the Church. The spiritual courts of the Church often reject applications of people who hold civil divorce and seek the religious decree in order to remarry. Many times the efforts of the Church succeed in reconciling the separated spouses. Guided by the Church, they see their mistake in seeking divorce. Often, after receiving divorce from the civil courts, guided by the Church, they continue their marital life. Also, even after the issuance of the religious divorce there are cases of reconciliation. In happy cases like these, though the sacrament of marriage is not repeated, a prayer is recited by the priest in church or in the home for the enlightenment, protection, forgiveness, salvation of the spouses, and peace.[2]

Dr H. S. Alivisatos, for many years Professor of Canon Law in the University of Athens, in his lecture, *Marriage and Divorce, in accordance with the Canon Law of the Orthodox Church* (London 1948) gives a similar, though not identical, list of reasons for divorce. The one major additional cause cited is "serious shaking of the matrimonial union as caused by one of the parties and proved to make the continuation of common life insupportable".[3] There is, however, a great difference in regard to the authority considered competent to grant the divorce. In the United States, as we have seen, the diocesan court acts independently of the civil court. In Greece, on the other hand, where the overwhelming majority of the population belong to the Orthodox Church, and the links between Church and State are very close, jurisdiction in divorce cases lies with the civil authorities.

On the basis of one of the above-mentioned reasons, a petition is filed with the civil court, which has exclusive jurisdiction on matrimonial causes. The part the Church plays in divorce procedure is very limited. Before the process and within a period of three months, the bishop tries through spiritual means to persuade the parties to reconcile. During this period the bishop allows separation *a mensa et*

---

[1] Op. cit., p. 50.   [2] Ibid.   [3] Op. cit., p. 15.

thoro, this kind of separation being known only in this case in the Orthodox Church. If the bishop's efforts fail, the suit is in the ordinary way continued before the civil court and, if the plaintiff's petition in divorce is accepted, the marriage is declared dissolved. The decision is communicated to the bishop, who, basing himself on it, declares the marriage also as "spiritually" dissolved. From then on, the two parties are regarded as having no matrimonial relationship between each other, and they are allowed to remarry.[1]

[1] Op. cit., pp. 15–16.

4

Marriage as Illustrating Some Christian Doctrines

by Helen Oppenheimer

Naturally, a report on the Christian doctrine of marriage has sought to illuminate the human reality of marriage by the light of the Christian gospel. But it has also been suggested[1] that the illumination may be two-way, that Christian theology, in turn, can be illuminated by the human reality of marriage. It could be useful to expand on this suggestion a little, with particular reference to three theological themes.

Marriage and Grace

A happily married Christian will tend to think of his marriage as a real "means of grace", a channel through which the grace of God is effectively communicated to him and his wife in their daily lives. If without at all belittling this thought he can put the divine dimension on one side for the time being, and consider marriage as a non-Christian humanist might for what it is in its earthly reality, he may still find that something very like the concept of "grace" has a use. It could be a less amorphous word than "love" to characterize what he and his wife have to offer one another, the substance of their relationship. It draw's one's attention to the sustaining and upholding strength of a good marriage, to the "mutual society, help, and comfort, that the one ought to have of the other, both in prosperity and adversity".

Since Oman's *Grace and Personality* churchmen have understood much better the inadequacy of thinking of grace as a supernatural substance which flows into people like petrol into a motor car, giving them a source of energy, constantly renewed, which they burn up in going the way they should go. They have learnt to think of grace primarily in terms of relationship between persons; and it is worth while to have the courage of one's convictions here, to speak boldly of human grace as well as divine, in the hope both of talking sense about human beings and also of illuminating divine grace more usefully in the end. The whole approach of Chapter 2 of this report, the description of what husband and wife can be and do for each other and of their complementarity to one another, could be summed up by using the word "grace", meaning here human grace, to characterize their relationship.

[1] For example, paras. 31, 66.

Having taken account of all this, one can go on to make the theological application, to think in turn of marriage as a useful finite model of divine realities. There is a central theological problem here: the difficulty of understanding "how man's will can be free and yet man be assisted by the grace of God";[1] indeed how persons can become "one" with each other without losing their separate identities. The problem has been sharply brought into focus in recent years by thinkers with a profound understanding of the religious issues involved. Professor Maclagan in *The Theological Frontier of Ethics*[2] insists that in the last resort the will which makes the moral choice must be one's very own. Whatever external help or encouragement, human or divine, we may have, the moral struggle must be "all our own work". It is "up to us" in the last resort to be good, and even to be perfect, for ourselves. Likewise, Professor H. D. Lewis in *Our Experience of God* declares that in moral experience "we are thrown altogether on our own resources and required to function in a way which owes nothing directly to either man or God".[3] Neither philosopher is by any means a cold legalist, belittling relationship in the name of theory; yet neither would allow one to envisage the grace of God entering into the very will of a human being in the way that St Paul seems to do with his "I but not I".

The logic appears inescapable, and many of the standard human analogies only serve to confirm it. Kings, parents, teachers, and friends become tyrannical when they impinge upon the independent wills of other people, however much help and even guidance of an external kind they may hope, in all good will, to give. But it is not special pleading to affirm that the analogy of marriage, though still of course imperfect, is different in kind, not only in degree. It is not a fiction for the law of the land to treat a married couple as one person in a way in which two close friends simply are not; it answers to the reality of their experience. In becoming united in marriage two people essentially impinge upon each other's will in a way which is not an intrusion, but part of the achievement of a good marriage. There is no necessary limit of influence beyond which each of them has to be thrown upon his own resources; and to think in terms of "all my own work" is apt to be simply inadequate and artificial. Often they do not know what is of one and what is of the other; yet the reality and personality of each is not diminished but enhanced. The experience of responding to the grace of the other and so becoming one is a maturing not an infantile one.

The inevitable imperfection of a human union is twofold: it will fall short of completeness on the one hand, and on the other hand in some directions it will overstep, with elements of infringement not of proper unity about it. Yet even in quite ordinary marriages one can begin to see what it can mean to say that two wills can be made one while still remaining two, a valid though small-scale analogy for the grace of God entering into the very will of a human being. Such "unity-in-plurality" can be given loftier application yet, for one could even dare to look at the mysteries of the Trinity and

[1] Report, para. 35.
[2] Ch. IV (Allen & Unwin 1961: Muirhead Library of Philosophy).
[3] P. 270 (Allen & Unwin 1959).

of the Incarnation in its light. If man is made in the image of God, it cannot be irrelevant to look hopefully at the kinds of unity which are possible to man's nature for elementary illustrations of the kinds of unity which one has been taught belong to the nature of God.

If it begins to be felt that the difference between marriage and other close human relationships has been overdrawn and that there is after all no need to deny the presence of a uniting grace in some of these other relationships also, so much the better. But Professor Maclagan's austere concept of the inevitably bare human will into which no outside influence can enter is too convincing to be refuted by simply alleging the contrary, but only by showing likely examples of wills becoming one without either being lost; and the analogy of marriage seems to be the clearest and therefore the most promising here.

The part played in all this by the physical, the analogy between the role of sex in married life and the role of the sacraments, the physical "means of grace" in Christian life, has been brought out in the text of the report.[1] Granted that grace is not some sort of material thing handed out to us but a relationship, all relationships need some physical means of expression. If words, gestures, smiles, handshakes, kisses can mediate good will between one person and another, then all the more can the physical act of sex in marriage mediate total commitment between husband and wife. O. C. Quick's "principle of representative dedication",[2] worthy of more attention than it has in fact received, could be exceedingly illuminating here. Total commitment belongs to the whole of marriage, not only to its physical expression; but, as in primitive sacrifice, the part represents the whole.[3]

Marriage and Faith

In marriage faith can be seen as an experienced mystery. It is therefore promising to look to this faith of marriage as a working model for faith in God, for the benefit of those for whom religious faith seems a mystery more looked for than experienced.

The demand for faith in God is apt to appear blindly irrational, coldly rational, or (in reaction against these) to collapse into "faithfulness" without cognitive content. Faithfulness is evidently a virtue, but it would be self-deception to imagine that it can bear the full weight of the New Testament insistence on faith as belief in God: not only a virtue but the ground of human justification.

It can seem that in being asked to "have faith" one is being asked for something completely beyond one's experience, and which on closer investigation is going to turn out to be impossible, irresponsible, or spurious. It is well worth looking at the human experience of marriage (where one can see both sides of the relationship) to find that here likewise faith means more than "faithfulness"; that it is or comes to be based on knowledge; and that it need be neither blind nor calculating, though

---

[1] Para. 31 above.
[2] *Essays in Orthodoxy* (Macmillan 1916), pp. 281–4.
[3] I have expanded further upon the theme of marriage and grace in an article in *Theology* (December 1969).

maybe still mysterious. The point is that it has a character of *response*. First, something is given (in this case human love) eliciting a response which potentially grows into a total relationship. In Christian faith what is given and elicits response is the life, death, and resurrection of Christ.[1]

For faith to "justify" it is the response which is wanted, not any particular deeds as such without the response. When the response is genuine the appropriate behaviour, the "good works", follow naturally and unforced as "the fruit of the spirit". In marriage it is particularly easy to see that the idea of "merit" can become irrelevant, that love is neither earned nor credited to one's account but in a more profound sense "rewarded".

But, on the other hand, even in a good marriage this sequence can sometimes break down. People can be "good to" their wives or husbands in a grim or dreary spirit of behaving properly, setting themselves to do their duty or acquire merit, not as a response. In doing what they ought, not "with a good grace" but with conscious virtue, they may be doing positive injustice to those they think to serve. Some will find it easier to recognize this truth in the religious, some in the human context, but the analogy can equally well go either way. Either in Christian life or in married life one can come to recognize the primacy of faith over works, which may sometimes mean that it is more constructive to stop struggling, even to admit when duty is defeated, and ask honestly for help rather than press on against the grain.

It is worth pointing out that faith as here understood is not the same thing as trusting the other person, negatively, *not* to do certain things; or it will still have something either illogical or provisional about it. It may well be presumptuous to say "I know he would never do that". Faith is rather a positive trust that the person in whom one has faith is and will be the person one is coming to know him as, and a valuing of this person for his own sake. Faith of this kind in a human being is compatible with the other person having failings; faith in God is compatible with his not seeming to succour one on a particular occasion. Both are faith in who the person is rather than in exactly what he does.

From this understanding of faith one could move on to a better understanding of *worship* as its fitting expression, taking worship of God as unique in degree but not in kind. "Worship here signifies not self-abasing praise, but the expression of adoration, wonder, and love." In marriage the real but finite worship which a husband offers his wife is neither idolatrous nor out of date, but a good model in miniature of the infinite worship one owes to God.

Marriage and Creation

It is contrary to the spirit of this report to make procreation the primary purpose of marriage. Yet still a Christian who is a parent may try in all diffidence to lay hold upon some kind of "theology of parenthood" which may allow procreation and Christian doctrine to shed light upon one

---

[1] This is a rough statement which needs much philosophy and apologetics to make precise and defend.

another in the same way as a "theology of sex" can allow marriage and Christian doctrine to shed light upon one another. One may dare to fly very high here, and draw one's understanding from no lesser doctrines than the Trinity and the creation. For present purposes the doctrine of the Trinity means that God's love is complete in itself and needs no finite object. The doctrine of creation is that God's love has none the less so abounded as to overflow and call into existence a whole universe, offering eternal life to created free beings and so making itself vulnerable.

So one can see human married love as, again in miniature, the image of God's; expressed in the union of whole persons, and overflowing, not from incompleteness but from abundance, to create real human beings to enter into the life of their parents. To want offspring is not just a matter of liking babies or having a gift with little ones, but of a much more long-term aspiration to make something abiding out of what means most to one.

The resulting vulnerability is evident; a parent can be more hurt by his children than by almost anybody. For many people the comparison of parental love with the love of God has called to mind first of all a love which is willing to endure. Yet marriage is not all parenthood, and parenthood is much more than endurance. It is worth laying the main stress on another aspect of the comparison. The doctrine of the Trinity draws one's attention to the primary sufficiency in relationship of the Creator; and on the human side of the analogy this concept not only allows one to put proper emphasis on the full reality of childless marriages, it can also illuminate the meaning of parenthood more completely than an exclusive emphasis on vulnerability. If parents live for their children they have nothing secure to offer to each other nor even, in the last resort, to their children; if their love for their children is based upon their love for each other the whole structure is firmly founded. To acquire creatures because one needs someone to love is to use them, not to treat them as beings in their own right; this is why Christians are glad to insist that God does not "need" our love, though he puts himself in want of it. So we may say he values us for our sake not his.

Likewise, the most awe-inspiring aspect of parenthood is the reality in its own right of what has been created. Even more than artistic creation, procreation can illuminate what it means to be responsible for the existence of beings with a life of their own. The ultimate aspiration for a human parent is not to enter into the meaning of the cross, though he may do this on the way, but to enter into the Creator's delight in his creation: "and God saw that it was good".

5

Vows

by Helen Oppenheimer
and Hugh Montefiore

There are various degrees to which a person may commit himself for the future or leave himself uncommitted. He may speculate about possible courses of action without expressing any kind of superiority for a particular option. Or he may make a prognostication, hazarding an opinion about what his future action will be. He may go further and state a preference for one specific line without necessarily giving reasons for this preference. None of these activities commits a person to undertake a particular course of action.

The point at which commitment begins is the point at which an utterance begins to count not just as a *statement* (true or false) but as an *action* (sincere or insincere, effective or ineffective); when, in J. L. Austin's terminology, it becomes a *performative*. Austin was apologetic about introducing a new and ugly word,[1] but under cover of a lighthearted approach he was making it easier to be clear about how people commit themselves, by helping to demolish the prejudice that the job done by a sentence in the indicative mood must be "always and simply to state something".[2] "When I say 'I name this ship the *Queen Elizabeth*' I do not describe the christening ceremony, I actually perform the christening; and when I say 'I do' . . . I am not reporting on a marriage, I am indulging in it".[3] Indeed the book in which he analysed the distinction in detail is called *How to do things with Words*.[4] The words themselves, granted the right context, *are* actions, not just statements about actions, so that when, for instance, an undertaking has been given, something has really happened. We do not have to look for some inward and spiritual act, over and above the uttered words, to be the "real" undertaking which the words simply report. To do so might seem more "solemn" but would only "open a loophole to perjurers and welshers and bigamists and so on. . . . It is better perhaps to stick to the old saying that our word is our bond."[5]

An utterance can be a "performative" without performing anything very earthshaking. Austin's examples[6] range from the "I do" of marriage to "I

[1] "Performative Utterances", a Third Programme talk printed in *Philosophical Papers*, ed. J. O. Urmson and G. J. Warnock (O.U.P. 1961), p. 220.
[2] *How to do things with Words*, p. 12.   [3] "Performative Utterances", p. 222.
[4] Posthumously published from lecture notes (O.U.P. 1962).
[5] "Performative Utterances", p. 223.   [6] *How to do things with Words*, p. 5.

bet you sixpence". The degree of commitment will differ with the seriousness with which someone has spoken and the importance of the action
indicated. A person who undertakes casually to look in on a friend while
passing is not thereby irrevocably committed to so doing, so long as both
parties accept this. He would be justified in not calling if other circumstances intervened. It would be wrong to give a casual undertaking about a
really serious matter ("Put me in your will as guardian if you like; you may
as well if you feel that way"). Such an undertaking, however, should be
honoured, if it is made and accepted.

A person may say, neither solemnly nor casually, that he will give someone
a lift home in his car. Is he thereby irrevocably committed to so doing?
Suppose he finds and suggests an alternative means of transport for his
intended passenger? Even if this suggestion were not welcomed, he would
not in such a case be under strong obligation to carry out his initial undertaking. In any case the arrangement may be terminated by mutual agreement without any difficulty. (The person concerned may prefer to walk
home.) What happens if the car breaks down? The undertaking is then
frustrated by events. Is the driver under any obligation in such a case to
provide an alternative means of transport? Not unless his undertaking was
unconditional. "I'll see you get home somehow" is unconditional. "I'll see
you home in my car" is an undertaking limited to my car. If my car is
incapable of being safely driven, then the undertaking lapses since it is
impossible of fulfilment. The concept of *frustration*, as applied to more
formal legal undertakings, is a technical term of considerable importance.
The Shorter Oxford English Dictionary gives as one of the meanings of the
verb "to make null and void". The concept of such invalidity, not absolutely intrinsic but arising out of insurmountable circumstances, has the
clear commonsense rationale that people cannot be expected to do the
impossible, that "I ought" implies "I can".

Some moral commitments in process of being carried out take on a
different character from an obligation required *of* one person *by* another.
Whether originally given gladly or reluctantly, an undertaking to a third
party can merge into a joint enterprise. "I" and "You" can become "We".
When such an enterprise looks like failing there can indeed be "frustration"
but in the everyday, not in the legal, sense. It is not a matter of "Well, I
can't be expected now . . ." but of "What *are* we to do?"

To what extent does a *promise* differ from an undertaking? It increases
its solemnity. "I will lend you a tenner" is an offer which may easily be
frustrated by the lack of availability of ten pounds. "I promise to lend you
ten pounds" is more serious. If a person has not got ten pounds of ready
cash to hand, he ought to take steps to provide himself with it, as soon as
possible. What if he has promised to lend someone more than he has in
ready cash, or in his bank account? "I will lend you a thousand pounds",
he may say in a moment of compassion; and on the strength of this his
friend may take out a mortgage. Ought he to sell capital of some kind (if he
has it) in order to honour his promise? Is his conscience to be clear by
admitting that he has been foolish or thoughtless? The promise must still
stand unless it has been voluntarily released by the beneficiary. This is a

case of one who "sweareth unto his neighbour, and disappointeth him not: though it were to his own hindrance" (Ps. 15.5).

What difference does it make if he has sworn an *oath* about the matter? An oath calls God to witness that a solemn promise is being made. The object is to show the seriousness of the undertaking by calling on God to punish the person who takes it if he does not keep it. This brings home to all concerned the solemnity of the promise, but it does not in itself make the promise more binding. Jesus, according to St Matthew, taught that oaths were not only unnecessary but potentially blasphemous, for God is not ours to swear by and nor are his creatures. (Matt. 5.37).[1] "Let what you say be simply 'Yes' or 'No': anything more than this comes from evil" (Matt. 5.33–6). On the whole, the New Testament does not bear out the idea that this means a plain prohibition of all oaths.[2] One's word should be one's bond; but in situations where it is not so accepted, it may be necessary and permissible to add the solemnity of an oath, so long as one is clear that it is one's credibility to others, not one's honourable intent, which the oath puts into the situation. This at least is one way of understanding the matter.

A *vow* has been defined[3] as "a solemn engagement, undertaking or resolve to act in a certain way", and vows as "solemn and voluntary promises to perform something not otherwise required but believed to be acceptable to the person to whom the vows are made".[4] In the Old Testament it was realized that it was wrong to fulfil an immoral vow,[5] although (with the culture of his day) this did not deter Jephthah from killing his own daughter in order to keep his word.[6] Jesus strongly condemned the use of a vow which allowed a person to escape his duty to his parents,[7] and implied that such a vow should not be binding. Vows taken in accordance with Old Testament practice were considered binding in the early Church. St Paul, for example, fulfilled one at Cenchrea[8] and was actually arrested in the Jerusalem Temple while assisting others to carry out a vow.[9]

Even when made in all sincerity, vows sometimes prove impossible to keep. If performance was in fact completely impossible at the time when the vow was made, the vow can be said to have been void from the outset, as when unwittingly a man goes through a form of marriage with his own sister. What is more to the present purpose, a vow may in course of time become impossible to fulfil; and such a vow must fail to have effect under the principle of frustration. No sin can be attached to the person involved for non-performance, although sin may well be involved in the circumstances which have arisen to make it impossible to fulfil.

In situations of this kind it is natural for Christians to turn to the Church not simply for forgiveness but for some kind of regularization of their position. This need not be sought in a coldly legal spirit but with a sincere longing that somehow what has gone wrong and is on a bad footing should

---

[1] Cf. Jas. 5.12.
[2] Cf., for example, Matt. 23.16–22; 26.63; Rom. 1.9; 9.1; 2 Cor. 1.23; 11.31; Phil. 1.8; Heb. 6.16–17.
[3] Shorter Oxford English Dictionary.
[4] Oxford Dictionary of the Christian Church.   [5] Deut. 23.18.
[6] Judg. 11.30–9.   [7] Mark 7.9–13.   [8] Acts 18.18.   [9] Acts 21.26ff.

be set straight so that a fresh start can be made. What they seek is *dispensation*, whether they call it by this technical name or not; and of course it is useless for anyone to seek to quieten his troubled conscience in this way unless he believes that the body to whom he goes in his need has indeed authority in his case. Compassion is not enough; what is required is the right to act in, or pronounce upon, the situation.

It has been generally agreed by the Church that a dispensing power should not be lightly used. On the whole, the history of its use has not been such as to give much encouragement to those who hope that dispensation may be a straightforward answer to the problem of broken marriage vows. Dispensations have been defined[1] as "licences granted by ecclesiastical authority to do some act otherwise canonically illegal, or for the remittance of a penalty for breaking such a rule". The Church has used its dispensing power chiefly in connection with the ordination of the clergy, the translation of bishops, monastic vows, vows of virginity, and legal matters arising out of marriage, nullity, and separation. In the question of dispensing from vows, since the thirteenth century a distinction has been made between simple vows and solemn vows. A simple vow may be broken under pain of sin; but a breach of solemn vows, such as lifelong profession, has been regarded as invalid. For example, the marriage of a nun under solemn vows is regarded as void. In the Roman Catholic Church solemn vows and vows to the advantage of a third party who is not willing to relinquish them are dispensed only by the Pope or an agent appointed by him for the purpose. In the Church of England dispensations are granted by archbishops and bishops.

It might seem that the dispensing power of the Church, if it exists, should extend over all fields of life and not be confined only to these ecclesiastical matters. "Verily I say unto you, Whatsoever ye shall bind on earth shall be bound in heaven: and whatsoever ye shall loose on earth shall be loosed in heaven" (Matt. 18.18; cf. 16.19). Why then has the Church made such restricted use of these great powers delegated to it? Binding and loosing here may refer to condemning and acquitting sins.[2] It may conceivably refer to excommunication.[3] It is, however, most easily explained as a translation into Greek of the technical Aramaic terms used by a teacher of the law who, as a result of his expert knowledge, declares some action or thing "bound" (i.e. forbidden) or "loosed" (i.e. permitted). According to St Matthew, decisions made by Peter or by the disciples in the name of the *ecclesia* will be endorsed by God. This does not give them the right to take God's name in vain. Both Matthaean passages occur in strictly ecclesiastical contexts. How after all could the Church aspire to dispense from God's law, and change what God has ordained? It may be said, because it speaks in God's own name, and what it truly "dispenses", on behalf of God, is God's grace. Of course: but grace perfects nature. It does not make it a different thing altogether. The fact has to be faced that for the Church to attempt to give dispensation from the moral law would be to grant people permission to sin. For instance, it cannot dispense from

[1] *Oxford Dictionary of the Christian Church.*
[2] Cf. John 20.23.   [3] Cf. Josephus, *Jewish Wars*, 1. v. 2.

the seventh commandment, and give people a licence to commit adultery. How do marriage vows stand in this connection? A marriage made in a register office is valid and recognized as such by the Church. The two partners take each other as man and wife, and it is pointed out to them that according to the laws of this land marriage is a lifelong union between one man and one woman. The register office setting is formal and solemn; the undertaking of marriage is explicit and binding. Because marriage is not a mere contract, the marriage is not voidable by mutual consent. If marriage vows can be dissolved at all, they cannot be dissolved, even legally, by . mere permission of the other person. Marriage effects a status, and this status is not voidable at will. This holds good for anyone married according to the laws of this land, whether or not the Church comes into it at all.

In the case of a Christian there is an added reason why marriage vows should be kept. He has a double obligation, firstly to keep his humanly pledged word, not just formally but in loyalty to his wife; and secondly to obey the teaching of Christ, not just formally but in loyalty to his Master and Lord. When two people are married in church, the vows themselves are far more explicit than in a register office ceremony: "for better for worse", "till death us do part". The reply to the betrothal question "Wilt thou have this woman to thy wedded wife . . .?" is "I will". This could be ambiguous. It can mean "I shall have her" or "It is my will to have her". The reply could be either a vow or a solemn intention—and intentions, however solemnly expressed, may change. But the marriage vow is explicit and unconditional: "I . . . take thee . . ." More than intention is expressed. The words create an unconditional and lifelong solemn undertaking made more graphic and solemn by being embodied in phrases covering different aspects of life (for example, "for richer for poorer"; "in sickness and in health"). These vows are made in church. The couple "have consented together in holy wedlock, and have witnessed the same before God and this company". To "witness before God" is not the same as to "swear by God" or "to call God to witness". God is omnipresent, and to come to a church building to make marriage vows does not make God *more* present; it emphasizes his presence in a special way. It is hard to imagine promises taken in a more solemn manner, and it is not surprising that they are often engraved deep in the consciences of those who make them in a way that is unlikely to be the case after a register office marriage.

When a marriage irretrievably breaks down, some parts of these vows are impossible of fulfilment. For example, they are no longer able "to have and to hold" each other. They cannot any longer cherish each other, because to cherish someone needs the co-operation of the person to be cherished. Those vows which are impossible of fulfilment can no longer be binding. The principle of frustration operates. A person cannot be under an obligation to carry out what cannot be performed.

Not all parts of the marriage vow, however, are still impossible of performance after a marriage has irretrievably broken down. It would still be possible for either partner to continue "forsaking all other" for so long as they both shall live. If this means the prospect of future loneliness and suffering, then this could be seen as a way of keeping faithful to the phrase "for better for worse". Is there still an obligation to keep those residual parts of the marriage vow in the case of irretrievable marriage breakdown? A closer examination of the vow reveals that it refers wholly to the married state. Indeed, it can only be construed in connection with it. The wording of the promise is "forsaking all other, *keep thee only unto her*, so long as ye both shall live". A man says "*I take thee – to my wedded wife . . .* for better for worse . . .*"

The vows are dependent grammatically and actually on the marriage. Those who believe that marriages are indissoluble, even when there is to all outward appearances an irretrievable breakdown, will also believe that those parts of the vow are still binding if they can still be kept. But for those who believe that when the outward appearances point to irretrievable breakdown then there is nothing further left to a marriage, it logically follows that those parts of the original vow which could still be kept if they had stood on their own are without further effect if there is now no marriage. This is an extension of the principle of frustration.

Is it a legitimate extension, which people may wholeheartedly acknowledge, or a debating point of which Christians at least ought to be rather ashamed to take advantage? There is such a thing as giving up too easily, counting one's purposes as "frustrated" too soon when a little perseverance would be more honourable and might even do wonders: true. But it is also true that there is such a thing as pig-headed obstinacy, a clinging to a previous situation against the facts and against all reason; and it is more than doubtful whether it is the part of the Christian Church to encourage people in this. If a person whose marriage has broken down is still genuinely directed in fidelity towards the other person, however badly he or she may have behaved, such faithfulness can only be honoured. In such a case people are inclined to say such things as, "You know, she still loves him really". But there can be cases where the fidelity is directed, not towards the other person but to the idea of fidelity, to the promise itself in abstraction from the person to whom the promise was made, and from the married life which was supposed to give the promise its context. Human motivation is mixed and cases shade into each other, but there could be times when the principle of frustration might be not just a convenient excuse but a wholesome release. It is not likely to be wise to encourage people to direct their lives towards a blank.

Many married Christians will half agree with all this but will instinctively add, "But in such a case I should never feel free myself." It needs to be asked, What does "should never feel" amount to here? Often one can work out what one would do or advise someone else to do in a hypothetical situation; but the case of marriage is special. One may say, "*I* should always feel I must be faithful", but the question is, To whom? To one's existing faithful spouse? Of course. Or to some imaginary person one has never married? But if one had married someone else, one would be a different person oneself. It cannot make sense to ask what one "would" do if one were a different, unspecified, person. The logical inevitability of this kind of lack of understanding of other people's problems in the case of remarriage after divorce must cast a particular doubt on the right of the happily married to bind burdens for other people's shoulders, even when they are suggesting only that these burdens should be taken up voluntarily.

The question arises whether it would ever be possible to make fresh vows of marriage to another person, or even exactly the same vows; and whether such vows could properly be made in a church building. The latter question is not really a separate problem. If it can be right to make such vows, and if the Church acknowledges this right, and if it believes that the benefits of fresh vows in church (for example, helping to ensure the new marriage is permanent) outweigh the dangers involved (for example, eroding its public image of believing in the permanence of marriage), then such vows can be made in church.

But what of the persons concerned? Should a person's sense of integrity prevent him from making a second marriage vow? Certainly many people feel that they would never be able to do this, however much they were convinced of the rightness of a second marriage. But if the foregoing arguments are correct, the first set of vows have ceased to have any further effect when the marriage to which they belonged has irretrievably broken down. If the previous union has been dissolved by due process of law, and if the Church gives permission for remarriage in church (and this permission itself would be a form of dispensation), then such scruples, while they should be respected, would not be soundly based. For if the first set of vows are no longer binding, and if the person thinks it right to marry again, presumably he wants this second marriage to be more real, not less, as a lifelong and unconditional commitment before God. Vows are the best way of effecting this; they do not just *state* an intention, they perform an action; and if the present Prayer Book vows are the best for this purpose, they should be used again. Whether or not such persons should get married is another matter, one for the consciences of both; and it is a decision which could only be taken by Christians after great heart-searching in view of the reported words of Jesus. It follows from our argument that the role of a church counsellor in such a matter would be not negative, but, in the best sense, non-directive, helping a person to reach his own conscientious decision in his own particular situation.

If analogies are required of the failure of the residual marriage vows to continue to have effect, two possibilities suggest themselves, one from religion, and the other from law. At confirmation, you make a vow "ratifying and confirming the same in your own persons, and acknowledging yourself bound to believe, and to do, all those things, which your Godfathers and Godmothers then undertook for you". This renewal of the baptismal vow refers to the practice of the Christian life. It often unfortunately happens that the person concerned loses his faith and ceases to lead a Christian life. He obviously cannot continue to "believe all those things" which his godparents undertook on his behalf. This part of the vow fails on the principle of frustration. But it would be theoretically possible for such a person to continue to "do all those things" which his godparents had undertaken. However, he would properly be regarded as hypocritical if he went through all the actions of Christianity without Christian faith or perhaps even contrary to his present convictions. Therefore the residual part of the vow, which, if it stood on its own, theoretically could still bind, in fact has no further effect. There is an important difference here from the situation of total marriage breakdown. There is always the possibility that faith may revive, in which case the vow would again have effect. But if a marriage really has irretrievably broken down, this is not going to happen.

A second illustration could be taken from the Non-juring Schism. The clergy of the Church of England had sworn their allegiance to King James II and his heirs and lawful successors. When William and Mary were declared king and queen, a delicate matter of conscience arose. James, a fugitive in France, had not abdicated and was still alive. How could allegiance in conscience be given to William and Mary in his place? Since King James was no longer *de facto* king, did the vow of allegiance to him as king still have effect? Most of the clergy thought that it did not. Some, greatly honoured, whose consciences forbade them to swear their allegiance, were deprived of their posts in the Church of England and formed the Non-juring Schism. For them James ought still to have been king, and so their vow was still binding. But when James II died, should their earlier vow still have had effect? James II had no *lawful* successor to whom this allegiance could be given. The vow therefore could be said to have lost its binding force because the former king had died; and the majority of the schismatics felt free to vow a new vow to the existing monarch. (But there were some with tender consciences who could not do even this.) Once again the analogy is by no means exact, because in this case there were political motives mixed up with religious ones, and a further oath was required to abjure the person falsely called the Prince of Wales. Nevertheless, there is a sufficient analogy to the second vows of a "remarriage" to make it worth using.

There remains a danger that this argument may have proved too much. Has it, in trying to set up the possibility of second marriage vows, merely eroded the meaning of the first, not only in cases where the first marriage has failed but in the still far more numerous cases where it undoubtedly remains in being? If in the event of a breakdown the vows can be treated as if they had been conditional, what right has the Church to assure successive generations of young people that the vows they hope to pledge to one another are indeed permanent and unconditional? Are they being asked only to utter platitudes: "I will love and cherish you as long as I do love and cherish you"? Or is there a concealed condition which ought in honesty to be made explicit: "I will love and cherish you as long as you love and cherish me"? The marriage service would be wrecked; but have we any right to hang on to an impressive ceremony unless we really intend it to be taken in its straightforward meaning? It is the first service in church, not the second, which is jeopardized by the facts of marriage breakdown.

It is sometimes suggested in irony that the vows ought to be worded "until death or divorce us do part". More seriously, it is proposed that the vow from ordination might be used, "I will, the Lord being my helper". Perhaps if this had been the form of words in the wedding service all along, the problem might not have come so sharply to a head, but it is doubtful whether a change now would help. Would such a change render the vows conditional or not? Would it represent a seemly humility or a substantial alteration in marriage doctrine? As an innovation, at a time when the permanence of vows is being particularly questioned, it would look like either a concession or an attempt to sit on the fence. If it were a concession, it would be rather a strange one; to make the vows conditional upon the receipt of the grace of God would introduce theological complications of a far from soothing kind.

It is more promising to try to answer the criticisms which are being made of the vows in their present form: that it is wrong to ask so much of people in demanding the pledge of permanence for an indefinite future; or that, since we all know the vows are conditional upon the marriage not breaking down, we ought to say so; or that they do not really amount to anything but an impressive but presumptuous way of affirming present feelings.

The criticism that they ask too much has been only too well met by the whole present line of argument which has sought to give people a way of release. The present difficulty is rather that the vows are then left with too little substance to do what is hoped of them. However unconditional they sound, it begins to look as if they can really only be conditional, though this is certainly not, on the face of it, what people want. Characteristically, people who seek to get married do not think of themselves primarily as conforming to the requirements of society, nor even as setting up claims upon each other, but as pledging themselves. People who love each other want, it seems, to commit themselves deeply and permanently, and this is not seen as a condition they have to meet, but a major part of what they find attractive about the idea of marriage. For such a pledge the present marriage service purports to supply the opportunity, except that an increasingly persistent voice seems to say that those who think in this way are just being sentimental and unrealistic, that they ought to content themselves with present devotion and not make claims upon the future.

To give way here and settle for a less demanding form of pledge would be no light matter. It would be to give up not only the apparently harsh demands of the Christian doctrine of marriage, but also some of the most convincing human insights into the capabilities of human beings. "Love is not love which alters when it alteration finds." Fidelity is not just a requirement somewhat arbitrarily laid upon Christians, but is integral to human life.

Faithfulness [said Austin Farrer] is the thing which most forcibly convinces us of personal identity. If we rely on a friend's words, we know that he will not become a different person; for if he did, he might change his mind and let us down. He may become a different person in many ways; he may change his tastes and occupations, many of his opinions; but he will not become a different person in this particular way; not, that is, in respect of his faithfulness to me.[1]

In defence of this concept of continuing pledgeable faithfulness it needs to be said that the exception need not disprove the rule. The concept of infidelity is what philosophers like to call "parasitic" upon the concept of fidelity, in the same way as lying is "parasitic" upon truth-telling. The

[1] *Said or Sung* (Faith Press 1960), p. 162.

imaginary island of the riddle, where one tribe always told the truth and the other tribe always told lies, is strictly inconceivable logically, for language is essentially a means of communication and is a meaningless concept unless truth-telling is the norm. We do not have to disbelieve each other until we have tested each other's truthfulness; rather, we believe each other until we have reason for suspicion, and that is how it is possible for us to be language-using beings. Once we are such, the concept of language can "carry" a certain amount, though not an unlimited amount, of lying.

Likewise, the making of vows is an activity which takes advantage of the fact that there are circumstances in which human beings are normally trustworthy;[1] that an element of fidelity is somehow built into the concept of a characteristic human being. Infidelity is no more inconceivable than lying, but it is not, so to speak, on equal terms with fidelity, any more than lying is with telling the truth. All sorts of things can go wrong with human vows, "infelicities" in J. L. Austin's phrase, but it is still proper to take vows at their face value, not to be on the look-out for trouble. If indeed the infelicities became so frequent as to swamp the "normal" occasions, then the institution of vow-making would founder. However much individuals might long to pledge eternal faith, they would lack the context of trust within which they could meaningfully be said to make marriage vows.

To use another piece of philosophical jargon, it is "conceptually necessary" that, for beings who work with the concept of fidelity at all, fidelity should be the norm; and "norm" is an interestingly slippery term, with a foot in both camps of statistics and ideals. The argument is not a purely numerical one: "most people keep their vows, therefore it is still worth making them". Nor does it merely underwrite unrealistic aspirations: "human beings are such that they need to make vows, therefore let them continue even if they don't keep them". Either of these would be far too easily overthrown. What is needed is some kind of interplay between the two, based on the peculiar and useful (some might say shifty) character of the word "normal". The argument is something like this: "as long as we have reason to think that fidelity can be said to be a 'normal' feature of human nature, let people engage in making and accepting vows wholeheartedly, with responsible care indeed but not with hypochrondriacal or sceptical doubtfulness."

It has to be recognized that a vow evaded but counted as not "broken" will undercut the institution of marriage more dangerously than a vow plainly broken. One therefore needs to be very clear that the circumstances in which a vow is to be counted as of none effect are not just evasions, if vows in general are to keep their significance; but it has been the argument of this whole appendix that to abandon a vow when its keeping is genuinely "frustrated" does not constitute a mere evasion. In other words, neither the fact that a vow may be broken, nor the fact that it may founder if its purposes are frustrated, make the vow "conditional" in itself. "Unconditional" is possibly not after all the most happy way to describe it, since

---

[1] The difference between a vow and an oath would then be that a vow depends upon such circumstances, an oath sets about creating them for a particular occasion; see p. 133 above. It follows that the "sacredness" of oaths would be impaired by any practice of dispensation much more than the "sacredness" of vows would be.

at the outset it is made to a particular chosen person not to just anybody; but it is not a bargain with limiting conditions.

If it is granted that our marriage vows are not too harsh, since a way out can be found, yet that they are not made "on conditions", has the argument not rendered them merely platitudinous? If I say "for better for worse", I seem to be saying something very momentous, but if the "worse" is entirely taken care of by the concept of frustration, one begins to wonder if it amounts to more than a rather exhilarating piece of showing off for the happily married. If the idea of an "ontological" bond is rejected, and if the concept of possible breakdown is, however reluctantly, accepted, how are people who have made vows more seriously committed to each other than two friends who sincerely hope not to lose touch with one another? What does this "performative" act perform?

The answer simply is that it brings into being a *marriage*, and that we do really know what a marriage is and how it differs from a friendship, in the sort of way in which we know what an animal is and how it differs from a plant, although we may still have all manner of trouble with the borderline cases. A marriage is the voluntary union for life of one man with one woman, and this remains something of profound significance, by no means a matter of the uttering of impressive platitudes. Nor is the "worse" entirely whittled away by the concept of frustration. Many circumstances can arise, wholly within the concept of marriage as a going concern, which can be and are looked upon as "worse" by one or both of the partners. What one is pledging oneself to is partly that one will choose even unhappiness together rather than any prospects of satisfaction apart. The difficulty of pinning down the "worse" is that within the context of a good marriage it has a way of transmuting itself in practice into something one would ultimately call worthwhile. If kept at all, the vow will tend not to need any conscious keeping. But this does not mean that it effects nothing: on the contrary.

6

Marital Breakdown

by J. Dominian

The twentieth century has seen an unprecedented rise in divorce. The figures from the Registrar General's *Statistical Review of England and Wales*[1] show that at the beginning of the century the total number of new petitions filed for dissolution and annulment were 4,062, a number which had increased to 55,007 in the latest detailed returns for the year 1968.

It has been calculated that from the 1861–65 period to 1937 the divorce rate increased by 319 per cent and that the Second World War was associated with a further increase of 337 per cent.[2]

Another study in the early 1960s has shown that between 8 and 14 per cent of the informants of a national sample of men and women had experienced marital problems which were severe enough to cause them to contemplate separation, actually to experience it, or to end in divorce.[3]

Sociological explanations have been put forward for this increased incidence. These include the intervention of two major world wars, the impact of increased financial and legal aid, and the extension of grounds for divorce.

Although these events are undoubtedly contributory, a more appropriate interpretation would be that at least two of these factors, namely the changes in the law of divorce and the financial assistance offered by the State, reflect the needs of a changing situation. In other words, it would be more accurate to interpret these social factors as following rather than causing marital breakdown. In a pluralistic society no longer absolutely committed to the principles of indissolubility, the social changes have followed the requirements of men and women whose marriage had broken down, needing a legal remedy.

For a deeper understanding of the causes of marital breakdown it is necessary to go beyond the actual changes of the law. Here social and psychological factors are delicately entwined in a complex structure. The identification and isolation of the significant elements is far from complete or certain and what follows is a tentative analysis.

One of the most significant changes that has occurred in this century is the rise in expectation of life. At the turn of the century the average expectation of life for a man was 48 years and for a woman a little longer, 52 years. As a result of the marked advances in medicine and social con-

[1] *Statistical Review of England and Wales* (1968), part II (H.M. Stationery Office, London).

[2] G. Rowntree and N. Carrier, *Population Studies 1958.*

[3] G. Rowntree, *Population Studies 1964*, 28, No. 2.

ditions of life, the average expectation of life has extended to 68 for men and 75 for women.

Not only do people live longer but they marry younger. The mean age of marriage at the turn of the century was 26·9 for bachelors and 25·37 for spinsters. Today the corresponding ages are 24·08 and 21·95. The combination of prolongation of life and earlier marriages means that marriages are extended at both ends and that couples will have, increasingly perhaps, fifty years of marriage or more to negotiate. Many marriages which would have faced difficulties in the past were dissolved by the death of one spouse before the crisis emerged.

Within this increased span of married life another element has changed radically, namely, the average size of the family. At the turn of the century this consisted of five children; today the number has been halved. This change has been influenced enormously by the advent of widespread and increasingly effective use of birth regulation practices. Birth control, coupled with modern obstetric practice, means that a mother today can choose the timing and spacing of her family with the justified expectation that her pregnancies will reach a successful conclusion and that neither she nor her children will suffer the ravages of pre- or post-natal mortality. In 1911 the total infant mortality (death under one year) was 129·4 per 1,000 live births; by 1968 it had dropped to 18. Thus the actual amount of time devoted to child-bearing has been drastically reduced, freeing wives for other activities and experiences, which means a return to work and a much greater emphasis on the quality of the relationship between the spouses.

To longevity and reduction in the size of the family has to be added the third and probably most important change, namely, the social and economic emancipation of women, bringing about, step by step, an equality in the relationship of the sexes which cannot be evaluated with statistical precision, but which has undoubtedly altered most radically the whole character of marriage. Millions of words have been used to describe the emancipation of women and this is not the place to enter into any detailed description. As far as marriage is concerned, however, it means that androcentricity is drawing to an end and that women no longer relate to their husbands on the basis of fear, subservience, and dependence of whatever nature—economic, social, or emotional.

These social changes have been paralleled by a qualitative change in the character of living. Increasingly age-long material threats such as hunger, poverty, lack of shelter, and unemployment have receded in significance in the West. Although far from eliminated they occupy far less the energies of men and women, who are now freer to concentrate on the next layer of their beings, the psychological, emotional, and sexual, opening new vistas of varied expectations in the personal encounter between spouses, while simultaneously making greater demands on them.

These changes form the social background against which marital breakdown needs to be understood. The sciences of sociology, psychology, psychiatry, and psychoanalysis began to undertake from the 1920s onwards more precise investigations into specific causes. This research has been carried out largely in the United States, but some of the findings have been confirmed in Britain.

Perhaps the single most important social factor related to marital break-down is age at marriage. Youthful marriages, particularly those entered into below the age of nineteen, run statistically a much higher risk of instability. Detailed research, both in the United States[1] and in Britain,[2] confirms this.

Pre-marital pregnancy has also an adverse effect, succinctly summarized by an American worker who studied this phenomenon extensively both in the United States and in Denmark thus: "The conclusion that pre-marital pregnancy is more likely to be followed by divorce than post-marital pregnancy, and that early post-marital is more likely to be followed by divorce than is delayed post-marital pregnancy seems almost inescapable."[3]

Mixed marriages, whether of religion, race, or social class, run a higher risk; but the significance of these factors is not as important as the two previous ones.

It should be stressed that the higher risk involved in all these groups is a statistical one and no prediction can be made for the individual marriage. This means that the success or failure of each and every marriage depends on much more than the environmental influences of age, colour, religion, and social class. In the final analysis it depends on the personality of the spouses and their capacity to initiate and sustain a relationship which satis-fies their minimum physical, emotional, social, and spiritual needs.

At this level the psychological sciences take over and make their own contribution to the understanding of the subject. The complexity of the psychological factors is so marked that in what follows only a few of the well-recognized issues will be considered.

The capacity to form an intimate personal relationship is one which the overwhelming majority of human beings possess. But not all, and there is a group of men and women who have been categorized in psychiatric terms as *psychopaths*. Psychopathic disorder was defined in the 1959 Mental Health Act for England and Wales as "a persistent disorder or disability of the mind (whether or not including subnormality of intelligence) which results in abnormally aggressive or seriously irresponsible conduct on the part of the patient and requires, or is susceptible to, medical treatment".

Psychopathic behaviour can and does play havoc with marriage as the impulsive, aggressive, unreliable, and callous characteristics of the sufferers make mockery of any vows taken to love their partners. These marriages end sooner or later by the unilateral or mutual inability of the person con-cerned to offer a minimum degree of reliable, non-aggressive, caring behaviour towards his or her spouse. The misery inflicted is immense and the details of individual marriages make incredible and tragic personal histories.[4]

Here is a serious defect of the personality, which leaves the rational,

[1] P. C. Glick, "Stability of Marriage to Age at Marriage", *Selected Studies in Marriage and the Family* (Holt Rinehart & Winston, New York, 1962).
[2] G. Rowntree, *Population Studies 1964*.
[3] H. T. Christensen, *Eugenics Quarterly 1963*, 10 (3), p. 127.
[4] J. Dominian, *Marital Breakdown* (Pelican 1968), p. 70.

cognitive aspect of man intact, allowing the making and receiving of the promises implied in the words of the marriage ceremony. Due to the defect present, the promises of care, love, and cherishing cannot be actualized in the actual relationship which is punctuated with infidelity, cruelty, and ultimately, with desertion. Psychopathy stands out *par excellence* as a condition which defies the traditional Western emphasis on reason. Reason is intact in these men and women but their behaviour is gravely defective, making it impossible for them to translate the promises given in their vows into the reality of everyday living.

Another major assault on the supremacy of reason has come from the work of Freud and other psychoanalysts who have emphasized the importance of the unconscious and the role of emotions and instincts in intra- and inter-personal relationships. Although there remains much that is open to dispute in these theories, there is a great deal that has stood the test of time and is of relevance to marital breakdown.

What is popularly remembered of Freud's work is his preoccupation with sexuality and aggression, the two basic instincts on which he believed the personality develops. Important as these discoveries were they lag behind currently in significance the other major discovery of Freud and other analysts, namely, the importance of the early years as laying the foundation of learned experiences governing all future intimate personal relationships.

In the first few years of life the child experiences in relation to his mother and father the basic feelings of trust, security, physical closeness, autonomy, acceptance, rejection, ambivalence (loving and hating the same person resulting from parents being one moment the source of good experience and the next frustrating, denying objects), frustration, fulfilment, anger, and envy. These are all experiences of one-to-one relationships; where the situation becomes triangular with both parents involved or the presence of siblings intervenes, then competition and jealousy are also encountered.

It is due to Freud's genius that we owe the concept of transference, namely, the capacity of a patient to displace on his or her analyst feelings and ideas derived from previous figures in life, usually the parents. But transference is not only experienced in psychoanalysis, it is experienced in any situation which allows for the presence of the same degree of emotional intimacy as that of the child and parents in childhood.

Generally speaking there are only two intimate relationships in life, that between the child and the parents and secondly that between husband and wife. The pattern of behaviour shown in marriage will correspond closely to the experience in childhood, and once again statistically there is good evidence to associate marital breakdown with an unhappy childhood.

This is not to say that every person who has experienced an unsatisfactory childhood is likely to suffer marital breakdown. The intimacy of the second relationship has the capacity to heal the wounds of the first by providing the ingredients of acceptance, trust, and care, which can repair the ravages of the past. But for this is needed a partner with a relatively intact personality who can make up for the past and is able to tolerate the limitations of the vulnerable spouse. Such relationships exist in abundance and provide the evidence for the healing capacity of marriage. Unfortunately they do not take the limelight as much as marriages that break down.

In these latter circumstances the limiting defects in the personality of the spouses make it impossible for the relationship to continue, as it flounders on the rocks of mistrust, jealousy, fear, hostility, rejection, lack of affection, sexual incompatibility, cruelty, adultery, and finally desertion.

There are one or two points that need underlining in connection with this description of the intimate emotional life. First, while it would be true to say that the details of transference and the significance of learned emotional patterns have been investigated for the first time this century, the phenomena themselves have existed as long as man has. What is new in our century is the change in the husband–wife relationship which has brought into prominence and focused attention on this deeper layer of the personality. In the past the energies of the spouses were taken up with child-bearing and survival and couples rejoiced in the avoidance of disease, the satisfaction of elementary material needs, and the successful raising of a family. Today this is no longer enough, as man delves into and touches the richness of the potential created in the image of God.

Secondly, an understanding of this layer of intimate emotional life will also explain why a husband and his wife will be at daggers drawn with each other but will frequently have simultaneously a number of other satisfactory friendships in which none of the stresses and strains encountered in the marriage will be present. It is the intimacy of the relationship which evokes expectations and patterns of behaviour which are only present in this unique relationship.

Another important contribution to marital breakdown is that of *emotional dependence*. The whole process of personality growth is one of gradual separation between child and parents, culminating in the second half of the second decade when physical, social, and emotional separation takes place and the young man or woman is ready to survive and relate as a separate person. This phase of adolescence, in which time is needed to consolidate an independent identity, leads on to courtship and marriage in the early twenties for the overwhelming majority of men and women. But not for all.

A certain number find this separation from home difficult, if not impossible, and psychiatrists are asked to help specifically with this problem. Some solve this problem in a different way and one that is potentially extremely hazardous for the marriage.

The dependent person marries a husband or wife who is felt to be sufficiently strong, organizing, capable, confident, or full of initiative to complement his/her own limitations. This dominant–submissive pattern is a frequent one and may in fact work out to the satisfaction of both parties. But in a small percentage of these marriages something quite different happens.

At some stage—five, ten, fifteen, or more years later—the dependent partner begins to change, to grow more confident and assured, and is now eager to take the initiative, to participate more fully in the decision-making moments of the marriage, and generally to have an equal say with his/her spouse.

If the change is not comprehended by the spouse, it will be resisted, and will lead to increased arguments, quarrels, and fights. The dependent partner will now begin to feel trapped, experiencing the spouse as a jailer, as someone impeding growth, denying what is due as a human being. If the situation continues unaltered, then sooner or later the dependent partner will find somebody else who will respond in the way he/she wishes to be treated now. This is what is meant when people refer to falling out of love with one's spouse and in love with somebody else. Very often, while all this is taking place, neither partner realizes what is at stake. The real emotional problem is lost in the maze of accusations and counter-accusations about cruelty, sexual incompatibility, infidelity, etc., etc. Only a very careful evaluation of the personality of the partners will give the appropriate understanding of this problem, which may emerge as late as twenty or more years after the inception of the marriage.[1]

Reference has already been made to sexual incompatibility in marital breakdown. It is very rare indeed for a marriage to be on the verge of breaking down without the presence of sexual difficulties. This is not to say, however, that sexual incompatibility is the principal reason or explanation for failure. Such a facile and naive interpretation would make a mockery of this complex topic.

Sexual difficulties need to be separated into three distinct categories. First, there are commonly difficulties of male potency, non-consummation of marriage, frigidity, and sexual deviations. Each of these difficulties presents distinct problems but none is in itself absolute, and marriages in which a good affectionate relationship exists can survive in the presence of these admittedly severe problems.

Secondly, and in this category belong the majority of sexual complaints, are the marriages in which the emotional relationship is rapidly deteriorating and almost invariably the first and most sensitive area to be hit is the sexual relationship. When spouses are angry with one another, as they frequently are when their emotional relationship is disturbed, this anger will be shown by the most delicate indicator, their sexual life. When this suffers for a prolonged period of months or years, then it will itself become the cause of bitter complaints, thus establishing a vicious circle. Affection and sexual life are intrinsically connected, and any attempt to deal with one and disregard the other is unlikely to be fruitful. Hence, the disastrous consequences of all philosophies, however sophisticated, which consider that sex is the cause of all evils in marriage and, if that is put right, all else will fall into place.

Thirdly, there is a small and highly important group of conditions which can diminish sexual interest and activity for either partner. The puerperium is a common period for the wife, and any physical or psychological illness (particularly a depression) for either partner. The true nature of the sexual withdrawal needs to be recognized and the cause treated in order to avoid a

---

[1] J. Dominian, op. cit., ch. 6.

F

secondary vicious circle, to avoid misunderstanding and tension arising from the primary cause.

Apart from the defects of personality and the consequent inter-personal clashes contributing to marital breakdown, actual psychiatric illness makes a small but decisive contribution. In terms of the major mental illnesses or psychoses, schizophrenia has the most serious adverse effect on marriage. But any illness, neurosis, or psychosis may handicap the sufferer to such an extent as to preclude the ability to meet his/her partner's minimum needs.

In this essentially truncated description of social and psychological factors contributing to marital breakdown the rudiments of marital pathology have been given. Christianity, however, may well respond to this by saying: "This is all very well but a contract is a contract and no difficulty, however pronounced, is an excuse for breaking up a marriage."

The answer to this very important objection is crucial. The concept of contract emanating from Roman jurisprudence and strongly upheld later on in the medieval Church is a very powerful one which has stood the test of time for hundreds of years. If marriage is viewed in this restricted sense of a contract, how do the modern social and psychological discoveries on marital breakdown influence it?

Both parties, in offering themselves, offer a self who undertakes to love, to provide help, to give sexual satisfaction, and to be a parent. These are commitments undertaken at the time of the contract, but, unlike other contracts, the ability to discharge the requirements resides in personality characteristics which are beyond the conscious grasp of the person. In other words, spouses offer to each other in perfect faith aspects of themselves which, in practice, in the actual existential reality, are found totally wanting, rendering the promises null and void.

"One cannot offer in a contract something one does not possess, and that which is lacking can only be seen in the actual relationship itself, not before."[1]

In terms of contract, contemporary understanding of the causes of breakdown suggests that the contract is null and void by the incapacity of the person to give effect to the promises made—an incapacity that existed before the marriage.

But the limited legal concept of contract does little justice to Christian marriage, a state which the Second Vatican Council calls a community of love.[2] In fact the concept of marriage visualized as a relationship is deeply rooted in the Old and the New Testaments in the notion of the covenant and St Paul's analogy of Christ and the Church. It is in this sense of relationship and community that Christian marriage can be understood more fully in all its aspects.

If the essence of marriage is to be found in its relational features, then Christian marriage can be described in the following terms:

Christian marriage is a God-given, freely entered, lifelong community, created to ensure the most appropriate conditions for the promotion of life, the life of the

---

[1] J. Dominian, "Marital Breakdown", *The Ampleforth Journal*, vol. LXXXIII, pt. I (1968).
[2] "Pastoral Constitution on the Church in the Modern World", *Documents of Vatican II* (Chapman 1966), p. 249.

children and that of the spouses. It is based on a series of relationships of love which, in a chronological order, are those of the spouses, the spouses and the children, the children among themselves, and the whole family with other members of society. It is upon the physical, psychological, and social integrity of these relationships, participating in the sacramental life of grace (the relationship between man and God) that the essence of marriage ultimately rests.[1]

If marriage is seen primarily as a relationship, then those entering the state must have the capacity to initiate and sustain a viable, physical, psychological, and social relationship for its whole duration.

Despite the far-reaching consequences of such changes, in my view they do not represent any radical break with tradition. The Pauline privilege[2] can be seen as the first manifestation in which the right to dissolve marriage and remarry was granted when the spiritual relationship of a couple was not viable, i.e. in the absence of a minimum spiritual relationship. In the middle ages the Church moved into the position of dissolving a marriage in which no physical consummation occurred, that is in the absence of a minimum physical relationship. Today we have reached a stage of recognizing the necessity for minimum psychological and social relationships which are probably the fundamentals on which visible marriage is formed. These are the factors which constitute the real validity or viability of a marriage. Seen in this light the task of the Church is to go on proclaiming the truth about indissolubility, the ideal of Christian marriage, and at the same time learn to distinguish what is viable from the non-viable so that no marriage will be held to be so in the name of Christ which in reality cannot be.[3]

But if the Christian Church is to go on proclaiming the lifelong indissolubility of marriage as the Christian ideal, then it needs to do more than state this in words. It must become the leader in comprehending, advising, and helping those entering marriage. Clearly the challenges of contemporary marriage are enormous and only a penetrating understanding of its complexity backed by widespread education and counselling will allow people to respond to the grace of God and persevere in the ideals offered in the Gospels.

The Church has an enormous responsibility to take the initiative and become an active force in bringing about the necessary research, education, guidance, and help to strengthen Christian marriage by an extended practical programme of service to the family which, coupled with its interest in education, will become the dual foundations of its concern for preserving the Christian ideals of the family.

Such a programme for research and service is too costly to be conducted on any basis other than on an ecumenical front, and a detailed description for an Institute for the Family has been given elsewhere.[4]

While Christianity has the responsibility of distinguishing viable from non-viable marriage, it has the further responsibility of actively helping marriage in all its stages to anticipate, negotiate, and overcome the difficulties that besiege contemporary marriage. If it is to remain faithful to Christ, it must continuously preserve the standards he set for us, so that his members have no doubt that the right goal is in their lives, and at the same

---

[1] J. Dominian, *Christian Marriage* (Librex Books 1968), p. 243 (slightly altered).
[2] 1. Cor. 7.12–15.   [3] J. Dominian, *The Tablet* (October 1969).
[4] J. Dominian, "To Serve the New Poor", *Theology*, vol. LXX (October 1967), p. 442.

time it must offer them the appropriate help that will sustain and strengthen their lofty motivation. This help has to be given today through the widespread use of the knowledge and skills which the disciplines of psychology and sociology have placed at our disposal. This in turn means that the Christian community has to become the spear-head of revolution in comprehending, assisting, and safeguarding all that is best in contemporary marriage.

Appended Note

AN INSTITUTE FOR THE FAMILY
by J. Dominian

The Christian ideal of marriage has always been and remains a lifelong indissoluble union within which children are born and nurtured in love. Until recently these aims could be expounded in familiar verbal and written exhortations of a general nature which seemed both appropriate and effective. An ever-increasing output of studies in depth from the behavioural sciences such as sociology, psychology, psychiatry, anthropology, and others, have revolutionized the way we can look at and understand the same phenomena such as marriage, sexuality, and the family. Christianity has not found it easy to integrate such new languages meaningfully within its own terms of reference, often treating the pioneers and the fruits of these sciences with suspicion and hostility. This is both regrettable and unnecessary. On the contrary, a proper understanding of this contribution will become an essential ingredient of the continuous translation of the Christian truths with recognizable and meaningful goals for a contemporary world acutely conscious and anxious to realize its human potential. In what way then can an Institute for the Family help to achieve the Christian aims of marriage?

The ideal composition for such an institute would be the combination of a research and a service team. The research team would be composed of psychologists, sociologists, and other experts whose task will be to study the evolving pattern of marriage as a relationship and as an institution. The sociologists would have the responsibility of examining the significance and impact of changing social factors. For example, within the last fifty years the trends towards earlier marriage, an increase in longevity, changes in fertility patterns, and the significant alteration of the status of women, have all made a vital impact on the nature and stability of marriage. It will be the tasks of the sociologists to examine and identify these changes both in global and more specific terms such as economic, social class, education, work factors operating for or against marital stability.

Within these broad social changes there is taking place a large-scale psychological revolution in our understanding of man. The factors which contribute to the psychological stability of an intimate relationship will become increasingly the crucial elements in the success of marriage. Only the most refined understanding of the needs and expectations of individual couples will allow the resolution of conflict. Here longitudinal and cross-sectional studies will be required to examine in detail the factors in the personality which act positively or negatively in initiating and maintaining a conjugal relationship. The psychological studies will have to draw their terms of reference widely both from dynamic and behavioural psychology.

Such detailed scientific information will not stand in a vacuum. It will be used to achieve something highly desirable and virtually non-existent at present, namely, the ability to anticipate and, if possible, to predict vulnerable marriages, thus offering effective help at the earliest possible moment.

The means of offering help have to develop further. Here the parish, the parishioners and its ministers, will have to act as a caring community that can identify and support those that cannot solve their problems for themselves. Infinite tact and understanding will be required, coupled with efficient and prompt professional support where needed.

This should be available from the second element in the Institute, namely, its service and teaching work. Here the Institute will actually be serving its own surrounding community and developing techniques of how such service can be developed in different settings. It will also be a teaching centre to communicate and spread such specialized knowledge.

Thus the research and service elements will form a two-tier system for the Institute which will become a centre for up-to-date, detailed, and reliable information. This information will give the Church and the community the means of understanding the evolving nature of marriage and will provide a continuous dialogue between the behavioural sciences and theology, offering the best means for implementing the message of the Good News.

7

Marriage and Divorce in the Anglican Communion

by Herbert Waddams

Dr A. R. Winnett's book *The Church and Divorce, a Factual Survey* (Mowbray 1968) provides all the essential information on the Anglican situation up to the date of its publication. As its first sentence states: "It is a survey of the teaching and practice of the Church of England and the other Churches of the Anglican Communion, and the Roman Catholic, Orthodox and Reformed Churches, in the matter of divorce and remarriage." This appendix is no more than an attempt to summarize the information for the readers of this report, and to add some notes about subsequent developments. For fuller treatment readers should refer to Dr Winnett's book.

When the Reformation was applied in its English form, the attitude of the Church of England was, as in other things, compounded of change and caution. Although it modified and added to the complicated medieval canon law and its accompanying procedures, it did not adopt the radically new approach of some of the continental reformers. The attempt to follow the continental pattern under Edward VI did not come to fruition and it was not subsequently revived.

Marriage continued to be dealt with by the church courts, which did not claim to have the power to dissolve marriages, but only to grant decrees of nullity and separation. Nevertheless, in accordance with their reading of the New Testament, many members of the Church considered that adultery dissolved the marriage bond and that remarriage was permissible for the innocent party. This particular view has persisted throughout the history of the Church of England up to present times, and has been the basis of attempts elsewhere in the Anglican Communion to frame regulations about marriage.

During the seventeenth century there were differing views about divorce and remarriage among leading churchmen, as may be seen from the short catena on the subject published in *Anglicanism* by More and Cross.[1] But since the church courts could not dissolve a marriage, the only way in which any person could be divorced and remarried was through a private Act of Parliament. This procedure was open to very few people, and the total number of such divorces over a period of 187 years was only 317. This remained the position in England until the middle of the nineteenth century.

[1] S.P.C.K. 1935.

In 1858 the Matrimonial Causes Act became law, and with this Act jurisdiction in matrimonial causes was transferred from the ecclesiastical courts to a newly constituted secular Court, whence later it passed to a division of the High Court. Although the old canon law continued in great part to be administered, and the old canonical procedure continued to be followed, their effect was radically altered by the introduction of dissolution of marriage on the ground of adultery.[1]

The 1857 Act gave an incumbent the freedom to refuse to solemnize a second marriage in church for a person whose previous marriage had been dissolved and whose partner was still living, though he was bound to permit the use of his church if another clergyman was willing to perform the ceremony.

At this time it would seem that the majority of churchmen believed that divorce was permissible in accordance with the Matthaean exception, including the right to remarriage of the innocent party, a view which a number of leading Tractarians shared.

Dr Winnett notices a new development at the start of the twentieth century.[2]

At the beginning of the present century a significant change occurred in the Anglican opinion on divorce and remarriage, and took the form of a strengthening of the indissolubilist position. Many factors contributed to this. New Testament criticism questioned the Exceptive Clause in St Matthew (not found in St Mark) as an authentic word of Jesus. The Anglo-Catholic movement, with a moral theology largely derived from Roman sources, had gained ground among the clergy. Divorce, moreover, was no longer an exceptional occurrence, but had come to be regarded as a major challenge to the Christian conception of marriage demanding an uncompromising stand on the part of the Church.

The justice of this judgement must be accepted, and the trend in the first decades of the twentieth century was for the Church of England to entrench itself in an uncompromising attitude and to forbid all second marriages in church to divorced persons whose partners were living. The most authoritative recent statement is to be found in Canon B 30 which reads:

1 The Church of England affirms, according to our Lord's teaching, that marriage is in its nature a union permanent and lifelong, for better for worse, till death them do part, of one man with one woman, to the exclusion of all others on either side, for the procreation and nurture of children, for the hallowing and right direction of the natural instincts and affections, and for the mutual society, help, and comfort which the one ought to have of the other, both in prosperity and adversity.

2 The teaching of our Lord affirmed by the Church of England is expressed and maintained in the Form of Solemnization of Matrimony contained in the Book of Common Prayer.

3 It shall be the duty of the minister, when application is made to him for matrimony to be solemnized in the church of which he is the minister, to explain to the two persons who desire to be married the Church's doctrine of marriage as

---

[1] *Putting Asunder: A Divorce Law for Contemporary Society, The Report of a Group appointed by the Archbishop of Canterbury in January 1964.* S.P.C.K. 1966.
[2] Op. cit., p. 7.

herein set forth, and the need of God's grace in order that they may discharge aright their obligations as married persons.[1]

This canon was designed as a basis for the discipline of the Church. Its first clause consists of a short descriptive account of the Christian doctrine of marriage as maintained in the Church of England, and provides the latest official expression of this doctrine. It was followed, soon after its promulgation, by the discussion in Convocation which resulted in a request for a statement of the Christian doctrine of marriage, of which this present report is the outcome. The short descriptive statement in the canon was in this way shown to need to be supported and interpreted by fuller theological exploration into its basis and its consequences for the Church's life.

The Church of England is therefore once more rightly examining the question in all its aspects. This begins from an already existing tension. On the one hand its resolutions have been increasingly rigid about remarriage of divorced persons in church, the rationale of which was admirably set out by the former Archbishop of Canterbury, now Lord Fisher of Lambeth, in his booklet *Problems òf Marriage and Divorce*;[2] on the other there have been increasing signs of uneasiness at the pastoral position created by these regulations. These signs may be seen in the continuing discussion about services of prayer in church for those who have been remarried in register offices, in the constantly recurring debate on remarriage in church, although the matter was technically settled, and also perhaps in attempts to find ways of mitigating the severity of the rule by exploring the possibility of the wider use of church recognition of nullity.[3]

The severity of the rules has been exacerbated because nullity suits were rarely brought in the civil courts, since it was easier to secure a straightforward divorce. There is therefore a number of people who have been divorced who could have successfully obtained a decree of nullity. The Church of England, not having courts of its own to inquire into such matters, had perforce to accept the situation as stated by the civil courts in their decrees.

The Lambeth Conferences have followed the pattern of attitudes in the Church of England on the whole. They began by recognizing divorce for adultery and the 1857 Act. They then narrowed their regulations to forbid all second marriages in church of those whose partners were still living, except in cases where nullity could be established (1948). In 1958 the same line was adopted but slightly less definitively, and in 1968 the resolution ran as follows:

23   The Conference recognizes that polygamy poses one of the sharpest conflicts between the faith and particular cultures.

The Church seeks to proclaim the will of God in setting out the clear implications of our Lord's teaching about marriage. Hence it bears witness to monogamous lifelong marriage as God's will for mankind.

The Conference believes that such marriage alone bears adequate witness to the equal sanctity of all human beings which lies at the heart of the Christian

---

[1] *The Canons of the Church of England* (S.P.C.K. 1969), p. 22.
[2] S.P.C.K. 1955.
[3] *The Church and the Law of Nullity of Marriage.* S.P.C.K. 1955.

revelation: yet recognizes that in every place many problems concerning marriages confront the Church.

The Conference therefore asks each province to re-examine its discipline in such problems in full consultation with other provinces in a similar situation.[1]

This resolution is vaguely worded and somewhat general, and it is therefore difficult to determine its precise meaning. Nevertheless, it does at least seem clearly to mean that the present practice was considered in need of rethinking and reordering, at least in some of the provinces. Since the Lambeth Conference of 1968 there have been important developments, from which it seems clear that the independent Churches of the Anglican Communion are abandoning the marriage discipline which they have adopted in the past. By no means all of the Churches of the Anglican Communion have reconsidered the situation, but there have been significant moves which seem to show that a new attitude is superseding the old. Some of the evidence is no more than preliminary, but it appears that the steps taken by the Church of Canada in 1967[2] are providing a pattern for other Churches to follow, with such modifications as suit their particular circumstances. In the British Isles no radical changes have taken place, but a report by a group of the diocese of Aberdeen and Orkney recommends that the former way of dealing with the remarriage of divorced persons be reconsidered. The Church of Canada passed a canon in 1967 which permitted the remarriage of divorced persons in church, laying down detailed and careful regulations as to how this was to be decided. The important point to be noted here is that the remarriage of divorced persons who have a partner of the former marriage still living is now permitted under certain conditions, and the complete ban on such marriages has been abandoned.

The influence of this step can be seen in the regulations adopted by the Church of the Province of New Zealand permitting the marriage in certain circumstances of divorced persons. The key provisions run as follows:

1 The Marriage of a divorced person may be solemnized by a Bishop or Priest notwithstanding that the other party to a prior marriage is still living, where there are good and sufficient grounds to believe that

   (a) Any divorced person intending marriage sincerely regrets that the promises made in any previous marriage were not kept, and

   (b) Both parties to an intended marriage have an avowed intention to abide by the lifelong intent of the proposed marriage.

Regulations follow as to the procedures in deciding whether such a marriage can take place in church or not. The right of any incumbent to refuse to solemnize such a marriage is safeguarded. In decisions about such remarriages the bishop is responsible for the key decisions, assisted by an advisory committee, and, if he wishes, he may delegate his powers and duties in the matter to a committee approved by the Standing Committee of his diocese.

Revisions of the regulations regarding remarriage of divorced persons are also under consideration in the Church of England in Australia. In the

[1] *The Lambeth Conference 1968*, Resolution 23.
[2] See appended note to this appendix for some of the details.

Church of the Province of Central Africa new rules have been adopted as
grounds of nullity, which consequently affect freedom to be married in
church; they also make provision for recognition of marital breakdown
and for the remarriage in church of those who meet the requirements
laid down in the canon.[1] The language of the canon demonstrates its
pastoral purpose. Paragraph 3 of this canon states:

No priest shall solemnize the marriage of any person whose marriage has been
dissolved by secular authority, during the lifetime of the partner to that marriage
unless either:

(a) The marriage was null and void and has been so declared as provided in these
canons, or
(b) The priest has obtained the prior authority of the Diocesan Bishop to solemnize such a marriage in a suitable manner. The bishop shall give such authority
only in accordance with the decision of a Board established as provided in the
Canon relating to the hearing of nullity proceedings and given after the Board
has investigated and satisfied itself on the following matters:

(i) That there is no hope of establishing or re-establishing a true marriage
relationship between the former marriage partners;
(ii) That the partner desiring to re-marry has done everything reasonably possible to effect a reconciliation, sufficiently understands the reasons for
the break-up of the previous marriage, and is genuinely forgiving and
repentant;
(iii) That the couple desiring to marry have the interests of the children (if any)
at heart, understand the Church's teaching concerning marriage, truly
intend to enter into a Christian marriage and have a good prospect of
achieving a permanent and stable union.

The above paragraph (a) covers the nullity provisions whereas (b)
introduces the additional consideration of irretrievable breakdown.

Canon 23 in Central Africa permits nullity to be based on the grounds
(among others) that the woman was pregnant at the time of the marriage by
another man without the knowledge of the husband, or that either of the
parties was suffering from venereal disease at the time of the marriage unknown to the other party, or "the clear establishment, by evidence relating
to behaviour before or after the marriage, of a lack of intention at the time
of the marriage, on the part of either or both of the parties, to fulfil the
basic obligations of the marital state".

The Free Churches of the British Isles have generally adopted a more
open attitude to the marriage of divorced persons in church than the
Church of England, partly owing to the fact that many of them were more
closely related to the continental Churches of the Protestant tradition and
made a more radical break with medieval canon law. Their regulations
have mainly been governed in the light of the New Testament by pastoral
considerations so that each case could be considered on its merits, taking

[1] The account of the Central African situation has been slightly modified in the
interests of clarity as compared with the first impression.

into account the facts of the divorce, the position of any children, the interests of the two desiring to be married, and any denominational issues which are relevant. Enactments of this kind have been passed in the General Assembly of the Presbyterian Church of England (1967), in that of Wales (1949), and in that of Ireland (1948) (normally for "innocent" parties only). The Congregational and Baptist Churches leave the matter to the discretion of their ministers with the assistance of reports and debates in their constitutional assemblies. The Methodist Conference (1948) allows for discretionary action and the Moravian Church (1956) grounds its permission for remarriage on the assurance of "sincere repentance for any previous marriage fault".

The attitude of the Church of Scotland to divorce is summarized in a report on personal relationships:

The General Assembly have accepted the Committee's proposals, discussed at Assembly level in 1968 and 1969, for reform of the law in ways different from, and the Committee believes more Christian than, those in the new law for England and Wales and in the new Bill, introduced for Scotland.[1]

The report recommended that the breakdown of marriage should be the only proper ground for divorce. The Church of Scotland's regulations state:

A Minister of the Church of Scotland may lawfully solemnize the marriage of a person whose former marriage has been dissolved by divorce and whose former spouse is still alive, provided that the said Minister adhere to the requirements stated hereunder.

These requirements insist that remarriage is not a matter of routine, but may only take place when a number of general considerations of a pastoral nature have had full weight. No Minister can be forced to solemnize a marriage against his conscience.

In the Roman Catholic Church a debate is proceeding as to the possibility of extending the conception of nullity in the light of the relationships between the persons concerned, a matter treated in another appendix by Dr J. Dominian. The Eastern Orthodox Churches continue to grant divorces and to remarry such persons as are divorced in accordance with their traditions. Another appendix by the Reverend A. M. Allchin deals with this historical background.

It may therefore be reasonably concluded that the attempt to deal with the problem of marriage discipline within the Anglican Churches by the rigid adherence to a refusal of second marriages in church is now proving unsatisfactory and its practice is being modified. The shift in the attitudes of church people has been part of a developing debate about marriage and the personal relationships within it in the secular world, changing points of view within the Church to some extent reflecting the insights which have been derived from this secular discussion. This is not surprising when the

---

[1] *Why Marriage? Report of the Church of Scotland Social and Moral Welfare Board to the General Assembly 1970* (St Andrew Press 1970), p. 26; see also an important report of 1957: *The Church of Scotland Report of the Special Committee on the Remarriage of Divorced Persons.*

Church is in touch with the civilization to which it is trying to minister, and in itself would not seem to be a matter for regret. If the movement of church opinion were to be characterized in two phrases, it would be near the mark to say that there is a growing opinion among Christians that marriage and remarriage ought to be considered first as a matter of personal relationships of those most nearly concerned, and that the rules which are adopted ought to reflect this priority. Breakdown of marriage is a fact and always a tragic reality when it occurs. Church practice should be measured by its success in helping people to avoid such breakdowns, and, when they do occur, it should help those concerned to mend their personal lives.

Appended Note

ANGLICAN CHURCH OF CANADA

CANON XXVII: ON MARRIAGE IN THE CHURCH
PREFACE

1. The Anglican Church of Canada affirms, according to our Lord's teaching as found in Holy Scripture and expressed in the Form of Solemnization of Matrimony in the Book of Common Prayer, that marriage is a lifelong union in faithful love, for better or for worse, to the exclusion of all others on either side. This union is established by God's grace when two duly qualified persons enter into a contract of marriage in which they declare their intention of fulfilling its purposes and exchange vows to be faithful to one another until they are separated by death. The purposes of marriage are mutual fellowship, support, and comfort, the procreation (if it may be) and nurture of children, and the creation of a relationship in which sexuality may serve personal fulfilment in a community of faithful love. This contract is made in the sight of God and in the presence of witnesses and of an authorized minister.

2. The Church affirms in like manner the goodness of the union of man and woman in marriage, this being of God's creation.[1] Marriage also is exalted as a sign[2] of the redeeming purpose of God to unite all things in Christ,[3] the purpose made known in the reunion of divided humanity in the Church.[4]

3. The Church throughout her history has recognized that not all marriages in human society conform, or are intended to conform, to the standard here described. For this reason, in the exercise of pastoral care as evidenced in the earliest documents of the New Testament, the Church has from the beginning made regulations for the support of family life especially among her own members.

4. Aspects of the regulation of marriage in the apostolic Church are recorded in the New Testament. A new standard of reciprocal love between

[1] Cf. Gen. 1.27–31.   [2] Eph. 5.31f.   [3] Eph. 1.9f.   [4] Eph. 2.11–16.

husband and wife was introduced leading towards an understanding of their equality.[1] In preparation for marriage Christians were directed to seek partners from among their fellow believers.[2] In Christ's name separated spouses were encouraged to seek reconciliation.[3] In His name also divorce was forbidden though not without exception.[4] In certain circumstances a believer already married to an unbeliever might be declared free from such a marriage bond;[5] in others, and here in the name of Christ, remarriage during the lifetime of a former spouse was described, with one exception, as an adulterous union.[6]

5. From these principles and precedents the Church, living in many cultures and in contact with many different systems of law, has sought in her rites and canons to uphold and maintain the Christian standard of marriage in the societies in which believers dwell. This standard and these rites and canons pertain to the selection of marriage partners, preparation for marriage, the formation of a true marriage bond, the solemnization of marriage, the duties of family life, the reconciliation of alienated spouses, and to the dissolution of marriage and its consequences.

DETERMINATION OF MARITAL STATUS UNDER THIS CANON

1. Definitions
(A) "Marriage" as defined by this Canon means that union described in the Preface of this Canon and further described in clause 2 of this Part. With respect to marriage so defined, a man and a woman may nevertheless, for reasons of age or health or other serious cause, agree to marry upon condition that there shall be no sexual intercourse between them permanently or for a limited time or from time to time.
(B) "Commission" as used in this Canon means the Ecclesiastical Matrimonial Commission established under Part VI of this Canon, and the effect of a decision of a Commission shall be as stated in clause 6 of Part VI.

2. Conditions of Valid Marriage under this Canon
The question whether a purported marriage constituted a marriage as defined by this Canon shall be determined by the Commission in accordance with the following principles:
(A) The parties to a marriage are not qualified for the purpose of this Canon to marry each other if—
　(1) Either of them is under the age of 16 years, except as provided in clause 4 of Part I of this Canon,
　(2) They are related to each other by blood or marriage within the prohibited degrees listed in the Table of Kindred and Affinity set out in clause 3 of Part I of this Canon,

[1] 1 Cor. 7.3f; 11.11f; Eph. 5.21–33; cf. Gal. 3.28.
[2] 1 Cor. 7.39; 2 Cor. 6.14; cf. 1 Thess. 4.2–8, RSV.
[3] 1 Cor. 7.10f.
[4] Matt. 5.31f; Mark 10.2–9; cf. Mal. 2.13–16.
[5] 1 Cor. 7.12–16.
[6] Matt. 19.9; Mark 10.11f; Luke 16.18; cf. Rom. 7.3.

(3) Either of them has gone through a ceremony of marriage with a person who is living at the time of the application, unless

    (a) The previous ceremony of marriage has been found, as provided in this Part, by the Commission not to have been a marriage as defined by this Canon and therefore not to be an impediment to marriage under the Canon Law of this Church, or

    (b) The previous marriage has been found by the Commission to have been dissolved or terminated according to the civil law applicable thereto and permission to marry has been given by the Commission, as provided by Part IV of this Canon.

(B) The contract of marriage requires the free and voluntary consent of the parties to marry each other upon the terms set out in the Preface of this Canon, based upon adequate understanding by each of them of the nature of the union and of the mutual relations of husband and wife and of parents and children.

(C) Consent to marry is not present where—

    (1) One of the parties is at the time of the contract of marriage incapable by reason of mental defect, mental illness, alcoholic intoxication, or the influence of a drug, of having the necessary understanding or giving the necessary consent,

    (2) One of the parties has been induced to consent by duress, by coercion, or by fear,

    (3) The woman gives consent after having been abducted and before being set free,

    (4) One of the parties is at the time of the contract of marriage mistaken with respect to the nature of the contract or of the union, or with respect to the identity of the other party,

    (5) One of the parties is at the time of the contract of marriage deceived by misrepresentation or concealment of facts seriously detrimental to the establishment of the contract, including among other things misrepresentation or concealment of

        (a) Venereal disease,

        (b) Addiction to drugs or alcohol,

        (c) Pregnancy, except as a result of intercourse with the man,

        (d) Addiction to homosexual practice, sadistic conduct, or other abnormal practice endangering the life or health of the other party,

    (6) The marriage has been agreed to upon a condition which is illegal, impossible or contrary to the nature of the union, as defined in this Canon,

    (7) The marriage is intended to be a sham or mere form,

    (8) Either party is incapable of consummating or unreasonably refuses to consummate the marriage by sexual intercourse, subject to clause 1 (A) of this Part,

    (9) One of the parties is not a Christian and there is a condition that the Christian party shall be entitled to adhere to and practise Christianity or to bring up any children of the union as Christians,

and the non-Christian party assents to the condition without intending that it shall be satisfied.

(D) In the cases mentioned in sub-paragraphs (2) (3) (4) (5) and (9) hereof, the party coerced, mistaken or deceived or otherwise imposed upon may by an act of will approbate the marriage and continue to cohabit with the other party when free to cease cohabitation after being freed from coercion, fear or abduction or after learning of the mistake, deception, concealment or other circumstance constituting the defect. What constitutes approbation is a question of fact in each case. The effect of approbation for the purpose of this Canon is to validate the marriage.

(E) Nothing contained in this Canon shall authorize the solemnization of a marriage known to the minister or either of the parties to be invalid by civil law.

3. *Conditions Governing Application regarding Canonical Status*

(A) An application for declaration of marital status under this Canon may be made where the applicant has gone through a ceremony of marriage with a person living at the time of the application and it is alleged that the ceremony did not constitute a marriage as defined by this Canon and where the marriage or purported marriage

    (1) Has been annulled or declared null and void, or dissolved or otherwise terminated by a legislature or court, or

    (2) Is alleged to have been dissolved or otherwise terminated according to the civil law properly applicable thereto, by an extra-judicial or non-judicial and non-legislative act or event.

(B) An application under this clause may be made by a person who has gone through a ceremony mentioned in sub-clause (A) of this clause and who is

    (1) A member of this Church, or

    (2) A person who desires to marry according to the rites of this Church.

(C) (1) An application under this clause not made in the course of or with a view to proceedings preliminary to a marriage shall be made to the incumbent of the parish or mission where the applicant resides or is accustomed to worship.

    (2) An application under this clause made in the course of or with a view to proceedings preliminary to a marriage shall be made to the incumbent of the parish or mission where it is desired that the intended marriage be celebrated.

    (3) The incumbent receiving the application shall investigate it to the best of his ability and forward the application, together with his report thereon, through the appropriate channels to the Commission having jurisdiction in the diocese.

PART IV

THE REMARRIAGE OF A DIVORCED PERSON
WHOSE FORMER PARTNER IS LIVING

1. Application for Permission to Remarry according to the Rites of the Church

(A) An application for permission to marry each other according to the rites of this Church may be made by two persons, one or both of whom has or have gone through a ceremony or ceremonies of marriage with a person or persons now living not a party or parties to the application, if the prior marriage or marriages is or are not questioned under this Canon in the application but has or have been dissolved or terminated by a legislature or legislatures or a court or courts or by another act or acts or event or events according to the law or laws applicable thereto. Where a marriage or purported marriage has been annulled for a defect not mentioned in clause 2 of Part III of this Canon, and no defect mentioned in that clause is alleged in respect thereof, it shall be deemed for the purposes of this Canon to have been dissolved.

(B) The application shall be made to the incumbent of the parish or mission where it is desired that the intended marriage be celebrated. The incumbent shall investigate the application to the best of his ability and forward it together with his report thereon, through the appropriate channels, to the Ecclesiastical Matrimonial Commission established under Part VI of this Canon having jurisdiction in the diocese.

(C) The application shall be made in writing and signed by both applicants and shall contain the information required by Schedule C.

2. Permission to Remarry according to the Rites of the Church

Permission to marry according to the rites of this Church may be granted by the Commission to the applicants notwithstanding the marriage or marriages of either or both of them to another person or persons now living, if the Commission is satisfied that—

(A) Any prior marriage in question has been validly dissolved or terminated in accordance with the law properly applicable thereto,

(B) The causes which led to the dissolution or termination were sufficiently grave to justify application under this Part,

(C) The applicant concerned tried in good faith before dissolution to effect reconciliation with the other party,

(D) If prior marriages of both applicants have been dissolved, there are grounds for special assurance of the probable stability of the intended marriage,

(E) If the applicants have committed adultery with each other, there is good reason for permitting the marriage other than an intention to enter into a mere *pro forma* marriage to legitimate a child or children,

(F) If a former wife of the male applicant is living, adequate provision has been made according to his means for the former wife, or there is good reason why the applicant should not be required to make that provision,

(G) Proper provision has been made for the care, maintenance, education and advancement of minor, disabled or otherwise dependent children of any prior marriage,

(H) If the children of a prior marriage are to live with the applicants, there is a reasonable prospect that the family relationship will be satisfactory,

(I) The applicants understand the Christian Doctrine of marriage as defined in this Canon, and intend to enter into such a marriage, and believe on reasonable grounds that they have the capacity to enter into and sustain the marriage during their joint lives.

3. *Refusal of Permission*

If permission is not granted, the Commission, subject to clause 4 (C) of this Part, shall dismiss the application which may not be renewed thereafter before any Commission unless further information is available.

4. *Special Cases*

(A) If the Commission is satisfied that efforts towards reconciliation between the parties to a former marriage would have been ineffective as a result of the fault of either party or for any other reason, the requirement of clause 2 (C) may be dispensed with.

(B) If either applicant has entered into two or more marriages that have been dissolved, the Commission shall not grant permission unless special circumstances justifying permission are proved.

(C) Notwithstanding the form of the application, if the Commission is of the opinion that a prior purported marriage of an applicant did not constitute a marriage as defined by this Canon, and the conditions of Part III clause 5 are satisfied, the Commission may make a declaration under that clause in respect of the marriage in question.

PART V

ADMISSION TO HOLY COMMUNION IN SPECIAL CASES

In every case where a person who has been remarried, except as provided above in this Canon, whose former and present partners are both living, desires a ruling with respect to admission to Holy Communion, the case must be referred by the incumbent to the bishop of the diocese.

Declaration to be made by those entering upon a second marriage when a former partner of one or both is still living

SCHEDULE A

DECLARATION

See Part 1, 2, and Schedule C, 5.

We,.............................and...................., hereby declare that we intend to enter into marriage which we acknowledge to be a union in faithful love, to the exclusion of all others on either side, for better or for worse, until we are separated by death.

We undertake to prepare ourselves for the exchange of vows at our wedding, recognizing that by this mutual exchange our union in marriage will be established.

We intend to strive thereafter to fulfill the purposes of marriage: the mutual fellowship, support, and comfort of one another, the procreation (if it may be) and the nurture of children, and the creation of a relationship in which sexuality may serve personal fulfilment in a community of faithful love.

8

Episcopal Discretion and the Clergy

prepared by the Commission
with legal assistance

The Divorce Reform Act 1969 raises some very difficult problems with regard to the discipline of the clergy. To a very large extent it undermines the Ecclesiastical Jurisdiction Measure 1963. Under this Measure a priest or deacon of the Church of England must, under section 55(1)(c), be deprived of his living and disqualified from holding a preferment if a decree of divorce or order of judicial separation is pronounced against him on the ground of adultery, desertion, cruelty, rape, sodomy, or bestiality.

By section 55(1)(d) similar action must be taken against him if he is found to have committed adultery in a divorce or matrimonial cause. There is a proviso in section 55 that, if the divorce be on the ground of desertion or cruelty, the bishop (after referral to the archbishop of the province) has discretion not to make this declaration of deprivation and disqualification.

By section 1 of the Divorce Reform Act 1969, the sole ground on which a petition for divorce may be presented to the court by either party to a marriage is that the marriage has broken down irretrievably. Therefore after 1 January 1971 there will never be a decree of divorce on any of the grounds mentioned in section 55(1)(c) of the Ecclesiastical Jurisdiction Measure.

Automatic deprivation and disqualification for matrimonial offences will, therefore, no longer apply except where one of the reasons for the breakdown of a marriage is proof of adultery. In practice it seems possible that petitioners will not try to prove that adultery has been committed, because there may be other evidence which is easier to adduce as proof that the marriage has broken down.

Disciplinary measures will be open to a bishop under Canon C 10 3b when the question of institution to a benefice arises. Under that canon a bishop may refuse to admit or to institute any priest to a benefice on the ground (among others) that the priest is unfit for the discharge of his duties by reason of "grave misconduct or neglect of duty in an ecclesiastical office, evil life, having by his conduct caused grave scandal concerning his moral life since his ordination". What constitutes a grave scandal is entirely within the episcopal discretion, although evidence of adultery, or an affiliation order, would automatically bring into operation section 55 of the Ecclesiastical Jurisdiction Measure.

If, however, adultery was not an issue in the divorce proceedings, then the bishop would not be in a position to take any automatic action whatsoever; he would have to rely on proceedings being taken under Section 14 (1)(b) of the Ecclesiastical Jurisdiction Measure for conduct unbecoming the office and work of a Clerk in Holy Orders. This would set in motion the whole cumbrous machinery of the Ecclesiastical Jurisdiction Measure. To this there would generally be no alternative, because Canon 3 B only operates where a man is to be instituted to a benefice and not where he is already instituted.

Canon law does not forbid a marriage in church between two persons, one of whom has a former spouse still living, since this is permitted under statute law; nor does the Ecclesiastical Jurisdiction Measure contain any reference to the standing of a clergyman who remarries in such circumstances. It may lie within the episcopal discretion to determine whether or not the clergyman may have thereby caused grave scandal, but this would not be a ground of deprivation or disqualification where the clergyman is already beneficed.

A situation could arise whereby a clergyman is divorced with his consent after a continuous separation of two years.[1] No action could arise under the Ecclesiastical Jurisdiction Measure, and the clergyman would be free to marry again with no sanctions if he is already beneficed. As neither the ecclesiastical law nor the statute law forbids his remarriage, it is an open question whether the courts would necessarily decide in an action under the Ecclesiastical Jurisdiction Measure that his conduct was unbecoming the office and work of a Clerk in Holy Orders.

The advent of the new Divorce Reform Act also means that there is a possibility that a clergyman may find that his marriage has been dissolved against his will. It is possible that such a clergyman may decide to remarry.

The question arises whether there are any circumstances in which a clergyman, whose marriage has irretrievably broken down and has been legally dissolved, may properly be remarried in church and still be in good standing to hold a benefice. This question raises matters concerning professional discipline and offence to Christian conscience, and it is also an area where the theology of the ministry overlaps with the theology of marriage.

This area needs thorough investigation in its theological and disciplinary aspects. It is to be hoped that this task will shortly be carried out by a competent body. Since it falls outside the terms of reference of this Commission, it is appropriate here to do no more than to point to these urgent problems and to suggest that such a body should be appointed without waiting upon the full consideration of the main Report.

[1] This period was wrongly stated as five years in the first impression.

9
Regulations Concerning Marriage and Divorce

Passed in the Upper House of the Convocation of Canterbury on 16 May 1956 and 23 May 1957 and in the Lower House on 21, 22, and 23 May 1957 and declared an Act of Convocation by His Grace the Lord Archbishop of Canterbury on 1 October 1957

(Added for information in the third impression)

1

"That this House reaffirms the following four Resolutions of 1938, and in place of Resolution 5 then provisionally adopted by the Upper House substitutes Resolution 2(A) below, which restates the procedure generally followed since 1938.

(1) "That this House affirms that according to God's will declared by our Lord, marriage is in its true principle a personal union, for better or for worse, of one man with one woman, exclusive of all others on either side, and indissoluble save by death."

(2) "That this House also affirms as a consequence that re-marriage after divorce during the lifetime of a former partner always involves a departure from the true principle of marriage as declared by our Lord."

(3) "That in order to maintain the principle of lifelong obligation which is inherent in every legally contracted marriage and is expressed in the plainest terms in the Marriage Service, the Church should not allow the use of that Service in the case of anyone who has a former partner still living."

(4) "That while affirming its adherence to our Lord's principle and standard of marriage as stated in the first and second of the above resolutions, this House recognizes that the actual discipline of particular Christian Communions in this matter has varied widely from time to time and place to place, and holds that the Church of England is competent to enact such a discipline of its own in regard to marriage as may from time to time appear most salutary and efficacious."

2(A)

"Recognizing that the Church's pastoral care for all people includes those who during the lifetime of a former partner contract a second union, this

House approves the following pastoral regulations as being the most salutary in present circumstances:

(*a*) When two persons have contracted a marriage in civil law during the lifetime of a former partner of either of them, and either or both desire to be baptized or confirmed or to partake of the Holy Communion, the incumbent or other priest having the cure of their souls shall refer the case to the Bishop of the diocese, with such information as he has and such recommendations as he may desire to make.

(*b*) The Bishop in considering the case shall give due weight to the preservation of the Church's witness to our Lord's standard of marriage and to the pastoral care of those who have departed from it.

(*c*) If the Bishop is satisfied that the parties concerned are in good faith and that their receiving of the Sacraments would be for the good of their souls and ought not to be a cause of offence to the Church, he shall signify his approval thereof both to the priest and to the party or parties concerned: this approval shall be given in writing and shall be accepted as authoritative both in the particular diocese and in all other dioceses of the province."

2(B)

"No public Service shall be held for those who have contracted a civil marriage after divorce. It is not within the competence of the Convocations to lay down what private prayers the curate in the exercise of his pastoral Ministry may say with the persons concerned, or to issue regulations as to where or when these prayers shall be said."

2(C)

"Recognizing that pastoral care may well avert the danger of divorce if it comes into play before legal proceedings have been started, this House urges all clergy in their preparation of couples for marriage to tell them, both for their own sakes and for that of their friends, that the good offices of the clergy are always available."

Regulations 1 (1), (2), (3), and (4) and 2(A) (*a*), (*b*), and (*c*) are substantially the same as those approved by the Convocation of York in June 1938.

Jesus on Divorce and Remarriage
Additional Note

Three articles, published since Appendix 1 was written, merit this additional note.

1 In "The Teaching of Jesus on Marriage and Divorce" (*Law in the New Testament* (London 1970) pp. 363–388), J. D. M. Derrett argues that Jesus reaffirmed the teaching of Genesis about the divine constitution of man and woman. Marriage is constituted by sexual intercourse, and the resultant "one-flesh" relationship is indissoluble. According to Derrett there is no contradiction between this teaching and the Mosaic concession of Deut. 24.1ff. The object of the Deuteronomic teaching was to prevent impurity. If a husband finds some immorality in his wife, she is unclean and he may not have intercourse with her. If he labours under the strain of combining abstinence with cohabitation, he may relieve it by divorce; but he may not remarry, and the "one-flesh" relationship remains. Jesus did not deny the use of this concession "for the hardness of men's hearts" (i.e. moral weakness) so long as there was no remarriage. The so-called "Matthaean exception" is consistent with this teaching. A man may properly divorce a wife for immorality to prevent his house being defiled.

Derrett's explanation assumes that there should never be any sexual intercourse in any second marriage. This, however, is unknown not only to Jewish tradition but also to Deut. 24.1ff; and so Derrett's explanation lacks credibility.

2 David Daube deals with the "Pauline privilege" in "Pauline contributions to a pluralistic culture" (*Jesus and Man's Hope*, vol. ii, ed. D. G. Miller and D. Y. Hadidian (Pittsburg Theological Seminary 1971), pp. 223–45). Daube holds that Paul faithfully followed the teaching of Jesus on the impermissibility of divorce. But on conversion a spouse became a "new creature"; and his marriage ended with his old life. It could be reconstituted by intercourse and cohabitation. Paul advises this course. "For God has called us in peace" (1 Cor. 7.15) refers, according to Daube, to the possibility that the pagan partner may be converted by the believing spouse. Thus the "Pauline privilege" merely deals with a marriage that has ended and which the unbelieving partner refuses to reconstitute.

But Christian marriage, according to Schillebeeckx, was in the early centuries "a secular matter with a Christian inspiration" (*Marriage,* vol. ii (London 1965), p. 18). The Church had not altered its doctrine of marriage during the apostolic age. Furthermore, if a marriage ended at conversion, why not other social ties? In 1 Cor. 7 Paul deals not only with sex but also with race (circumcision) and class (slavery). He concludes: "In whatever state each was called, there let him remain with God." Marriage no more than slavery ended on conversion. But for the sake of peace (a great Jewish ethical principle) a marriage could be dissolved if the pagan partner deserted.

3 The use of nuptial imagery to describe the relationship of the Church to Christ is said to demand an indissoluble view of marriage (*For Better For Worse*, ed. C. P. M. Jones (Church Union 1971), p. 33). But the most that can be proven from the use of this imagery is that marriage is intended by God to be permanent. What we have here is "an exalted portrait of marriage" (J. P. Sampley, '*And The Two Shall Become One Flesh*' (C.U.P. 1971), p. 157).

St Valentine's Day 1972   HUGH MONTEFIORE